THE MINNESOTA
Forgotten River

I do not know much about gods; but I think that the river
Is a strong brown god——sullen, untamed and intractable.
Patient to some degree, at first recognised as a frontier;
Useful, untrustworthy, as a conveyor of commerce;
Then only a problem confronting the builders of bridges.
The problem once solved, the brown god is almost forgotten
By the dwellers in cities——ever, however, implacable,
Keeping his seasons and rages, destroyer, reminder
Of what men choose to forget.

—T. S. Eliot

RIVERS OF AMERICA BOOKS

Already published are:

The Merrimack *by Raymond P. Holden*
The Minnesota: Forgotten River *by Evan Jones*
The Missouri *by Stanley Vestal*
The Mohawk *by Codman Hislop*
The Monongahela *by Richard Bissell*
The Ohio *by E. R. Banta*
The Potomac *by Frederick Gutheim*
Powder River *by Struthers Burt*
River of the Carolinas: The Santee *by Henry Savage, Jr.*
Rivers of the Eastern Shore *by Hulbert Footner*
The Sacramento *by Julian Dana*
The St. Johns *by Branch Cabell and A. J. Hanna*
The St. Lawrence *by Henry Beston*
The Salinas *by Anne B. Fisher*
Salt Rivers of the Massachusetts Shore *by Henry F. Howe*
The Sangamon *by Edgar Lee Masters*
The Saskatchewan *by Marjorie Wilkins Campbell*
The Savannah *by Thomas L. Stokes*
The Shenandoah *by Julia Davis*
The Susquehanna *by Carl Carmer*
Suwannee River *by Cecile Hulse Matschat*
The Tennessee: The New River, Civil War to TVA
   by Donald Davidson
The Tennessee: The Old River, Frontier to Secession
   by Donald Davidson
Twin Rivers: The Raritan and the Passaic
   by Harry Emerson Wildes
Upper Mississippi (New Revised Edition, 1944)
   by Walter Havighurst
The Wabash *by William E. Wilson*
The Winooski *by Ralph Nading Hill*
The Wisconsin *by August Derleth*
The Yazoo River *by Frank E. Smith*

Songs of the Rivers of America *edited by Carl Carmer*

RIVERS OF AMERICA

Edited by CARL CARMER

*As planned and started
by* Constance Lindsay Skinner

Associate Editor JEAN CRAWFORD
Art Editor BEN FEDER

EVAN JONES

THE MINNESOTA

Forgotten River

Illustrated by HARRY HEIM

HOLT, RINEHART AND WINSTON • *New York* • *Chicago* • *San Francisco*

977.6

Jones

cop. 1

Designer: Ernst Reichl

84713–0212

Printed in the United States of America

In memory of
ELIZABETH McLEOD JONES

Table of Contents

THE MINNESOTA
Forgotten River

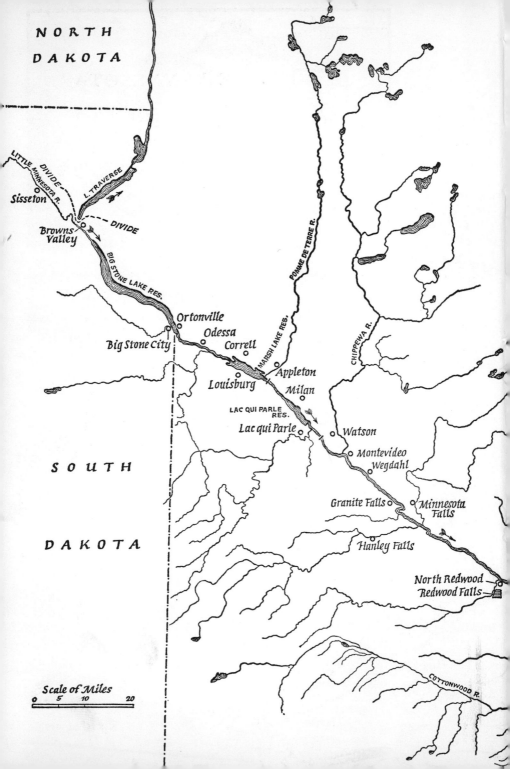

MINNESOTA RIVER

map by palacios

1

WHERE THE RIVER WARREN
FLOWED

By the sweet-tasting brooks of the blond country,
The country of snow and wheat,
Or west among the black mountains, the glacial springs,
Far North and West they lie. . . .

—STEPHEN VINCENT BENÉT

O UT OF THE vast water rimming the retreating glacier the
river flowed southeastward more than two hundred miles.
Diverted by massive deposits of earth and stone, it then swept
briefly north, seeking its level. Joined by lesser streams, the torrential waters turned again, racing eighteen hundred miles
through preglacial channels to the Gulf of Mexico. For thousands of years, during the slow melting of mountainous ice, the
rivers known as the Mississippi and the Minnesota were one.

Cyclonic winds whipped the vast water as it formed ancient
Lake Agassiz, an inland sea far larger than all the Great Lakes
combined. Spreading out north and west of the land from which
the Mississippi now springs, Lake Agassiz covered one hundred
and ten thousand square miles in Minnesota, North Dakota and
Manitoba, and it varied in depth from one hundred to seven
hundred feet. A wall of ice was its northern shore, the high
ground of preglacial time shaped the lake on east and west. In

5

the south, where the line dividing the two Dakotas meets the Minnesota boundary, the giant lake found its outlet—the Glacial River Warren.

As it drained Lake Agassiz, the Warren carved the wide valley that is now that of the Minnesota. It continued to feed the Upper Mississippi long after glacial waters ceased to pour into the little stream flowing out of Lake Itasca. Had there been men to give it a name, the River Warren might have been called the Father of Waters, the true upper branch of the Mississippi.

In carrying its turbulent burden, the Warren varied from one to five miles in width, from seventy-five to two hundred feet in depth, until the northern ice wall broke, opening a second drainage channel. The lake waters then began to seek the sea through Hudson Bay. As the ice age waned, the level of Lake Agassiz gradually dropped and retreated northward. The once vast inland sea is marked in Canada by Lakes Winnipeg and Winnipegosis, by the great Red River Valley spreading its rich farms across the American boundary, by Upper and Lower Red lakes, by Lakes Traverse and Big Stone lying head to head—one draining north, the other south. Out of the southern end of Big Stone flows the Minnesota, the meandering reminder of the River Warren.

The Warren channel remains to frame the lazy Minnesota in a wide, troughlike, loam-covered valley, sometimes richly black, sometimes chocolate-colored. Cutting into western prairies, into sandstone and granite terraces, the valley lies upon the lake-strewn map of Minnesota like the imprint of a boomerang.

Its earliest settlers are nameless, unknown. Hunters came and left. Only in a skeleton found in the long-dry bed of Lake Agassiz is there an inkling of the earliest human life. When the Minnesota Valley was filled with plunging waters moving southward, a nomadic tribe pitched a camp not far above this outlet of the lake. A teen-age girl (so the skeletal measurements indicate) tumbled into the water. Perhaps she was fishing, fashioning a crude vessel of logs bound with vines, paddling away from the

shore to find her quarry, losing her balance when she tried to spear the fish. She drowned more than ten thousand years ago, and long before the disappearance of Lake Agassiz her skeleton was buried in silt under the deep water.

In the summer of 1931, the grave of the nameless girl of unknown tribe was disturbed by a highway worker. Following a road grader, the worker saw an odd white substance shimmering in the afternoon sun. As he examined it, he found a deposit of crushed clam shells, and when he probed with his fingers, he came upon a human skull. In the careful digging that followed, a skeleton was uncovered and the highway crewmen notified Dr. A. E. Jenks, the state archaeologist. In 1945, Jenks called the find "the oldest human skeleton now known in the Western hemisphere." His prolonged examination indicated that the girl could not have looked like any modern Indian; the shape of her head was that of people who lived in Asia many thousand years ago, of nomads who crossed the Bering Sea land bridge to America.

Two years later "Brown's Valley Man" was unearthed at the head of Big Stone Lake, in an ancient burial pit near the shore of the River Warren. In the grave were beautifully carved and fluted arrowheads, which Jenks identified as Yuma points, thus dating this dead hunter of the early Minnesota Valley as having lived more than eight thousand years ago.

Brown's Valley is a lustreless village situated on the low continental divide that separates the waters flowing to Hudson Bay from those that flow to the Gulf of Mexico. The brook called the Little Minnesota slips by the town and disappears three miles to the south in the long, clear lake the Indians described as *Eatakeka*. Its name has never changed. When the French came they simply translated: *Lac des grosses roches*. The English-speaking Americans did the same. And so today from Big Stone Lake the Minnesota River rises to begin its gentle glide toward Minneapolis and St. Paul. For a hundred miles—from Ortonville at the foot of the lake to the quiet riverside at Franklin—the Minnesota moves past stupendous granite outcroppings, worn smooth and round as boulders to stud the fields above the stream. Sometimes these mammoth rocks seem grotesque against the prairie landscape, existing as incongruous mementos of vanished glaciers. Below them, at Odessa, the modern river is small as it flows through the glacial channel that once carried three streams separated by islands that now rise high and dry above the valley floor.

Serpentlike, the Minnesota wiggles its way downstream. Lazily, it accepts its first tributaries: Spirit Mountain River, the Whetstone, the Yellow Bank, and the Pomme de Terre. Twenty-five miles along its way it widens and the seven-mile lake thus made has a lovely name—Lac qui Parle; called "talking water" by the Indians because of the sound of waves against the shore. The Lac qui Parle River enters then, and the Chippewa, and the Yel-

low Medicine. The Minnesota flows over igneous and metamor-
phic rocks and breaks into its only waterfalls at Granite Falls,
still gentle as it laps at the backdoors of the town's main street
and the green lawns stretching away from the opposite bank.

There was a time when the sea covered the Minnesota Valley
and surrounded an island that is still a landmark. Known as Old
Redstone, it is now a conspicuous hill on the rim of the valley
near New Ulm. Here it rises one hundred and seventy-five feet
above the river, turning the waters from a direct course. Harder
than the hardest granite, this quartzite eminence has pointed to
the sky since before the river was born. From the heart of the
earth it protrudes over two square miles, surrounded now by
terraces left by glacial waters. Opposite Old Redstone, rising in
the distant, sloping Coteau des Prairies of South Dakota, the
Cottonwood joins the Minnesota. A few miles farther downstream, at Mankato, the Blue Earth enters, and there the river
begins its northeastward sweep. As the Minnesota flows toward
the Twin Cities, its banks are distinguished by rock terraces
that were left as perfect town sites by the River Warren. At
Shakopee the Minnesota no longer follows the Warren channel
due eastward to the Mississippi. Glacial retreat blocked the old
valley that led to Pine Bend with hills of boulders, clay, gravel,
and sand. So, as the Minnesota was forced northward toward
St. Paul, it curved the limestone promontory from which old Fort
Snelling long guarded the entrance to the valley.

The independent Minnesota is far longer than it looks on the
map. It is four hundred and seventy-five miles by water from
Big Stone to the fort. Dropping only two hundred and seventy
feet in the total distance, the river takes its time. Its meanders
are luxuriantly shaded with ashes and cottonwoods, box elders
and scrub oaks; in the sunlight-dappled bends and under the
low bridges there are crappies, bullheads, bass; and the river is
dotted with fishermen, good weather and bad. Through the wide
valley it winds like a leafy ribbon, gentle and generous, thread-
ing through peaceful life.

2

"SNAKES IN THE GRASS"

Soon in the wide wilderness,
On a branch blown over a creek,
Up a trail of the wild coon,
In a lair of the wild bee. . . .

—JAMES OPPENHEIMER

It may be true that life on the Minnesota has been peaceful less often than not. There is no way of knowing what wars occurred during the short life of the girl who drowned in Lake Agassiz; no knowledge, in fact, of Indian life until the coming of the French in the seventeenth century. Certainly strife flared along the river centuries before the Chippewa forced the Sioux out of the northern forests to the Minnesota Valley. In their turn, the Sioux drove the Iowa tribe southwest, and the valley became the holding ground from which the Sioux mounted predatory raids to the north. War was tradition.

Traditional, too, was the Sioux belief that the world had once been one vast sea. Casting a black ball upon the water, the Great Spirit Wahkon-Tonkah created the earth, and from a second black ball he created every kind of living thing. Memory lost details, but many Sioux believed their ancestors had come from the Arctic north, land of the Esquimos whom they referred to as "eaters of raw food." More recently, some anthropologists say, the Minnesota Sioux had lived peaceful lives along the Ohio

River. Not long before Columbus' time, war broke the Ohio tribes in two parts. Some were forced east to Virginia and the Carolinas, while others went to the Mississippi where they again divided. The Sioux were first mentioned in history by the *Jesuit Relations* of 1640, when they were encountered by the French at Sault Ste.-Marie.

Here again they had separated in splinter groups. They became the tribes of "the seven council fires," calling themselves Dakota, which means friend or ally. The Chippewa, however, gave them another name: *Nadouësse*, meaning snake in the grass; and it was in this unkind guise—in an epithet so capriciously spelled, or misspelled—that the Dakota were introduced to the French. The *voyageurs* promptly made the name plural by writing it "Nadouësioux," and then the new word was shortened to its last syllable. When the French arrived they had found the seven tribes—the Yanktons, the Yanktonai, the Tetons, and the four Santee branches—all with headquarters in northern Minnesota. Already the Tetons must have begun to leave the forests, for their name means prairie dweller. And soon the Chippewa—equipped with French guns—drove the Tetons, the Yanktons, and the Yanktonai southward.

In the Minnesota Valley the three retreating tribes parted company. The Yanktons and part of the Tetons went west toward the Dakota plains. Along the river a group split off to become known as the Oglala (the Sioux word meaning "scatter one's people") and began hunting buffalo in the Blue Earth country near the Minnesota's great bend. By 1730, when the long war with the Chippewa took its long lasting shape and the Santee tribes were being driven to the Minnesota, the Oglala were living on the western plains and the Yanktons and the Tetons had moved to the vicinity of Big Stone Lake.

By 1767, when Jonathan Carver visited the river and was moved to write about the Sioux, he asserted that they paid "a greater attention to their dress and to the ornaments with which they decorate their persons, than to the accommodations of their huts or tents." The dress moccasins of the men were decorated with porcupine quills, beads, and ribbons, and most of their other garments were similarly embellished by the women. They painted their faces, treasuring the clay from the Blue Earth country, braided their hair, and wore bangs above the eyebrows. "Not a few," an early American missionary wrote, "had curly hair, but neither males nor females patronized curls." Such showy items as decorated breech cloths, leggings, and knife pouches were prized only by the young.

In winter, the men wore buffalo skins while traveling, or sometimes blankets made of deer skins. They wore buckskin leggings cut to fit the contour of the top of the foot, and fastened inside the moccasins with a strap. Fur mittens were worn except when the fingers were needed for shooting or cutting up game. When hunting or traveling, each man carried with him a bag made of the skin of a mink, skunk, or some other small animal, tanned with the hair on. The bag was made by removing the entire carcass through a hole cut in the animal's throat. It was carried on the hip with the tanned head thrust under the girdle. After the Sioux came to know the white man, the bag carried pipe and tobacco, touchwood, flint, and fire steel. No single item was more important to the Indian than his bag. "They were as careful of it," it was said, "as an elephant is of his trunk."

In summer, the Sioux lived in houses framed with poles and covered with bark, sometimes large enough for two or more families, sometimes accommodating only one. Peeled saplings, set in the ground a foot or two apart, were squared at the top and at several lower levels with horizontal poles tied on with strips of basswood. Strong forked posts at each end of the house —and, if necessary, one in the center—supported the ridgepole to which rafters were tied. The covering for the house was taken from standing elms in pieces of bark five or six feet long and as wide as the circumference of the tree. Most of the labor was done by the women, but the roofing was supervised by men, who saw to it that the overhead bark was lapped like shingles and

BLACK DOG VILLAGE

that an aperture in it permitted smoke from the fire laid in the center of the earthen floor to escape.

There was a single doorway, and along the three other walls ran a continuous platform, about two feet high and covered with bark and buffalo robes to serve as a place for eating, sleeping, resting, and loafing.

The traveling home of the Sioux buffalo hunters was the tepee, and this skin lodge also was the winter shelter of the Indians along the Minnesota. Women began the erection of a tepee by tying together the ends of three long poles and setting them up as a tripod. Against this, nine other poles were rested, forming a conical skeleton. Eight to twelve good-sized buffalo skins, sewn together with sinews and shaped like a half-circle, were lashed to the frame of poles to make a snug tent that two nimble women could put together in five minutes. When new, the tanned skin covering was nearly white and translucent. Banked with hay and fur robes along the ground, and heated by a fire of dry wood, the skin tepee provided considerable comfort in the bitterest Minnesota winter.

Another important structure was the bathhouse, a hemispherical framework three or four feet high and also covered with skins. Inside, the Sioux steamed themselves in vapor created by pouring water on hot cobblestones. Cleanliness was a Sioux fetish. "At break of day," an early chronicle relates in some surprise, "the Nadouaissioux bathe, even to the youngest." The waters of the Minnesota, moving relentlessly past, drew homage before the bathers entered the bath. At dawn a Sioux chief took his children to the riverbank and, as he lifted his arms to pray, gave them presents to throw into the stream as offerings to the gods.

In spring when the wild strawberries had ripened in soil made rich and mellow by the growth of wild artichokes, the Sioux women planted maize; they soaked their seed until it sprouted, planted it with their hands, and when it shot up through the ground, they hilled it with primitive hoes. Sometimes they preserved maize by boiling it, scraping it from the cob with mussel shells, then leaving it to dry. They made barrels of bark to contain the dry kernels, and buried them until the end of the January deer hunt. But the greatest part of their diet was found among the foods that thrived naturally along the river. About the headwaters of the Minnesota they found native turnips scattered over the prairie, and they laboriously dug these one by one with a sharp stick. On the bottoms of the saucer lakes left in the valley by the glacier, they found other roots called *psincha* and *psinchincha*. They gathered wild rice and maple sap to supplement the deer and buffalo meat brought in by the hunters. And in summer or winter they used bone hooks and spears to catch fish and turtles.

Sioux life was communal. In general the chiefs inherited their offices, but they had no power to make laws nor to execute them. The tribesmen maintained the right of deciding all questions in council. Long and animated debate frequently preceded a vote; an effective chief, therefore, had to be a persuasive speaker. In time of war, his leadership was turned over to the "chief soldier," who led the Sioux warriors against their ancient enemy, the Chippewa.

The Sioux, according to a seventeenth-century report, "have very fine forms, but the women are not comely, and they look upon them as slaves. They are jealous and suspicious about them, and they are the cause of quarrels and blood-shedding." A husband might punish his wife for unfaithfulness by cutting off the end of her nose, thus rendering her less attractive. "The Sioux are very dexterous with their canoes," the old account continues, "and they fight unto death if surrounded. . . . One must be a Nadouaissioux, to find the way to their villages."

LAC QUI PARLE MISSION

On the banks of the Minnesota the superstitious Sioux worshiped Unkteri, the mammoth who had grazed in the valley before the coming of the glaciers. Samuel W. Pond and his brother Gideon worked as the valley's first missionaries. Samuel wrote: "They held many erroneous opinions concerning that extinct species of elephant, and did not know that the race was extinct. . . . As they worshipped many other animals, it was natural that the mammoth, which so exceeded the others in size, should be adopted as their chief god. To his worship their most solemn religious festivals were dedicated. . . . [Elephant] bones were highly prized for magical powers, and were perhaps as valuable to them as relics of a saint are to a devout Catholic. A Dakota told me that he had discovered some [mammoth] fossil bones in the lake opposite Shakopee, but was unable to raise them without some boat larger than a canoe."

In honor of such gods, Pond said, the Sioux were willing "to do any amount of praying and dancing . . . provided a good feast at the end made amends for all their fatigue; but, except when mourning for the dead, they seldom afflicted themselves with bodily tortures. . . ." An exception was the sun dance in which the participants performed with their faces toward the sun until their strength was exhausted. They inserted sticks under the muscles of the arms or body and fastened one end of a cord to these sticks and the other end to a post or some heavy weight, pulling until the flesh gave way.

Even more than most Indians, the Sioux insisted on personal courage, but they were also realistic about themselves. In an oft-repeated proverb, they would say, "The elbow is the bravest part of the body, the eye the most cowardly." They were easily frightened by the sight of something they could not understand. When Pierre Radisson and his brother-in-law Groseilliers began trading with the Sioux in 1661, Radisson threw gunpowder into a fire as a dramatic show of French power, and the watching Indians fled as one man. After the French managed to reassure the frightened Sioux, the natives feasted the traders and gave thanks to the sun for sending men whose words could make the earth shake.

Twenty years later they had no fear at all when they captured Father Hennepin and two others just below the place they called *Mendota*, "the meeting of waters," where the Minnesota flows into the Mississippi. "They first seized all our property, and broke our canoe to pieces, for fear we should return to their enemies. . . ." Hennepin failed to mention the Minnesota, but as he says, "they compelled us to go sixty leagues by land," a fact that may account for his ignorance of the stream called the Wattapaw Menesotor by the Sioux. Mendota, the Sioux mythology maintained, was immediately over the center of the earth and just below the center of the heavens. Therefore the control of the river and of its confluence with the Mississippi made the Sioux superior to all other people. Certainly that must have seemed reason enough to deny Father Hennepin even a passing glance at the river of sky blue waters.

The denial doesn't now seem to matter so much. In less than a decade the French not only had found the river, they had given it a name the Sioux were unable to understand. The French called it Rivière St. Pierre—for reasons that do not appear in the record.

3

FOUR THOUSAND POUNDS
OF BLUE EARTH

And down the river's dim expanse—
Like some bold seër in a trance.
Seeing all his own mischance—

—ALFRED LORD TENNYSON

PAGEANTRY was the necessary art. The ancient trees, the set-tled hills, the thousands of lakes and the rivers they fed had become Louis XIV's America. Frenchmen in the wilderness were emissaries of the king; their every considered act was a *bourrée* in the choreography of conquest. Costumed in the black robes of the Jesuits and Recollects, in the plumed velvet hats, the curled wigs, the velvet breeches, the lace, the ruffled knees and elbows of the king's gentlemen, or in the blazing vermillions, yellows, pur-ples of the traders' habits—they strode upon the forest stage and took command.

In the crystalline Midwest spring of 1689, a French procession moved through the gate in a log palisade; chanting stirred the air, swords caught the sun in splinters. The king's standard with the gold fleur-de-lis was white against the dark forest of the Sioux. The cross was held on high, and a hymn was sung. Indian witnesses stared from gaudily painted faces. Nicolas Perrot, com-manding for the king, listened as Father Joseph James Marest

18

blessed the cross. Then the proclamation was read. The great phrases rang in the air above the tribal delegation: ". . . to manage the interests of Commerce . . . of all the places where he has heretofore been . . . the mouth of the river St. Pierre . . . to take possession for and in the name of the King of the countries and rivers inhabited. . . ."

Nicolas Perrot, with Pierre Charles Le Sueur standing nearby, had claimed, by name, the valley of the Rivière St. Pierre—the Waddapaw Menesotor of the Sioux. He had claimed it all, the fur trade that furnished the means to pay for exploration, the rumored minerals—copper, iron, maybe even gold; he claimed the rivers that might lead to the Western Sea, for the king's colonial empire had been founded on the belief that a water route across North America was still to be discovered.

Eleven years were to pass before Pierre Le Sueur established himself in the Minnesota Valley, but on that day in 1689, on the Upper Mississippi, Perrot's proclamation made it clear that he and his friend Le Sueur already had dipped their paddles in the Minnesota's sky-reflecting waters.

Sturdy Pierre Le Sueur had spent his boyhood along the salmon and trout streams of ancient Artois, and had come to New France with his parents when he was about fifteen. Since he arrived in the period when every boy in Canada dreamed of becoming a *voyageur*, it was little short of inevitable that he should become a fur trader along the streams flowing into the Mississippi. He joined Perrot while still in his twenties.

In 1693, Count Frontenac appointed Le Sueur a commandant, with instructions to maintain peace between the Sioux and the Chippewa in the Wisconsin-Minnesota beaver country. After two years of trading for furs among those tribes, Le Sueur arrived in Montreal accompanied by a group of Chippewa and a rival chief named Teeoshkahtay, the first Sioux ever seen in Lower Canada. Peace might be possible in the region of the Rivière St. Pierre, he thought, if the French supplied the Sioux, as well as the Chippewa, with iron.

As a formal presentation of the Indian embassies was made to Governor Frontenac, Teeoshkahtay threw down a beaver robe and placed upon it twenty-two arrows, symbols of his villages. Pointing out that other tribes received iron tools and ammunition from the French, the Sioux chief asked Frontenac to give his people similar trading privileges. "Le Sueur, who understands our language, and has seen all our villages," said Teeoshkahtay, "will next year inform you what will have been achieved by the Sioux nations represented by these arrows before you."

Peace was important to Le Sueur because he was intent that year on finding copper in the Minnesota Valley. He left Montreal for Paris to get the government's sanction. Court intrigues kept him waiting until 1697 before his license was granted, and luck continued to run against him when, while crossing the Atlantic, he was captured by the English and thrown into prison. His dreamed-of mines continued to remain undiscovered.

It was 1700 before the expedition to exploit the valley got under way. After languishing in England, Le Sueur went again to Paris where he found his influential kinsman, Pierre le Moyne, Sieur d'Iberville, governor of all Louisiana and founder of Biloxi. The two men set sail for the Gulf, and from Iberville's southern colony Le Sueur started for the Sioux country at the end of April, 1700. He had recruited men in his own province of Artois, and in Paris, St. Jean d'Angley, Langres, and La Rochelle. One of the Rochellois was a young ship's carpenter named André Penicaut, who, along with Le Sueur, was to give the first descriptions of the river.

Le Sueur and his crew spent all summer struggling up the Mississippi in two canoes and a small sloop, the first sailboat to enter the Sioux country. The would-be miner knew where he was going, Penicaut reported, because he had been told, on earlier trading ventures, of copper to be found on the Minnesota. The expedition headed for "a stream that empties into the Missicipy from the left"—not far from St. Anthony Falls—"which we named *Rivière St. Pierre*. We then made our way through the mouth of

this river and ascended it for forty leagues and found another river on the left. . . . We entered this and named it *Rivière Verte* on account of clay that, loosened from the copper mines, dissolves and turns the water green." Although it was only the end of autumn, Penicaut added, ice had formed on the stream now called the Blue Earth.

Late though it was for mining, Le Sueur lost no time in building the valley's first fort—a stockade surrounding some log huts and a storehouse in which he piled the merchandise brought for barter with the Indians. He sent some of his men to hunt buffalo, which Penicaut seemed somewhat surprised to find different from the cattle of France. "They are very vicious," he wrote, "especially when the cows are calving. When you hunt buffalo, you must get down wind otherwise they catch your scent a quarter league away and flee." Le Sueur's men profited by this trick. "We killed four hundred buffaloes," the young carpenter said proudly, "which were our provisions for our winter. We put them on scaffolds within our fort after skinning, gutting, and quartering them."

The wilderness establishment was named Fort l'Huillier, in honor of a royal contractor who had helped organize Le Sueur's "Compagnie des Sioux." Yet even before the construction was finished a delegation of Sioux from the east arrived to protest. They said that because the fort had been built in territory belonging to the Sioux of the West, they thought they could not themselves engage in trade with Le Sueur without fear of attack from the Iowas, the Otos, and the western Sioux. Great weepers, these Sioux in time-honored fashion leaned over Le Sueur's head, letting their tears fall on him as they asked him to move to Mendota—the meeting of waters. *"Oueaechisson ouaepanimanabo,"* they cried; "have pity on us."

Le Sueur was wary, but was not moved to change his mind. ("These weepings," a contemporary wrote, "do not weaken their souls. They are very good warriors, and reported the bravest in that region.") Thinking of the copper he hoped to find beneath his feet, Le Sueur argued that it was too late in the season to find another location. He sent the Indian ambassadors off with powder, balls, knives, and an armload of tobacco. "The Sioux are all great smokers," he commented, "but their manner of smoking differs from that of other Indians. There are some Sioux who swallow all the smoke of the tobacco, and others who, after having kept it some time in their mouths, cause it to issue from the nose."

The prospector for copper soon learned that others of his countrymen had found their way into the valley. Seven naked Frenchmen turned up one chilly day. They had been caught by the dissatisfied Sioux of the East, stripped and robbed of all their possessions. Le Sueur recognized one of them—a Canadian named D'Eraque, whom he welcomed as a seasoned trader in the Minnesota country. Adding the newcomers to his party, he sent two of them to invite the Iowas and the Ottawas to establish a village near the fort, hoping that these agriculturally inclined natives might be induced to work in the mine when spring came. The visions of great industry along the river were fast taking shape.

When it turned out that only Sioux hunters, uninterested in steady employment, could be found, Le Sueur settled down to wait for warm weather within the security of his stockade. His men had their first taste of buffalo meat. "In the beginning," Penicaut wrote, "for the first two weeks, we had trouble enough getting used to it: we had diarrhea and fever and became so squeamish that we could not taste it; but little by little our bodies became so accustomed to it that after six weeks there was not one of us who did not eat more than ten pounds of it daily and drink four bowls of the broth. When we got used to that kind of food, it made us quite fat, and there were no more sick among us."

Winter in the valley interested Penicaut at least as much as his employer's dream of ore. "The cold is even more severe in these regions than it is in Canada," he wrote. "During the winter we spent in our fort, we heard trees snap like the reports of guns —split by the rigor of the cold. Ice is as thick as the fresh water in the river, and snow piles up there to a height of five feet on the ground." Penicaut's preoccupation with winter along the Minnesota would be repeated many times when the river had rolled on for another one hundred and fifty years and the settlers began to write of their experiences in the middle of the nineteenth century.

The bears hibernating in trees near the Blue Earth moved Penicaut to give his uninitiated readers in France a vivid description: "Wishing to kill a bear, a person leans a tree against the tree the bear is in, so that it mounts to the hole the bear went through. He climbs up the leaning tree and throws pieces of blazing wood through the hole in the hollow of the bear tree, forcing the animal to come out . . . and when he starts through the hole . . . he backs out as a man would do. As he comes climbing down, he is shot with a gun. This is very dangerous . . . for, although wounded sometimes by three or four shots . . . this animal will not fail to charge the first person he meets, and with one single blow of tooth and claw, he will tear you to pieces instantly. There are bears as big as coach horses. . . ."

Spring came finally, putting an end to such idle observations. Le Sueur assigned twelve men as diggers and four as hunters, and started mining. The strike, according to Penicaut, was "in the beginning of a very long mountain that is on the bank of the river. Boats can go right up to a point underneath the mine. The stratum where the ore is found is a green clay that is a foot and a half thick. Above, there is dirt as solid and as hard as a rock, which is black and charred, like a coal, from the fumes coming from the mine." A little doubt, but not much, crept into the carpenter's account of Le Sueur's project. "If this mine proves to be good, a fine business can be made of it, since the mountain contains more than ten unbroken leagues of the same formation. According to our observations, it seems that during the finest weather in the world there is always a fog on this mountain."

By the twentieth century the only thing approximating a mountain in the part of the valley Penicaut described was a large natural mound, about sixty to seventy-five feet high, which was topped by a few acres of level land that afforded a magnificent view. In 1835, the scoffing British geologist, George W. Featherstonhaugh, found no traces of either the fort Penicaut had helped to build or the copper ore Le Sueur had sought. "A fable" was his unromantic verdict on the testimony of both the ship's carpenter and his enterprising leader.

Penicaut is a convincing corroborator of Le Sueur's own account. The young artisan later traveled in French Louisiana for twenty-one years. He was known by Iberville, Bienville, Cadillac, and other prominent men; and his narrative has proved to be reliable in describing his role in the building of Biloxi, Natchitoches, Natchez, and New Orleans.

Penicaut did not assert that what Le Sueur and his men found was actually copper. "In twenty-two days," he wrote, "we took from this mine more than thirty thousand pounds of ore. We selected only four thousand pounds of the finest of it, which M. Le Sueure, who was well informed in such matters, sent to the fort; later, it was shipped to France."

After pointedly noting that he had not learned what happened when the ore was tested, he described the trade with the Indians who greeted them on their return to the fort from the mine. Le Sueur devoted a week that spring to barter, acquiring among many other pelts more than four hundred beaver robes, each made of nine skins stitched together. Preparing to leave, he told the Sioux that he was putting D'Eraque in charge of future trade, and that he expected them to settle down near Fort L'Huillier and remember their commitments to the French. Promising to send D'Eraque two thousand pounds of lead and powder, he loaded the sloop with four thousand pounds of "that green clay we had taken from the mine," filled three canoes with furs, and set off for Biloxi with Penicaut and a dozen men.

The venture at Fort L'Huillier collapsed totally in the spring of 1702 when a war party of Fox Indians chased D'Eraque out of the valley. Angry that the French were trading with the Sioux, the Foxes came shrieking in and murdered three men. D'Eraque was out of ammunition, out of supplies, and he chose to abandon the valley's first fort, stopping only to hide what remained of his trade goods.

By this time Le Sueur had sailed off to France. No report of what the chemists of the time thought of his ore has been found, but George Featherstonhaugh dismissed it as "a silicate of iron of a bluish green colour." Le Sueur found consolation for the failure on the Minnesota when he was named lieutenant general of the jurisdiction of Mobile. But in 1704 he was dead. He had contracted yellow fever on a transatlantic voyage that brought the first marriageable French girls to Louisiana.

The saga of Fort L'Huillier evoked the curiosity of settlers who came to make the valley their own in the nineteenth century. There were many stories about the brief French occupation, and most of them were fanciful. Perhaps the most persistent tale told of "an ancient and magnificent cave . . . hewn into the solid rock in the sides of the high bluff." Of course the entrance to the cave was so small that a man would have to crawl in on hands and knees. Once underground he would find "an immense chamber, whose sides and ceilings glitter with the sheen of a peculiar metal." The classic skeleton stood guard over a chest that held the French valuables hidden by D'Eraque. Sometimes the story included heaps of other treasure, concealed by Indians. And always the spinner of the yarn ended on the sad note that soon after his exploration a landslide had covered up the entrance.

But no authentic vestiges of the two winters spent by the fur traders were found until the summer of 1904 when a local committee was enlisted to explore the site near the junction of the Blue Earth and the Minnesota. The members paced the terrain in studious demeanor, sometimes holding aloft a black umbrella to ward off the Midwest sun. Among them was Judge Thomas Hughes, who noted in his report: "As the fort consisted of three or four log cabins inclosed by a log palisade, the timber used in its construction must have been conveniently obtained, since Le Sueur's party had no means to transport it except by hand." Hughes was deadly serious as he collated all the descriptions to be found in the Le Sueur and Penicaut narratives.

On a farm then owned by J. H. Ray, Hughes and his friends found a steep grass-covered hill on which grew a scattering of burr oaks. Here, it was noted, early settlers remembered noticing indications of an old excavation, and there was a bed of blue or green clay, which the Indians had used for pigment a couple of miles farther up the stream. Perhaps even a trained archaeological team could have come no closer to pinpointing the site, considering the lack of physical evidence. "In fact," Hughes summed up, "the top of this mound tallies exactly with all the data we possess regarding the fort's location, while no other spot tallies with any of them."

But that was not to be the last word on Le Sueur's enterprise on the river. Three years later Judge Hughes looked into an accidental discovery made by a Blue Earth County farmer. William Mitchell dug into a mound on his farm one day in June 1907 and turned up seventeen headless human skeletons." Two flint arrowheads were found among the bones, and the careful judge drew the inference from the decapitations and the presence of arrowheads that the deed had been done by some savage foe. The bodies, he observed, had been buried in dug graves and laid out in the manner of European burial. "Each body had been laid on its back, with the arms close to its sides and both legs stretched side by side. . . . The dug graves, the laying out of the bodies, and the absence of aboriginal implements and trinkets, indicate very strongly that the burial was the work of white men."

The good judge marshaled his facts to present an airtight courtroom argument. The bones "looked very old." The soil was "well adapted for their preservation." In the century preceding the find, soldiers, Indian agents, fur traders and missionaries— "each furnishing regular written reports"—had found nothing to explain the mass burial. The incident involved too many people, the judge said, to have happened in the nineteenth century "and we not know of it."

With his ready pen the judge reconstructed the episode: A warring band of Foxes and their allies had ambushed the Sioux who were trading at the fort. Then the victors had carried away the heads of their foes as trophies, and Le Sueur's garrison of miners had gone out with their picks and shovels and buried the bodies. Hughes asserted that "even common humanity aside from friendship would dictate to the simple miners the propriety of giving their red friends the rite of burial." None of D'Eraque's men were among those buried, he reasoned, because they all reported in at Iberville's colony in the south. But Hughes noted that other traders frequented the fort, and the three Frenchmen reported by Penicaut to have been killed might have been another incentive for the burial.

In thus analyzing the mass burial, discovered more than two centuries after Le Sueur became disenchanted with his Minnesota Valley "copper," Judge Hughes said he had arrived at the only theory which could fully accord with all the facts. His logic is beguiling: "Such a massacre, so close to Fort L'Huillier, and inspired partly as a protest to its establishment, would naturally terrify the miners and give good reason for their sudden abandonment of it."

The good judge wrote the final chapter in the chronicle of the *voyageur's* quest for copper in the valley of the Minnesota. Thousands of travelers on U.S. 14—who cut through the valley at the great bend where Le Sueur started his shipment of blue earth on its journey to France—would be amazed to learn that any but Indians traced Minnesota waters before the nineteenth century.

4

ROGERS SENDS A RANGER
TOWARD THE WESTERN SEA

And westward took my way to see the sun. . . .

—WILLIAM WORDSWORTH

AFTER THE French and Indian War, while Captain Jonathan Carver tarried "at the mouth of the River St. Pierre," he made a disconcerting discovery. The French had begun to convince the Indians that the English, "who were but a petty people," had stolen the savage land from "their Great Father the king of France whilst he was asleep; but that he would soon awake, and take them again under his protection."

Along the river itself, however, the French never had shown much official interest. Since the departure of Le Sueur and D'Eraque the river Sioux had been visited only by vagrant *coureurs de bois,* the free-lancing Montreal traders who took to the wilderness life like ducks to water. One other traveler claimed to have seen the country. He was a soldier-explorer named Louis Armand de Lom d'Arce, Baron de Lahontan—a frontier Münchausen. In his *New Voyages to North America,* first issued in 1703, Lahontan did not mention the Sioux by name; he told—in an account liberally dosed with fiction—of a journey along a river peopled by "great nations" of Indians. He called his stream the Rivière Longue.

Because Lahontan said he had followed the long river for five hundred miles, readers of his book for a generation believed that he had found the much coveted River of the West, the water route to the Pacific. Historians puzzled over his descriptions, and could not make them fit with knowledge of the Mississippi tributaries that by the eighteenth century was well established. Lahontan's stream came out of the west below the Falls of St. Anthony, neither crooked enough nor short enough to coincide with either of the known rivers in the region he described. Finally, in the nineteenth century, there was an uneasy agreement that Rivière Longue (if it had any existence outside Lahontan's imagination) compared most closely with the Cannon River, just south of the Minnesota. But it may have been—as others fervently argued—the latter.

As he paused at the river's mouth in 1766, Jonathan Carver pondered the Lahontan problem. The possibility of a Northwest Passage, of a water highway to the Orient, stirred many men. Fifty years before, the great map maker Guillaume Delisle had received from an amateur geographer a letter asserting that the writer had the word of La Motte Cadillac that "if the Rivière St. Pierre is ascended to its source explorers will, according to all appearance, find in the highland another river leading to the Western Ocean." The letter writer admitted to having "tormented" the authorities in Canada in his enthusiasm for the accomplishment of a Northwest Passage.

Increasing conflict between the French and the English frustrated many such dreams of finding an inland waterway. The Minnesota River remained unexplored. When at last the French forfeited New France and the river became part of the Louisiana Territory ceded to Spain, there was little interest from the new owners. It was the British, moving relentlessly westward from the Atlantic, who fixed their sights on the region drained by the Minnesota.

A reward of £20,000 for the discovery of the Northwest Passage was offered by the Admiralty in London. In Detroit—after fighting his way through Pontiac's siege—the audacious Robert Rogers lost interest in his Rangers and began to dream of greater glory. Appointed governor of Mackinac, he tried first for a royal subsidy to explore the West, and then, with the encouragement of influential men he had met in London, he determined to make the search for the Western Sea a private enterprise.

Returning from London, Rogers hired a former Ranger, Jonathan Carver, who was a New England cobbler with a knack for drawing maps. Rogers had projected a transcontinental journey, and Carver was sent ahead "to ascertain the Breadth of that vast continent . . . from the Atlantic to the Pacific Ocean, in its broadest part between 43 and 46 Degrees Northern Latitude." Carver said he was convinced that this would greatly facilitate the discovery of a Northwest Passage, that it would open a passage for "conveying intelligence to China," and that men fortunate enough to succeed would reap "exclusive of the national advantages that must ensue, Emoluments beyond their most sanguine expectations." Carver was not averse to becoming either wealthy or famous. He headed with high hopes for the river lying between the 44th and 45th parallels.

Carver, an aging adventurer in his fifty-seventh year, was provided by Rogers with an allowance of eight shillings a day "together with other incidental Charges" when he set out from Mackinac. Heavy-set, double-chinned, with large, strange, bulbous eyes, and a florid complexion, he had left behind a wife and seven children and a record of service both as a selectman in Weymouth, Massachusetts and as a soldier who had fought with Wolfe at Quebec and with Amherst at Montreal. Accompanied by several *coureurs de bois,* Carver began his journey to the Mississippi tributary that would take him west.

On November 14, 1766, he slipped his canoe into the Minnesota's waters. "Ten miles below the Falls of St. Anthony," Carver wrote, "the River St. Pierre, called by the natives the *Waddapawmensotor,* falls into the Mississippi from the west. It is not mentioned by Father Hennipin, although a large fair river: this ommission I conclude, must have proceeded from a small island that is situated exactly at its entrance, by which the sight of it is intercepted." Although he was unhampered by hostile Sioux, as Hennepin had been, Carver confessed: "I should not have discovered this river myself, had I not taken a view, when I was searching for it, from the highlands opposite, which rise to a great height."

For eleven days he explored the country on foot and found it extremely beautiful. He was delighted by its "many gentle accents, which in the summer are covered with the finest verdure, and interspersed with little groves, that give a pleasing variety to the prospect." He described the river as broad and deep; when he had paddled along it for three days he discovered a small branch to which he was pleased to give his own name. Forty miles farther upstream Carver entered the Blue Earth country, passing the spot where Le Sueur had dug for copper. He had seen neither the account of Penicaut nor that of Le Sueur, and he arrived at his own conclusions. He reported that the country abounded in blue clay that served the Indians for paint. "Those that can get the blue clay," he said, "paint themselves very much with it; particularly when they are about to begin their sports and pastimes. It is also esteemed by them a mark of peace, as it has a resemblance of a blue sky, which with them is a symbol of [peace]." Making these observations as his men nosed the canoe westward, Carver at last sighted, not far from where the valley now protects the city of New Ulm, three canoes paddled by "Nadouwessies of the Plains." He was anxious to meet them, to learn all they might know about the Northwest Passage.

The plainsmen, however, were less than eager to reciprocate. They paddled frantically toward shore, leaping overboard "with precipitation," and abandoned their canoes to the river current. A few minutes later another group appeared, and seemed equally disturbed by Carver's strange canoe. Proceeding with caution, Carver took the side of the river opposite to that on which the Indians had landed, reassuring himself that "the pipe of Peace which was fixed at the head of my canoe, and the English colours that were flying at the stern, would prove my security."

Paddling around a sharp bend, he saw spread out on the prairie a village of many tepees "and more than a thousand Indians" whose friendship, at a glance, seemed in doubt. As Carver recounted the incident, there was only one possible course of action. "Being now nearly opposite them," he wrote, "I ordered my men to pull directly over, as I was willing to convince the Indians by such a step, that I placed some confidence in them."

Even though these were Sioux—and prairie Sioux at that— the tactic worked. Whether they mistook him for a trader loaded down with guns, blankets, and other articles for barter, Carver didn't bother to explain. As soon as he stepped from his canoe, he said, the Sioux spread out the welcome mat. Two chiefs came forward and "presented their hands" to the white stranger. Then "amidst the astonished multitude, who had most of them never seen a white man before," the explorer was led to a tent where the pipe of peace was lighted, and everybody smoked. "Having gratified the curiosity of the common people, their wonder abated, and ever afterward they treated me with great respect."

Carver stayed through the winter—stretching his legs in long walks, searching the western periphery of the prairie. He was fascinated by the endless perspective that glazed the horizon in the months when snow lay on the flat land like a frozen sea, like the vast expanse of water for which he searched. Did he find the promontory known as Old Redstone, the lone survivor of the deluge, from which he might have looked west, tracing in his mind the curl of the Minnesota's beginning? Perhaps he walked with one of the chiefs who, he said, became his friends, combing the horizon for the route to Cathay, the Northwest Passage. The prairie horizon in winter, even more than in the long-grass months of summer, is beckoning. Beyond lies the dream most sought.

"I have reason to believe," said Carver, "that the River St. Pierre and the Messorie . . . take their rise in the same neighborhood; and this within the space of a mile." This great misjudgment was not based on snow blindness. The Sioux, wrote the explorer, told him everything they knew. His ear was cocked for any "information relative to the chief point I had constantly in view": Did the Minnesota lead to the Western Sea? He hunted with men who should have known. The northernmost branch of the Minnesota, his informants made him believe, "rises from a number of lakes near the shining mountains." As Carver worked it out on the map he later published, the mountains that shone were the backbone of America that was yet to be discovered—the Rockies.

Winter on the prairie could be bitter enough for an active man to stay within the warmth of a tepee banked with hay and buffalo furs. Around the central fire, with smoke drifting reluctantly toward the peak and the windy cold above, the talk could swing to battle prowess, and Carver said that he regaled his hosts with many a lively anecdote involving himself and General Wolfe in the siege of Quebec. He listened to some even more gory accounts in return. He did, however—and who can doubt him?—make friends. Did the Minnesota, he asked his fireside cronies, lead on to the Western Sea? In answer, the Sioux drew maps on birch bark with charcoal taken from the hearth. "Their sketches are made in a rude manner," the New England cartographer reported rather primly, "but they seem to give as just an idea of a country, although the plan is not so exact, as more experienced draughtsmen could do."

In April, accompanied by three hundred Sioux friends, Carver took these sketches and pointed his canoe downriver, intending to pick up supplies promised him by Rogers. "At this season these bands annually go to the Great Cave," he wrote, "to hold a grand council with all the other bands; wherein they settle their operations for the ensuing year." Among the delegation was a burial party, carrying the dead to traditional ground at the river's mouth. As they passed Mendota, Carver noted a promontory "as white as the driven snow," which he thought might "have a very noble effect in architecture." Across from the snow-white hill, Carver edged his canoe around the island that had intercepted Hennepin's view of the Minnesota, and crossed the Mississippi to the opposite bluff where the glacier had lashed the terrain.

Here was the "remarkable cave of an amazing depth." It has ever since borne Carver's name, although his hosts called it the Dwelling of the Great Spirit. Carver described a lake within the cave, "the water of which is transparent, and extends to an un-searchable distance." When Carver threw a pebble with his

"utmost strength," it caused "an astonishing and horrible noise." Less playfully, the explorer then joined the Indian council and made a long speech to the Sioux in their own language.

He quoted himself: ". . . the other day when you were camping on the river of sky-tinted water, the black clouds, the wind, the fire, the stupendous noise, the horrible cracks, and the trembling of the earth . . . then alarmed you, and gave you reason to think your gods were angry with you; not unlike these are the warlike implements of the English when they are fighting the battles of their great King." After drawing this picture of a thunderstorm in the valley, Carver promised to tell George III of the tribe's desire for traders, and agreed to escort several Indian ambassadors to Mackinac, assuring them "a straight road, smooth waters, and a clear sky." In response, the Sioux chief was very grateful, and said he wanted the king to know how much the tribesmen hoped to be counted among the monarch's good children, and how great was their wish for "such fine things as we need" from traders who would live among them. Thus, said the chief, the hearts of his young men, their wives and children would be made glad.

After this exchange of affection and desire, Carver set down his view of the valley in general: "The River St. Pierre . . . flows through a most delightful country, abounding with all the necessaries of life, that grow spontaneously; and with a little cultivation it might be made to produce even the luxuries of life. Wild rice grows here in great abundance; and every part is filled with trees bending under their loads of fruits, such as plums, grapes, and apples; the meadows are covered with hops, and many sorts of vegetables; whilst the ground is stored with useful roots, with angelica, spikenard, and ground-nuts as large as hens eggs. At a little distance from the sides of the river are eminences, from which you have views that cannot be exceeded even by the most beautiful of those I have already described; amidst these are delightful groves, and such amazing quantities of maples, that they would produce sugar sufficient for any number of inhabitants."

Here at Mendota he also made notes on the Indian custom of burying their dead in communal mounds, and so gracefully recorded a death dirge he heard that Schiller—after reading Carver's book—turned it into verse that later was translated from the German by Sir Edward Bulwer-Lytton. The first two stanzas give a glimpse of the Indian mysticism that Carver had tried to interpret:

> See on his mat—as if of yore,
>   All life-like sits he here!
> With that same aspect which he wore
>   When light to him was dear.
>
> But where the right hand's strength? and where
>   The breath that loved to breathe
> To the Great Spirit, aloft in air,
>   The peace pipe's lusty wreath?

At the end of the Indian proceedings, Carver discovered that the promised supplies had not arrived, and he went south to find out why. Enroute he met Captain James Tute, whom Rogers had named to guide the Northwest Passage expedition in a more northerly direction. Together, the two former Rangers advanced to the Chippewa country, intending to strike west from Lake Winnipeg. But on the shore of Lake Superior they learned that Rogers had been accused of exceeding his authority and that they could expect no further support. With the prospect of hostility rather than help from the northern Indians, the party disbanded. Carver slowly worked his way east, abandoned his wife and children in Boston, and went to England in the hope of interesting new sponsors while he wrote his *Travels through the Interior Parts of North America, in the Years 1766, 1767, and 1768.*

The try for the Western Sea by way of the Minnesota was not quite over. Robert Rogers made a second petition for backing to find the "River Ourigan," the fabled River of the West that was so vital a part of his Northwest Passage. He planned to go to the source of the Minnesota River, "to cross a twenty-mile Portage into a branch of the Missouri, and to stem that northwesterly to the Source: To cross thence a Portage of about thirty Miles into the great River Ourigan; to follow this great River through a vast and most poplous Tract of Indian Country to the [Pacific]." The intrepid Ranger might have realized his scheme had sponsors been as courageous as he. The Minnesota was navigable by canoe to Big Stone Lake, where a portage of less than fifty miles might have been made to the Big Sioux River, an affluent of the mighty Missouri. He might have followed the portage made later by Lewis and Clark from the Big Muddy to the Columbia, the fabled "Ourigan."

Because Rogers soon was in disgrace, Carver wrote his book and did not mention his former leader. And soon he himself was in disgrace. The fact that he had quoted liberally—and sometimes without credit—from the books of Lahontan and Father Charlevoix cast unearned discredit on descriptions of what he had actually seen. In giving the first detailed account of the Minnesota country, he became the subject of controversy. He settled in England and tried to beat down his critics. He married again and fathered a child named Martha. He talked constantly of new expeditions. In an appendix to the third edition of his book he summed up his thoughts on the great quest. He had evoked the interest of a member of parliament named Richard Whitworth, who "designed to have pursued nearly the same route that I did . . . to have proceeded up the River St. Pierre, and from thence up a branch of the River Messorie, till having discovered the source of the Oregan . . . he would have sailed down that river to the [Pacific]."

Whitworth was to be as frustrated as Carver because the American Revolution had begun, and the war "put a stop," said Carver, "to an enterprize that promised to be of inconceivable advantage to the British dominions." But though no one was to find the Western Sea by way of the Minnesota Valley, the book Carver wrote about his days on the river went through thirty-two editions—one of the most popular narratives of adventure ever written. That scholars of the day undertook to minimize the book's worth may seem a little mysterious, or it may be explained by the persistent notion that nothing so popular could be authentic. Before the third edition appeared in 1781 Carver died in want—and left behind another mystery begun at the mouth of the Minnesota.

Forty years after his death a deed was read before a committee of the United States Senate:

"To Jonathan Carver, a chief under the most mighty and potent George the Third, King of the English and other nations, the fame of whose courageous warriors have reached our ears, and has been more fully told us by our good brother Jonathan aforesaid, whom we rejoice to see come among us, and bring us good news from his country. We, chiefs of the Naudowissies, who have hereto set our seals, do by these presents for ourselves and heirs for ever, in return for the many presents, and other good services done by the said Jonathan to ourselves and allies, give, grant, and convey to him the said Jonathan, and to his heirs and assigns for ever, the whole of a certain tract or territory of land, bounded as follows: (viz.) from the fall of St. Anthony, running on the east banks of the Mississippi, nearly south-east, as far as the south end of Lake Pepin, where the Chippeway river joins the Mississippi, and from thence eastward five days travel, accounting twenty English miles per day, and from thence north six days travel, at twenty English miles per day, and from thence again to the fall of St. Anthony, on a direct straight line. We do for ourselves, heirs, and assigns, for ever, give unto the said Jonathan, his heirs and assigns, for ever, all the said lands, with all the trees, rocks, and rivers therein, reserving for ourselves and heirs the sole liberty of hunting and fishing on land not planted or improved by the said Jonathan, his heirs and assigns, to which we have affixed our respective seals, at the great cave, May the first, one thousand seven hundred and sixty-seven.

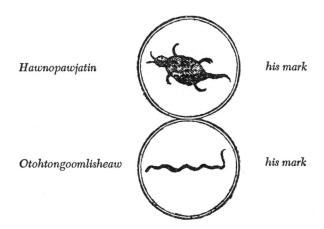

Hawnopawjatin .... *his mark*

Otohtongoomlisheaw .... *his mark*

Nothing had been heard of this grant of some two hundred thousand square miles of land until Martha Carver was married after her father's death. A London mercantile firm then bargained with her for the rights to the remarkable deed. In January, 1806, the affair became a matter of public record when Samuel Peters appeared to testify before a Senate committee in the interests of all the Carver heirs—both his English and American families. Peters managed to keep the case open for two decades. On January 29, 1822, the House of Representatives sent a formal request to President Monroe for all available information. The President asserted that because Carver had been a British officer he was forbidden by a royal proclamation from accepting any such gift. An investigation among the Sioux brought the statement that no chiefs bearing the names signed to the deed were known. The petition of the family was tabled. But for fifty years "Carver's Grant" continued to be outlined on maps, delineating an area encompassing the present sites of Minneapolis and St.

Paul—a chunk of real estate that would have made Carver's heirs fabulously wealthy. Confidence men found the story made to their order, and they sold shares in the grant to the unsuspecting. Even in the twentieth century the governors of Minnesota occasionally have been required to deal with the claims of those persuaded to invest in an unexplained mystery more than a century and a half old.

5

PETER POND—
"NOT ENEY THING
EXTRODNEREY"

Villon among the birds is he,
A bold, bright rover . . .

—LOUISE DRISCOLL

JONATHAN CARVER, said Peter Pond, "gave a good a Count of the Small Part of the Western Countrey he saw But when he a Leudes to Hearsase he flies from the facts in two Maney Instances." Carver's account of the Minnesota Valley was something Pond might have judged more objectively, for he himself spent two trading seasons on the river while his fellow New Englanders were staging the Boston Tea Party and Patrick Henry was calling for liberty or death.

Peter Pond had had his war. "From the fifth gineration downward we were all waryers," he wrote, declaring that at sixteen he had exercised a "Strong Desire to be a Solge" when he volunteered for service in the French and Indian War. When peace came, Pond's father was among the first Englishmen who went west to take over the fur trade the French had been forced to leave. Young Pond was soon in the West himself, a master fur trader by the time he was thirty-one. But though his keen intel-

42

ligence had no trouble learning French and several Indian dialects, he would not bother with the regulations of written language. He may have been the most persistent phonetic speller who ever lived.

He described his journey to the Minnesota Valley thus: "I went In to the Entearer Part of the Countrey first to Mishlemackanack from thenst to the Mississippey and up Sant Peters River & into the Plaines Betwene the Mississippey & the Miseura and Past my Winter among the Nattawaysease on such food as they made youse of themselves which was Verey darteyaly Cooked."

Aside from the flamboyance of Peter Pond's orthography, his memoirs, set down after his retirement, are unique for the way in which the narrative was saved for posterity. In 1868 the manuscript was found in a kitchen (of Pond's nephew, a former governor of Connecticut) where the housekeeper was using it to start her morning fires. Mrs. Nathan Gillet Pond stepped into the kitchen just in time to retrieve the early episodes of Pond's fur trading days along the Minnesota; the descriptions of his later years on the Canadian frontier already had gone up in smoke.

But not Peter Pond's vitriolic dismissal of Carver's visit to the valley. "His Hole tour I with One Canoe Well Maned Could make in Six weeks," said Pond thirty years after the event. A century later, when these words were read in his legible hand they served to give new comfort to Carver's detractors. Yet it is now almost two hundred years since Carver wintered on the Minnesota, and careful comparison of his observations with those of others of the period indicate that he was a trustworthy reporter of the "Western Countrey he saw."

By the time he saw the Western Country, the Europeans' name for the Minnesota had been anglicized, like many things in the wilderness; the river was being called the St. Peter's, and it may even have had a degree of fame among those fur traders who might have known Jonathan Carver. Pond, for one, does not indicate (although both were in the region at the same time) that he met Carver at Detroit or Mackinac, or anywhere else; nor does he explain what led him to the Minnesota Valley. He could only have heard about Carver's exploits through word of mouth; he could not have read Carver's book because it was not to be published until five years after Pond's first sight of the St. Peter's. Still, irascible Peter Pond pursued the fashion of belittling his predecessor when, in his bitter old age, he wrote his memoirs. On his first trip, "as we Past up the St. Peter's River about fourteen miles we Stopt to Sea Carvers Hut," wrote Pond. "It was a Log House about Sixteen feet long Covered with Bark —with a fireplase But one Room and no flore. This was the extent of his travels."

The disdain seems all too easy. If in later years he got around to reading Carver's *Travels,* Pond missed the fact that nowhere in the text does Carver say he actually built any sort of shelter; his account gives the impression that he was the guest of the Sioux. Carver wrote that he "met with every accommodation their manner of living could afford"; and, in describing his departure, he said he "left the habitations of these hospitable Indians." Aside from this, Carver drew tepees on his map to show where "the Author Winter'd in 1766."

Perhaps Pond found it hard to believe that another might have found the Sioux more hospitable than he himself did. Seven years after Carver, Pond started up the Mississippi from Prairie du Chien in October, 1773, and proceeded "sloley" because, he made clear, he wanted to let the Sioux "Git Into the Plains"; he wanted no trouble with them "as they are Bad Pay Marsters." He entered the St. Peter's and paddled up it "as far as we thought Best Without Seaing an Indian Except what we toock with us."

He passed through country radiant with fall foliage and generous with wild food. "The banks of Ye River aforded plenty of Crab Apels which was Verey Good when the frost had touched them at a Sutabel tim." The woods were full of deer and bear; ducks and geese were easy targets on the water; they had plenty of flour, tea, coffee, sugar, butter, spirits and wine, and they "faird as well as Voigers." Pond observed the land and timber and pronounced it "Exalent—fit for Eney Improvement." He noted the glacial walls of the valley and picked a high bluff on which to winter so that his party would "not be Overflone in the Spring at the Brakeing up of the Ice."

On December 2, with the snow deep around his wilderness post, Pond told a couple of passing Indians that he was ready for business. His trade goods were snugly under cover and he was more than willing to exchange them for any furs the native trappers might bring. Business was good in January. Indians began turning up with armloads of skins and furs—beaver, otter, deer, fox, wolf, and raccoon; they also brought "Dried and Grean Meet." But the wily Pond soon discovered that there were tricks he hadn't learned about the fur trade. "I had a french man for my Nighbor Who had Winterd among the Nottawase Several Winters in this River," and the neighbor was therefore well known by the various native bands. As Pond began to realize that his rival was doing better than he, he said it was not to be wondered at "as he had Bin Long a Quanted."

Pond's French friend—long acquainted with the savages—had learned to put out bait for his clients. Indians, especially women, said the Frenchman, liked to steal; so he habitually left small trinkets, beads, knives, needles, or bells, on his counter. "For the sake of Stealing these trifels," Pond reported, "thay Com to Sea him and what thay Had for trade he Got." As a good Yankee, Pond put the idea to use immediately, and soon he was doing as well as the cheerful *coureur de bois*. In other ways, however, Pond found little to report on his snowbound life. "Well," he put down in his manuscript, "thare was not Eney thing Extrodnerey Hapened Dureing the Winter."

The profits of that season may not have been extraordinary, but they were substantial enough to bring Pond back to the Minnesota after he had disposed of his furs in Prairie du Chien. He had counted there one hundred and thirty canoes from Mackinac, and others from New Orleans. French-Spanish com-

binations from St. Louis had been formed to compete with the
English, and their traders would soon be on the Minnesota.
Peter Pond was not a man to retreat from any rich territory until
he had acquired all the furs he wanted.

At the same time, he said in his memoirs, news came of rising
unrest between the Sioux and their arch enemies, the Chippewa.
In counsel with Pond and other traders, the British commander
at Fort Detroit in August 1774 agreed to call the tribes to a meeting the following summer. The traders put together six belts of
wampum to be presented to influential chiefs, and "the counsel
with ye commander thought proper to give me ye charge of thre
belts," said Pond, "and traders to Lake Superior were charged
with others. The import of the bisness was that I should send out
carrears into the planes and—all the chefes to repare to my
tradeing house on the banks of the St. Peters river in the spring."
Pond was to escort the Indians to Mackinac for the next year's
council, but first he was to see that the chiefs "hear and obsarve"
the contents of a proclamation issued by the commander in the
interest of peace. The chiefs were to "look at the belts" and, in
accepting the gift, understand the obligation to maintain peace
and thereby help the English fur trade.

Back on the Minnesota, the Yankee trader was scarcely settled in when he saw a horse galloping along the river bluff. The
horseman was a chief of the western Sioux, with a stern invitation to Pond to travel two hundred miles up the river where the
Yankton tribe was eager to offer their furs in exchange for
European goods. To make sure that his invitation was accepted,
the stalwart chief told Pond he would ride along the banks while
the trader and his two men paddled their canoe and its burden
of trading items. With the threats of snow in the air and ice in
the river, the journey took nine days. On a "larg Sand flat by the
River Side . . . about three miles from the Indians camp and it
beaing weat weather and cold I incampt and turned up my canoe
which made us a grand shelter. At night it began to snow and
frease and blowe hard." The wind scooped "the Canew up in the

Air—Leat hir fall on the frozen flat and Broke hir in Pecis. I was then in a Sad Situation," Pond recalled.

Help came about noon when "I Perseaved a Number of the Natives on Ye Opaset Sid of the River Aproaching me—Sum on Horsback—Others on foot." The Indians forded the river, loaded the trade goods on their horses, and the combined party marched on toward the Yankton village. When they stopped to rest, Pond observed four newcomers trudging across the prairie, bearing a beaver blanket ornamented with painted designs, and another carrying a handsome peace pipe "Verey finely Drest with Differant feathers [and] Panted Haire." The four blanket bearers sat down while the man with the pipe lighted it "with a Grate dele of Sarremoney," pointing the stem to the north, the south, the east, the west, then to the sky, and finally to the earth. Pond found only signs of friendship as they smoked the calumet in turn.

"Then thay Lade me Down on the Blanket—One Hold of Each Corner and Cared me to the Camp in a Lodg among a Verey Venarable Asembley of Old men." Pond was seated in the place of honor beside an earthen hearth, raised about five inches and about five feet by two and a half feet in dimension, over which hung three brass kettles of simmering food. After the Sioux had copiously wept the characteristic tears over Pond's head, an old man fed him three ceremonial spoonsful of gruel made from corn meal. Given a bark dish and a spoon carved from a buffalo horn, the trader then joined his hosts in a feast, the first of three meals he had to eat in rapid succession as he was carried on a blanket from one lodge to another.

At four o'clock he was brought to the lodge set aside for trading, where he found his two clerks and his merchandise. In the excitement of the various feasts, Pond had lost track of the man who had urged him to come. "The Chefe who Came Down the River to Envite me . . . Gave me to understand that my trade was to Begin at Sundown But he was absent When thay Compelled me to Begin Befoar time." Six spearmen had been assigned as guards for the trade goods, but "ye Croud was so Grate" the guard had to be doubled before Pond could continue his business in safety. "My People ware Bystanders—Not a word —Not a Word to Say or Acte." At sundown the lost chief finally turned up and took charge. For what Pond called "imperdence" the chief ordered a lance thrown at an overly eager Indian, and there was then a marked improvement in the general behavior. Pond kept at his bargaining table until there was the hint of dawn across the river and the Indians had exhausted their supply of pelts.

Having no canoe, he decided to cache his newly acquired furs, and he set out to walk two hundred miles through the frozen valley to his trading post. When spring came he sent his clerks to retrieve the result of his bargaining. "The men cut down small saplens and made the frames of two boats—sowed the skins [of buffalo they had killed] togather and made bottoms to thare frames." They caulked their skin crafts with tallow "which made them tite anuf to bring the furs down to me where I had canoes to receive them." The winter on the Minnesota had been a rewarding one. Pond recorded that his profit for the season ending with the spring of 1775 was almost twenty thousand dollars.

He had good reason to speak well of the valley. "On account of the face of the Countrey . . . the Entervales of the River St. Peter is Exsalent . . . and the Soile thin and lite." He betrayed his ineptitude as an angler by continuing: "The River is Destatute of fish, But the Wood and Meadowes have an abundans of Annamels, Sum turkeas; Buffaloes are Verey Plentey, the Common Dear are Plentey, and Larg. . . ." He counted many red deer and moose, "Espeshaley the former. I have seen forty Killed in One day By Surrounding a drove on a low spot by the River side in the Winter Season. Raccoons are Verey Large. No Snakes But Small ones which are not Pisenes. Wolves are Plentey—They follow the Buffaloes and often Destroy thare Young and Olde Ones. In Winter the Natives near the Mouth of the River Rase Plentey of Corn for thare [principal food]."

Peter Pond turned toward Mendota for the last time in April, 1775. "The Spring is now advansing fast. The Chefes Cuming with a Number of the Natives to Go with me to Mackenac to Sea and Hear what thare farther Had to Say. . . ." On this inconclusive note the manuscript was retrieved from the kitchen fire that had consumed the narrative of Pond's northern experience. From the Minnesota he had gone on to become one of the founders of the great North West Company and to inspire the youthful Alexander Mackenzie to complete the first overland crossing of northern America—not by way of the Minnesota and the Missouri, but through the hazardous peaks of the Canadian Rockies.

Peter Pond mapped the unknown lands through which he traveled. After the Revolutionary War, a boundary commission sought to draw a line between the United States and British Canada and to remove English traders from the Minnesota Valley and other fur regions in the Old Northwest. One of Pond's maps, it is said, was used by Benjamin Franklin when he helped to settle the boundary dispute.

6

"SOME LIQUOR
TO CLEAR YOUR THROATS"

And still from solemn councils set
  On every hill and plain,
The smoke of many a calumet
  Ascends. . . .

—JOHN BANNISTER TABB

IN SPITE OF the predilections of map makers, the Minnesota
flowed on through the wide walls of its glacial valley—known
intimately only by traders who moved across the Great Lakes
from Canada or from the depleted fur country of New England.
Three hundred miles below the river's mouth lay the village of
Prairie du Chien, thriving at the turn of the eighteenth century
with a population of almost four hundred and a firm hold on the
Canadian fur trade. Farther south was roistering St. Louis, a
French-Spanish boom town that sent its flatboats north with trade
goods for barter at Prairie du Chien.

Noting these towns as he pored over his charts, aware that the
Canadian British remained south of the Great Lakes in spite of
the Revolutionary War, Thomas Jefferson examined the vast expanse of the sprawling Louisiana Territory. When it became
apparent that Napoleon and his Spanish allies needed money for
war with England, Jefferson moved quickly. The Louisiana Pur-

50

chase made the rivers flowing east into the Mississippi part of the United States; and it made the confluence of the Minnesota and Mississippi a vital point in plans for defense of the newly acquired territory. The mouth of the Minnesota commanded the headwaters of the Mississippi, just as south of it the Missouri led the way west to the Pacific, and the Wichita and Red rivers probed toward Spanish holdings.

Jefferson sent Lewis and Clark northwest from St. Louis, and William Dunbar into the Arkansas country; in 1805—as part of the same three-pronged plan of exploration—a United States Army expedition pushed its way up the Mississippi under orders to persuade the Indians to approve the establishment of military posts "at the mouth of the river St. Pierre . . . and [at] every other critical point which may fall under your observation."

It was the end of September—the first year of Jefferson's second administration. It was the week that Merriwether Lewis and William Clark were stranded, starved and sick, along the banks of Idaho's Clearwater River, not yet close to the "Ocian in view" that Jefferson had sent them to report on. Six months later, again implementing the President's instructions, Captain Clark wrote a letter to Hugh Heney, a trader among the Sioux, in which he urged Heney to counteract the influence of the British trading on the Minnesota River. The newly acquired Louisiana Territory was to be made American in every sense.

On the last day of that golden autumn week Lieutenant Zebulon Montgomery Pike, twenty-six years old and a veteran of eleven years in the United States Army, stopped his Minnesota expedition at the island in the river's mouth that now bears his name. On Pike's order, Sergeant Henry Kennerman, and Corporals William E. Mack and Samuel Bradley, directed seventeen privates in pitching camp on the island's western shore. The next day, Sunday, September 22, Pike went a short distance upriver from Mendota to pay a social call on trader Murdoch Cameron and his family. Late in the afternoon of that wilderness Sunday, a party of one hundred and fifty painted Sioux warriors aban-

ZEBULON PIKE

doned a planned raid on the Chippewa in favor of investigating what loot they might acquire from the white strangers. They turned their war canoes into the muddy island shores. Zeb Pike, lean, high-cheekboned, darkly handsome in his braided blue uniform, turned to his interpreter and said he wanted a parley. He invited Le Petit Corbeau, the war party's chief, to come back the next day.

On Monday at noon, while insects floated on the tepid river waters, Pike was ready for the Indians. He had had his men spread the sails from the keelboat in which he had come north from St. Louis. The cloth was suspended horizontally on poles to form a "bower" under which the gathered tribesmen might sit.

He had summoned Murdoch Cameron and a Vermont trader named Frazer as witnesses.

"Brothers," the young lieutenant said, "we having but lately acquired from the Spanish the extensive territory of Louisiana . . . wish you to grant to the United States nine square miles . . . at this place. . . ." It was the intention of his government, he said, to establish not only a fort but a trading station at which the natives could acquire the things they needed at cheaper rates than from British traders, "as they are single men who come from far in small boats." He promised that the United States would see to it that the traders on the river were good men. "Brothers, I now present you with some of your father's tobacco," Pike finished, "and some other trifling things, as a memorandum of my good will, and before my departure I will give you some liquor to clear your throats."

The quiet Minnesota lapped at the island, and the September sun glinted in the poplar leaves. Cameron and Frazer sat beside Pike, watching the impassive Indians. They knew that Pike had privately dined with Le Petit Corbeau and his fellow chief, Way Aga Enagee, before the council met; but they also knew that the Sioux chiefs thought their honor impugned in having to sign a paper that merely repeated what had already been agreed to verbally. Pike won over the chiefs by simply asking them to sign as a favor to himself. As a result of so ingenuous a ruse, Le Petit Corbeau and Way Aga Enagee set their "hands and seals, at the mouth of the St. Peter's River on the twenty-third day of September, one thousand eight hundred and five," to the first land treaty signed in Minnesota.

The treaty had some loopholes that were to come to light later. Pike went north on the Mississippi to spend the winter searching for its source and talking peace with the Chippewa. Wherever he went, he announced that British authority was no longer valid. When he found the Union Jack flying over a trading post at Leech Lake, he ordered his men to shoot it down. He encountered the wily British trader, Robert Dickson, struck up a persuasive friendship, and in April brought Dickson, with some Chippewa peace pipes, down to Mendota. April offered no balm that year; Pike reported it was snowing very hard when he sent a messenger to gather the Sioux for another parley.

But Pike's aim was to instill in all the Indians a feeling of the gentleness of spring. Chippewa chiefs had assured him that—if the Sioux drew the calumet on the trunks of the trees around the island—there would not have to be warfare when the northern Indians chose to pass the Minnesota. Knowing that the summer before, in their first message to Jefferson, Lewis and Clark had reported the untrustworthiness of the western Sioux, Pike was intent on impressing the tenants of the Minnesota country with his firmness.

At Mendota a half-breed Sioux called Fils de Pinchon offered to make arrangements for Pike's parley. That evening the lieutenant was sent for and introduced into a council-house large enough to seat three hundred men. There were chiefs from the Sissetons, the Wahpetons, the Mdewakantons; but the Yanktons had not come in from the West. "They were all waiting for my arrival," said Pike. "There were about one hundred lodges, or six hundred people . . . forty chiefs, and as many pipes set against the poles, alongside of which I had the [Chippewa] pipes arranged." Pike got the chiefs to smoke the calumet— "excepting three, who were painted black" and in mourning. He told them the Chippewa had promised peace, and he expected the same promise from the Sioux. He invited Fils de Pinchon, and the son of the Killeur Rouge, to have a meal with him. Trusting Dickson, Pike used him as an interpreter as he announced to his guests that he wanted to be able to make a better report of the Sioux present than Captain Lewis had been forced to make on their western brothers.

Pike made a fetish of firmness—with temporary effect. When, later, another chief was refused a kettle of liquor and threatened to go to war that summer, Pike assured the Indians that if he returned to the river with troops, he would make short work of the matter, and he got Le Petit Corbeau to apologize for the incident. Then, with his treaty safely tucked away, Pike left the river.

He had acquired the site of a citadel, a United States Army post that was for decades to be the only permanently fortified position in the Upper Midwest. But, although the Senate ratified the treaty signed under the flapping sailcloth, the two thousand dollars to be paid for the site of a fort at the mouth of the Minnesota was not delivered. Discovering this omission during the War of 1812, Robert Dickson had some second thoughts about his friendship with Pike, and he persuaded the Sioux that all Americans were of bad faith. He lined up all but one of the tribes to fight with the British against the United States. A new chapter in the life of the river had begun at Pike's island.

7

RIVER BASTION

Sometimes we see a cloud that's dragonish;
A vapour sometimes like a bear or lion,
A tower'd citadel, a pendant rock. . . .

—WILLIAM SHAKESPEARE

ABOVE PIKE's island in the mid-1820's a lofty stone citadel cast its medieval image. It rose from the white promontory Jonathan Carver had singled out, and was carved from the limestone he had recommended to architecture. Hundreds of square miles of wilderness lay between the fort and any other point of civilization. The striped flag with its twenty-four stars stirred in the clear air over the strongest United States bastion west of the Mississippi. It was a citadel indeed—as defiant and isolated as Coeur de Lion's Chateau Gaillard, his saucy castle on the Seine.

The new fort grew out of the bluff where the rivers joined, its walls thrusting upward almost one hundred and twenty feet above the landing, where frail canoes drifted in the Minnesota. Obliquely upward from the river ran a wagon road, cut out of the cliff where nesting swallows flew in and out. The road passed a commissary, four stories high, built into the great wall and large enough to contain four years' supply of provisions; it swung away from the river past a hexagonal tower guarding the Minnesota waters. A limestone tower looked out over the

FORT SNELLING FROM
PIKE ISLAND

rolling prairie behind the fort, a pentagonal tower thrust up from the Mississippi shore. The stone walls quarried from the nearby ground enclosed the towers in a diamond-shaped area seven hundred by four hundred and fifty feet, an island of strength designed to give pause to the audacious Sioux.

Josiah Snelling built the fort, and he was often as bold as his handiwork. Once when he spotted an Indian raising a rifle behind a tree, he sprang at the savage, knocked the gun from his hand, and skewered the man's neck with his sword. When his commander surrendered Fort Detroit during the War of 1812, young Snelling refused to help run up a white pennant. "No, sir," he said indignantly, "I will not soil my hands with that flag." He had flashing eyes, and thinning red hair that caused his men, behind his back, to nickname him "the prairie hen."

Josiah Snelling's younger son said his father showed "a character and standing among the wild men of the forest that alone could restore peace and keep their turbulent nature under control." No doubt he did. He was thirty-eight when he came up from St. Louis as a newly commissioned colonel assigned to command a detachment that had encamped at the river's mouth the summer before.

The first soldiers had arrived in 1819 under Lieutenant Colonel Henry Leavenworth's command, and they had spent a tragic winter. Leavenworth had put his men to work immediately, building a stockade which was first called Camp New Hope and later Fort St. Peter's. The site was on low ground on the right bank of the Minnesota, and it proved to be full of trouble. An officer's daughter years later recalled weather so severe that "the roof of our cabin blew off, and the walls seemed about to fall in. My father . . . held up the chimney to prevent a total downfall; while the baby, who had been pushed under the bed in her cradle, lay there . . . until the wind subsided. . . ."

Lack of proper provisions caused trials far greater than wind storms. Bread was "two inches in the barrels thick with mould"; there were no vegetables; the Indians refused to sell game. A

boat sent to get new provisions was frozen in on the Mississippi.
Then malignant scurvy broke out. Men who went to bed in good
health were found dead in the morning. The disease was at-
tributed to the villainy of St. Louis contractors, who drew the
brine from barrels of pork to lighten the load, and then had the
barrels refilled with river water before delivery.

Early in the following summer Snelling's predecessor moved
his survivors across the Minnesota to a temporary camp on higher
ground. He began plans to build a square fortress on the nearby
bluff of the Mississippi. He named one of the adjacent lakes for
his wife, Harriet, who had accompanied him, and another for
Secretary of War Calhoun, who had sent him upriver. But Leavenworth was soon to be relieved. When Josiah Snelling paced the
terrain of the summer encampment, he threw out Leavenworth's
plans for a conventional fortress. He "infused system and energy
among men and officers," it was said, and on September 10, 1820,
with the band playing and salutes being fired, he laid the corner-
stone. Four years later, General Winfield Scott arrived to inspect
the work, and was so impressed that he persuaded the War
Department to name the post for its "meritorious" commander.

Fort Snelling had become, a traveler said, the finest site on
the Mississippi River. The view from the lookout, another wrote
"is highly romantic. To your left lies the broad deep valley of
the Mississippi, with the opposite heights descending precipitously to the water's edge; and to the right and in front, the St.
Peter's, a broad stream, worthy from its size, length of course,
and the number of tributaries which it receives, to be called
the Western Fork of the Great River itself. It is seen flowing
through a comparatively open vale, with swelling hills and
intermingling forest and prairie, for many miles above the point
of junction. As it approaches the Mississippi, the volume of
water divides into two branches . . . directly under the walls
of the fort. . . ."

Snelling's domain was not always so glowingly portrayed. A
carping inspector wrote that some of the "points of defence

against an enemy appear to have been in some respects sacrificed in the effort to secure the comfort and convenience of the troops in peace." He asserted that "The buildings are too large, too numerous, and extending over a space entirely too great; enclosing a uselessly large parade, five times greater than is at all desirable in that climate."

Fort Snelling never acquired the heroic literary profile that distinguishes bastions that have been besieged. The edifice was far more commanding than Fort Leavenworth, erected on the Missouri by Snelling's predecessor, but it did not have the Oregon and Santa Fe trails to make it famous; emigration also solidified the fame of such outposts as Laramie and Bent's Fort. Yet though Snelling's fortress was an aid to the fur trade, no legendary bravado related it to the folklore of the mountain men or the Wild West of publicists like Buffalo Bill. By its very awesome architecture the citadel curbed the audacity of Indian warmakers—and that virtue made it seem tame, sometimes almost uninteresting.

Snelling's soldiers wanted more action and less drudgery. They found it monotonous to have their three-o'clock dinner invariably followed by a sunset band concert and a full-dress parade just before bed. And the commandant came up with even less gladitorial duties. "We *can* and *ought* to supply our own rations," he wrote headquarters, and he had the men plant acres of wheat, oats, and corn procured from the Sioux. His lack of total success as a farmer is indicated in the fact that his 1821 corn crop was virtually destroyed by blackbirds. Although Snelling kept his soldiers at their agrarian tasks, he at last found a better answer to his food problem in the unexpected arrival of some refugees —some bourgeois Swiss who had been lured to North America by way of Hudson Bay, only to seek softer climes by following the Red River and the Minnesota valleys southward.

The refugees had been members of Lord Selkirk's well-meant colony on the site of what is now Winnipeg. Unable to cope with problems of life cut off from all communication, they had abandoned the north in hope of establishing themselves in central United States. Snelling's military reservation and its river connection with Prairie du Chien and St. Louis offered a haven that Snelling did nothing to discourage. The Selkirkers proved to be adequate farmers, and their presence as squatters was welcomed for more than a decade.

Yet the new families contributed little to the relief of boredom on the reservation. The soldiers got drunk frequently, and sometimes they disappeared, "supposed to have drowned by falling through the ice." Usually a gentle man, Snelling was just as violent a discipliner of drinkers as he was a fighting soldier. "He would take them into his room, and compel them to strip, when he would flog them unmercifully," said a young woman who lived in his household. "I have heard them beg him to spare them, 'for God's sake.' "

Most of the commandant's three hundred men were uneducated, almost undisciplinable. To escape Snelling's wrath, his soldiers sometimes deserted and consequently faced greater hazards. Four who escaped at one time were killed by Indians, and their bodies were found half eaten by birds. Others equally discontented were wise enough to wait for the end of their enlistments to become fur traders within the jurisdiction of the fort.

Snelling ruled his citadel for seven years. He built a sawmill, and had the men grind their own flour. He built a "commodious" log cabin as an off-duty sportsman's lodge where officers and their wives went frequently to picnic, and to fish. "Bass, perch, sunfish, pickerel, pike, cat and other fish abounded in the river and made the sport of angling very lively," his son reported. Sometimes, young Henry Snelling recalled, "each family brought a tent and pitched it as their residence in preference, the weather being beautifully serene and balmy. The sport was excellent, and all were in the height of enjoyment. . . ." Snelling's Indian agent recorded in his diary a scene in March: "Wild geese seen this day —gentlemen generally out Walking—The Ladies also."

Out riding one day, the colonel's lady stopped at the tepee of a handsome Sioux named Rising Sun, and found him so ill that she took him home and sent for the fort physician. When Rising Sun recovered, said Henry Snelling, "he was ever most grateful. The best of everything in the shape of game was always set aside for his benefactress. He would travel a hundred miles, or more, to lay at her feet some fresh token of his grateful heart." Two years later, Rising Sun was stricken again, and again he hastened to Mrs. Snelling. But this time the fort doctor was unable to cure him. "When assured that his recovery was out of the question, he desired to be taken to the great hall of the house, where my mother almost constantly sat during the warm summer days." Rising Sun was laid upon a buffalo robe where he could have "the face of his benefactress ever before him. . . . He took the hand of my mother, and in pressing it to his lips with an ecstacy of delight, and a grateful heart, his spirit fled."

Abigail Snelling's affinity for Indians sometimes met interesting challenges. One of her guests so coveted the bear-claw necklace of the great chief Wanata that the visitor persuaded Mrs. Snelling to intercede in his behalf. Her son said she had "a very beautiful head of hair, it being jet black, very silkey, fine and long, reaching nearly to the ground as she stood, and of which she was justly proud." The canny Wanata sensed her pride. When she relayed her visitor's request, the chief "with equal suavity of manner returned her compliments and replied. 'Madam, I will make you a present of this necklass on one condition only; that you will reciprocate the favor and grant me whatever I ask in return. I will give you this badge of my prowess if you will cut off your hair and braid it for me to wear in its place."

Ten years earlier Wanata had been among the Sioux recruited by Robert Dickson during the War of 1812, and as a reward for his services had been made a captain in the British army and given a trip to England. A tall, superlatively built young man, Wanata was a prime example of Sioux confidence, even arrogance. While the citadel was still unfinished and Snelling's command was ensconced at Fort St. Peter's log stockade, the young chief plotted its capture, promising to dance to the sun if he failed. The building of the stone fort, he had declared, was an infringement of Indian rights, and because his argument had failed to dislodge the troops, he determined to strike a decisive blow. "After endeavoring for some time to draw the garrison into an ambuscade," Henry Snelling wrote later, "he withdrew his warriors and made overtures of peace, and then formed a plan for its capture and massacre within the walls of the fort. With this design he sent messengers to Col. Snelling requesting permission to enter the fort with a few of his principal warriors, for the purpose of having a 'talk' to settle the differences between them. . . . The plot was well laid, and, had a less experienced officer been in command, would undoubtedly have been successful."

Wanata deployed his main strength in the woods at Mendota and—wearing his bear-claw necklace and a headdress of eagle feathers and wolf tails that showed how many enemies he had killed—he entered the fort at the head of fifty men. Convinced that his plan had been kept secret, he saluted the officer of the day with a peace pipe in one hand and a wampum belt in the other. His scheme was as audacious as it was simple. "During the sitting of the council," young Snelling said, "and in the midst of his speech, the presentation of the wampum belt was to be the signal for the commencement of the murderous work, for which purpose each warrior had his weapons concealed under his blanket. While the greater part were to rise and dispatch the officers within, the remainder were to rush out and, taking the guard by surprize, were to open the gates and admit the whole savage horde, who were to have approached during the conclave, when an indiscriminate slaughter was to take place."

The colonel's son emphasized that Snelling had been too long among aborigines to be deceived by this artifice. Wanata and his advance party were quickly disarmed and then ushered to the parade ground where three large fires had been kindled. They were then stripped of their flags, tomahawks, knives, and

FORT SNELLING FROM N.W.

everything else that had been presented to them by the United States government. Their prized mementos were burned, and they themselves were drummed out of the fort in disgrace.

Death would have been preferable, said the colonel's son. "They could not return to their tribe with this vile stain of disgrace upon them. . . . Blood alone could cleanse them [and] Wanata set the example. . . ." Slashing the skin of his breast and arms, Wanata prepared himself for the sun dance and four days of fast. He tied rawhide ropes to his slashed skin and secured the ends to a vertical pole. Dancing around this pole, the stalwart chief repeatedly swung himself into the air, pendant on the slashed skin of his arms and breast. Thus he danced on, taking no food until midmorning of the fourth day when the strip of skin on his breast gave way. At noon the strip on his left arm snapped. An elder then judged he had suffered enough and drew his knife to sever the last rope from the torture pole. Wanata collapsed and was left unconscious until nightfall, when food at last was offered him.

It was the business of Snelling's post to see that Indians were punished for aggressive acts, and his troops often were sent hundreds of miles away from the fort to maintain order or to restore peace between warring factions. Sometimes the Sioux and the Chippewa dared to do battle within sight of the citadel. Young Henry remembered climbing into the lookout tower to watch the Sioux cross the river and fall upon their enemies— made unwary by liquor—and butcher men, women, and children indiscriminately. He saw his father's soldiers sent out to round up Indians guilty of murder, returning with culprits singled out by the chiefs. Any pretext to go into Indian country was hailed by the bored men. The citadel then was filled with bustle, with the sound of swords being buckled, arms shouldered, and the excitement of wives and children watching the exit of the company.

Such occasions were described by Mary Eastman, wife of the painter, Captain Seth Eastman. In her book about Fort Snelling she caught the meaning of departure to those who never knew how many might return from the Sioux lands: "The battalion marches out to the sound of the drums and fife;—they are soon down the hill—they enter their boats; handkerchiefs are waved from the fort, caps are raised and flourished over the water—they are almost out of sight—they are gone." Mrs. Eastman made a good deal out of Fort Snelling's scenery, and said of a nearby cascade: "the Indians call them Mine-hah-hah, or 'laughing waters.'" Although the authenticity of the name has been roundly scouted by experts, Longfellow gave credit to Mrs. Eastman and to the writings of Henry R. Schoolcraft for the Indian lore he wove into his *Song of Hiawatha*. Mrs. Eastman was among numerous writers in the 1830's and 'forties who helped to evoke the interest of Easterners and Europeans in visiting the fort at the mouth of the Minnesota. When the steamboat age began, the fort was the terminal point of "the Fashionable Tour," that brought travelers as distinguished as the widow of Alexander Hamilton and former President Fillmore.

The first steamboat to reach the citadel in the wilderness turned into the landing on the Minnesota River on May 10, 1823. "The arrival of the *Virginia*," said the river's first historian, "is an era in the history of the Dakotah nation, and will probably be transmitted to their posterity as long as they exist as a people. They say their sacred men, the night before, dreamed of seeing some monster of the waters, which frightened them very much.

"As the boat neared the shore, men, women, and children beheld with silent astonishment, supposing that it was some enormous water-spirit, coughing, puffing out hot breath, and splashing water in every direction. When it touched the landing their fears prevailed, and they retreated some distance; but when the blowing off of steam commenced they were completely unnerved; mothers forgetting their children, with streaming hair, sought hiding-places; chiefs, renouncing their stoicism, scampered away like affrighted animals."

High above, a cannon boomed as Josiah Snelling ordered a welcome for this harbinger of things to come. Among the guests the colonel greeted from the boat was a man who was later to write: "I know not what impression the first sight of the Phoenician vessels might make on the inhabitants of the coasts of Greece . . . but I am sure it could not be stronger than that which I saw on the countenances of these savages at the arrival of our steam-boat."

The author of this generous description was a political exile who stepped off the *Virginia* and announced to all who would listen that he had come to trace the course of the Minnesota River and work his way north in a modest attempt to add his name to the list of great Italian discoverers.

8

DON JUAN ON THE RIVER

There is a pleasure in the pathless woods,
There is a rapture on the lonely shore. . . .

—LORD BYRON

AFTER THE failure of the Neopolitans on the Po in the crisp spring of 1821, a young gallant marching under the red, blue, and black banner of the *Carbonari* vanished from his native Italy. Two springs later he was on the Minnesota, writing in his diary: "Everything conspired against my poor notes. I had already perched myself on an eminence for the purpose of enriching them with an Indian battle, and behold I have nothing to write. . . . I almost suspected that the savages were in league with the gentlemen of the fort to disappoint me."

Count Giacomo Constantino Beltrami, lawyer, linguist, and defender of the House of Savoy, had discovered that "revolutions are not made of rose-water," and now his lust for action was frustrated by Josiah Snelling's unromantic insistence that the Sioux and the Chippewa hold to their frail truce.

Tall and commanding, a Piedmont version of Lord Byron, the count continually fretted under frustrations. He had arrived from St. Louis when the *Virginia* made its maiden landing underneath Fort Snelling. For six weeks he had dallied as Colonel Snelling's guest, displaying his classical knowledge in French conversations

68

with Mrs. Snelling, and gathering native curios to bequeath to museums in his native country. Young Henry Snelling was persuaded to part with a bow and quiver of arrows "of exquisite workmanship" because the Italian nobleman "fell so violently in love with it that I was obliged, very reluctantly, to give it up to him, as he said, to grace the halls of ancient Rome."

Beltrami also whiled away his time on the river bluff by writing elegantly to "My Dear Countess" a series of letters afterwards published as *A Pilgrimage in Europe and America* and dedicated to "the Fair Sex." Six weeks after his arrival he wrote that the Indian agent, Lawrence Talliaferro, "had led me to entertain the hope that we should have proceeded together up the river St. Peter, which had never yet been explored, the sources of which are occupied by the most wild and powerful tribes of the Sioux, and as yet only vaguely defined, while the surrounding territory abounds in buffaloes." He was itching for action. "It was my intention to proceed thence towards the sources of the Mississippi, which are still absolutely unknown; but Mr. Tagliawar [Talliaferro] now feels his health is weak, and can proceed no farther. I cannot help fancying that it is intended to lull my projects into lethargy." Beltrami refused to forget that he was the scion of a distinguished family. "I am not, however, so easily hushed into inaction and forgetfulness," he assured the Countess. "I feel as yet firm in the saddle and shall sustain many a shock and conflict before I surrender."

Henry Snelling reported that Beltrami soon found an opportunity to indulge his love of danger. The restless Italian went hunting with an acquaintance, and on the prairie four days away from the fort he found a herd of buffalo. In spite of stern warning that it was foolhardy to hunt the big beasts except with a large and well-organized party, the Count rode within a few hundred yards of the herd, and then, waving his handkerchief in the air, he put spurs to his horse and dashed into their midst. He brought his horse to the side of a bull, giving the buffalo a violent kick in the side, as he plunged his knife into his back.

Undaunted by the charge of the infuriated animal, the impetuous Beltrami jumped from his mount and again attacked his prey with his knife. Snelling reported that the bull summoned his remaining strength and made a violent plunge at the Count that sent the hunter reeling. He was saved only because his companion was a skillful shot.

For several days more the brash *Carbonaro* was "incessantly thwarted," but on July 2, 1823, when a party headed by Major Stephen H. Long of the United States Army appeared at the fort, the Italian saw his chance. He made a stirring request to be allowed to join Long, and immediately began to add to his self-made troubles.

Under orders from Secretary of War Calhoun, Long was on his way "to the source of the St. Peter's River, thence to the point of intersection between Red River and the forty-ninth parallel, thence along the northern boundary of the United States . . . to make a general survey of the country. . . ." He had with him William Hypolite Keating, a twenty-three-year-old geologist, and the first landscape painter sent by the government to record what he saw. Beltrami saw no reason why he should not be the first nobleman to accompany an official American expedition, but he had trouble convincing Snelling and Long.

He wrote the Countess that they "set before me the sufferings, the dangers &c. . . . but as I laughed at these childish terrors [they] next attacked me on what they thought my weak side— my purse." Beltrami overcame all the arguments, but he couldn't resist reporting that "Major Long did not cut a very noble figure in the affair;" and he added that he "foresaw all the disgusts and vexations I should have to experience . . . from littleness and jealousy."

After the bakers at Fort Snelling had provided four hundred and eighty pounds of hard biscuit for the expedition, Long prepared to march. He wrote in his diary for Wednesday, July 9 that Snelling had furnished him with thirty-two men and an "amateur traveller"—Beltrami. With Snelling's older son Joe, and

BELTRAMI

Joseph Renville, the French half-breed who had been an interpreter for Pike, Long's party set out with the main body traveling in a skiff and four canoes, the remainder marching along the south bank of the Minnesota. That night, young Keating wrote in the official story of the expedition, the explorers were gratified and at the same time melancholy to be leaving even the insular civilization of Fort Snelling. "Before us," Keating wrote, "we had nothing but a wide and untravelled land, where no white man resided, except such as had foresworn their country and the friends of their youth, who, either out of aversion to society, or for the sake of lucre, had withdrawn from its social circle, to dwell in the midst of the uncivilized tenants of the forest."

Keating made only one acknowledgment of Beltrami's presence in the expedition. In a footnote he said: "An Italian gentleman, whom we found at Fort Snelling, asked, and obtained leave to travel with the expedition: he continued with them until the 7th of August. This is the gentleman who has lately published an account of his discoveries of the Mississippi; we have read it."

Beltrami was considerably less restrained about the situation. He began complaining immediately. On the third night, when a storm broke and camp was made in what others considered the most favorable spot, the Italian made a great scene. He told the Countess that he "was more thoroughly drenched than any of the others, because the major, faithful to the rules of *bienséance* and politeness, which allot the place of honour to the stranger, had had the attention to place me on one of the two sides of the tent; in order, no doubt, that I might observe the weather at my ease, and reap the glory of struggling valiantly against the fury of the wind, rain, hail, thunder and lightning."

Beltrami's discomforts were minor compared to the logistical problems of the expedition's commander. A canoe had been overturned in the afternoon preceding the storm, resulting in the loss of all the tobacco intended as a gift for the Indians; worse yet, much of the ammunition was waterlogged. The rain deluged the biscuit, sugar, and coffee stores, and the soldiers had found no game to supplement the rations procured at Fort Snelling. Long ordered nine men back to the fort with the boats, thereby reducing the number of mouths to feed, and after a day spent drying the baggage the remaining party continued to explore the river from its banks.

As the assigned recorder of the expedition, Keating was interested not only in minerals but in all the other characteristics of the valley. He noted that the trail they followed was marked by "four adjoining trees" on which there was drawn a profile of an Indian, with wings "painted in red earth," and with a large number of lines that Renville interpreted as meaning that Chief Redwing had passed with a body guard worth boasting about. Keating also was observant of the soil, which he termed excellent and deep and of the best quality along the river, and he noted that the grass grew six feet high. His eye was caught by lush grape vines, and abundant yellow raspberries. He examined the Indians' fields of corn, in one of which "a dog was found suspended, his head decorated with feathers, and with horse-hair stained red; it was probably a sacrifice for the protection of the corn-fields, during the absence of the Indians." Herbs were collected, trees listed, and the future of the river itself was summed up by Keating:

"The St. Peter, in our opinion, probably never can be made a commodious stream; for although it flows over gradations . . . the expense of rendering it navigable, by damming and locking, would far exceed the importance of the object. The plan would doubtless be found very practicable, but the scarcity of water during the greater part of the year would render these works unavailing." Major Long, in his diary, had something to add: "It is a very serpentine river, of a sluggish current, and varying in width from 30 to 70 yards. The first forty miles from its mouth the river is deep, and navigable for batteaus." Long said its name was "supposed to have been corrupted from Sans Pierre, which had formerly been given by the French . . . from the circumstance that no stones are found in it for a considerable distance from its mouth."

Beltrami, of course, was the only member of the party who could truly appreciate the river's aesthetic attractions. "We now reached a valley of the most lovely and interesting character," he wrote. "I took advantage of the time which chance procured me, to survey this enchanted ground; but I went alone, that the delicious reverie it threw me into might not be broken by cold-heartedness or presumption."

While Keating was making minute geological observations, the dashing Italian was enraptured by the view. "Never did a more striking illusion transport my imagination back to the classic lands of Latium and Magna Grecia. Rocks scattered, as if by art, over the plane, and on the hills, were at a little distance perfect representations of every varied form of the ruins of antiquity. In one place you might think you saw thermal structures, or those of an amphitheatre, a circus, or a forum; in another, the remains of a temple, a cenotaph, a basilicon, or a triumphal arch. . . . My eyes continually met new images: at length they rested on a sort of tomb, which for some time held me motionless. A thousand afflicting recollections rushed to my heart: I thought I beheld the tomb of Virtue and of Friendship; I rested my head upon it, and tears filled my eyes." How could a mere officer of the United States Army appreciate such a vista? "The spot was of the kind to soften and embellish grief, and I should have long given myself up to its sweet influence had I not been with people who had no idea of stopping for anything but a broken saddle, or some such important incident."

Sitting astride the horse, Cadmus, given him by his friend Talliaferro, Beltrami concluded that "Nature seems to have lavished all her treasures on this beautiful valley . . . the immense blocks of granite scattered here and there with such picturesque negligence, might with small aid from the chisel be raised to rival the pyramids of Memphis or Palmyra. When I woke from the dream of all this favored valley might become, I was struck by feelings I cannot describe at its awful and desert stillness— feelings which perhaps no other scene could awaken. Here Zimmerman or la Fontaine might *indeed* have painted solitude, with less metaphysical refinement and more truth." Nor was the Countess allowed to think that her correspondent had forgotten Rome. He told her the rocks were so beautiful and

varied that "tricking dealers of the Piazza Navona would sell
them as oriental or Egyptian porphyry or basalt."

Keating was content to let the matter go with the observation
that, having studied the geology of Europe and having examined
all strange formations westward from Philadelphia, he had nothing with which to compare the giant granite outcroppings in the
Minnesota Valley.

On July 19, with the sun hot and dry in the long grass covering
the flat land above the river, the explorers met two friendly Indians who boasted that they had killed a buffalo the day before
and that there were many more in the vicinity. This was welcome news to Keating because for several days they had been on
short rations. With Joseph Renville interpreting, Long told the
Indians where he had decided to camp, and that evening the
hunters showed up with their tepees and their families, offering the expedition a feast "which we of course accepted." Keat
ing said there were some ingrates who found the dried buffalo
meat tough and tasteless.

The next day's journey brought them to Lac qui Parle, which
they agreed was beautiful, yet they were disappointed when
they found the lake produced no echoes to justify its name. They
rode on in the wake of fresh buffalo tracks, as Keating noted a
prediction that because of the heat ("nearly 90°") the wild rice
would be ripe in mid-August. He jotted descriptions of Indian
mounds, and of rocks covered with circles, crescents, and crosses,
all painted in red pigment.

On the twenty-second they reached Big Stone Lake and
Keating recorded that their route continued for three miles in
what appeared to have been an old watercourse, that led them
to the banks of Lake Traverse, where Brown's Valley now nestles
on the continental divide. "The water has been known, in times
of flood," Keating wrote, "to unite the two lakes. In fact, both
of these bodies of water are in the same valley; and it is within
the recollection of some persons, now in the country, that a boat

once floated from Lake Traverse into the St. Peter. . . . Here we behold the waters of two mighty streams, one of which empties itself into Hudson's Bay . . . and the other into the Gulf of Mexico." This seemed to Keating a phenomenon that disproved the theory that large basins of water must always be separated by great elevations.

Having traced the course of the river, they were feted by the natives. Their host was the famous Wanata whose village was established on the continental divide. He presided in a pavilion formed by uniting several large tepees, at the end of which he sat, clothed in moccasins and leggings of scarlet cloth, a blue breech-cloth, a printed muslin shirt, and a blue frock coat with scarlet facings, "somewhat similar to the undress uniform coat of a Prussian officer." The chief's blue bonnet reminded Keating of a German fatigue cap. The final touch in the costume was a handsome Mackinaw blanket, slightly ornamented with paint, which was thrown over Wanata's broad shoulders.

The traveler reported that the feast was worthy of the chief. There was food sufficient for one hundred rather than for ten, said Keating, including "the much esteemed dog meat" which tasted like "the finest Welch mutton." Feeling as stuffed as Roman banqueters, the Americans settled back to absorb an exhibition of dancing and singing by Wanata's warriors, and Major Long transcribed the music of the Dog Dance that was accompanied by "a few unmeaning words":

The notes marked thus ♀ *are performed with a tremulous voice sounded High-yi-yi &c.*

Beltrami appears to have enjoyed all this, but his bile rose again when Long gave a speech—". . . very good to his government—but very bad to the Indians, since it concluded with the information that he had nothing to give them, and accordingly neither the chief nor anybody else made the slightest answer. . . . His majesty did not even deign to look at him; and while the interpreter was explaining . . . he amused himself laughing, with an air of royal nonchalance. . . ."

Keating remembered the scene differently: "We have never seen a nobler face, or a more impressive character, than that of the Dakota chief, as he stood that afternoon . . . contemplating the dance . . ." A few presents were distributed after the dance, and the Indians were "apparently as much satisfied as we were."

Impatient Count Beltrami was just as bilious when he later had to spend a night with fur traders whose housing he considered worse than that of the Indians. He hung on ungraciously with Long's party until they had followed the Red River north to the Canadian line, and there he was so offended by the accommodations that he ordered his own tent set up for him. "But the major," he lamented to the Countess, "who wishes to train me to the virtue of patience, refused to have it pitched; and fleas and other vermin concurred with him in pushing the trial [of sleeping with the traders] to the point of martyrdom."

Finally, on August 7, Long's diary quietly records, "Mr B our Italian companion, having taken offense at the party, generally, and being highly provoked at my objecting to his turning an Indian out of our Lodge, left the party in a very hasty and angry manner."

That closed the book on Beltrami as far as the official explorers were concerned. But not so for the former *Carbonaro*. Highhandedly selling the horse Talliaferro had given him, he struck southeast through the forest with a half-breed and two Chippewa. Evoking the shades of Marco Polo and every other Italian explorer of fame, he anointed himself as the discoverer of the source of the Mississippi when he at last stood on the shore of a wilderness pool—a heart-shaped lake in the middle of which water was boiling up from a depth he was unable to sound. He called it Lake Julia—for a lady out of his past. Then he headed for the mouth of the Minnesota. "I took my bath in the river," he wrote the Countess, "and dressed myself as well as I was able. . . . My head was covered with the bark of a tree, formed into the shape of a hat and sewed with threads of bark; and shoes, a coat, and pantaloons . . . formed of [deer] skins sewed together by thread made from the muscles of that animal, completed the grotesque appearance of my person."

On September 15, he turned up again at Fort Snelling. His Indian guides announced their approach, he said, by shouting, chanting, firing guns, and by the sound of "harmonious drums." It seemed to Beltrami that everyone at the fort must have been sick to death from worry about his welfare, because young Joe Snelling had arrived beforehand to tell the story of his disappearance. But when the count removed his "skin covering" and was recognized, "surprise and affection" marked the faces of his welcomers. "The excellent Mr. Tagliawar embraced me in the most cordial manner, and the colonel, his respectable wife, and his children, received me with the demonstrations of the most lively joy." Emotional as always, Don Juan shed tears. Eighteen days later he left the river valley he had traversed, still indignant at Major Long. He found solace by enshrining himself in the mists of romance.

Stephen Long's concerns were more prosaic. Calm and judicious, he led his expedition eastward across the Great Lakes and reported in Washington to John C. Calhoun. His data were used by William Keating in the government-sponsored *Narrative of an Expedition to the Source of the St. Peter's River,* the first account for Americans of the splendors of the Minnesota Valley. Keating did his work well, but the would-be settlers had to wait. For another generation the river remained part of Suland, the last redoubt of Sioux village life.

9

MEETING OF WATERS

*In rivers, the water that you touch
is the last of what has passed and
the first of that which comes. . . .*

—LEONARDO DA VINCI

LITTLE BY LITTLE after the erection of Fort Snelling life in the valley began to change. There were beginnings of order, beginnings of extended enterprise. Though the land belonged to the Sioux, traders now came to the river to spend the rest of their lives. More squatters came from the ill-starred Selkirk colony and joined those who were already farming on land that Pike had bargained for. Below the fort there was another settlement to which Count Beltrami had caustically pointed as three or four houses on the riverbank where traders "live among the frogs."

Thriving among the frogs was Jean-Baptiste Faribault, who had come to the river from Quebec. With his half-breed wife, Pelagie, he had witnessed the arrival of the Pike flotilla, and because he knew so well how to manage the Sioux he had been urged by Henry Leavenworth to settle on Pike's island as a sort of liaison officer. When the Faribault buildings were destroyed in the flood of 1822, Pelagie packed up her children, and handsome Jean-Baptiste moved his family across the "meeting of waters" to the mainland in the long shadow of the fort. The mixed-blood daughter of the Faribaults persuaded a *voyageur* named Alexis Bailly to settle down, and the Faribault sons grew up to be traders, too.

Around the Faribaults grew a hamlet for which American names were tried and found wanting. The tiny community was known briefly as New Hope, after the first encampment of the soldiers who built the fort; some called it St. Peter's, after the river that separated the houses "among the frogs" from the citadel above. But the Indian name prevailed—Mendota marked the mouth of the river. Mendota, St. Peter's, New Hope—the hamlet was French-Canadian. Wine was poured, violins were played, and the *chansons* of *coureurs de bois* mingled at the fireside with the drifting smoke of long clay pipes. The names were French: Pierre Gervais, William Beaumette, Vetal Guerin, Antoine LeClaire. Mendotans were fur traders, and with Scots who followed them down from British Canada, they brought in the finest pelts from their outposts along the valley.

No longer was it essential to be a "runner in the woods" to succeed in the fur trade, for civilization, willy-nilly, was creeping along the river. Down from the citadel with his trader's license came nineteen-year-old William Joseph Snelling, who had flunked out of West Point. Back from exploring the valley with Major Long, young Joe began to deal in furs and gather Indian lore that he wove into short stories. When he published a book entitled *Tales of the Northwest*, he gave readers in the East their first sampling of the Sioux country as a literary background.

Joe sat on the steps of the Indian agency building and quizzed the half-breed interpreter who had been up the Missouri with Lewis and Clark. He dogged the steps of Alexander Faribault to learn the fur trade. He was a youngster of mercurial temperament, who fought a duel to defend his father's honor. In quieter moments he wrote long, somewhat tedious poems to interpret his understanding of the savage mind. He was not content when Keating described a massive rock as "cleft, as we thought, by

SIBLEY HOUSE, MENDOTA

lightning . . . blackened, and a few bushes and trees near it
bore signs of having been on fire." Joe knew the Sioux legend of
the birth of thunder at this very rock, and he spun it out in re-
sounding meter:

> About his burning brow a cloud,
>> Black as the raven's wing he wore;
> Thick tempests swept him like a shroud,
>> Red lightnings in his hand he bore. . . .

Snelling thought civilized readers should respond sympatheti-
cally to this ominous riverside nativity:

> At the first stride his foot he set;
>> The jarring world confessed the shock.
> Stranger! the track of Thunder yet
>> Remains upon the living rock.

Despite a leaning toward prolixity, Joe Snelling sent out his
poems and gained some fame. He went East, as the first literary
ambassador from Mendota, and his career brought the river out
of the shapeless gloom of the unknown West into the light cast
by magazines. Now preferring his pen to sidearms, he dueled
with authors whose work is more memorable. When he composed a satire called "Truth, a New Year's Gift for Scribblers,"
he caused the more talented N. P. Willis to wince, and Willis
turned on Joe with a lampoon that had no heart for the fur
trade:

> Oh, Smelling Joseph! Thou art like a cur.
> I'm told thou once did live by hunting fur:
>> Of bigger dogs thou smellest, and, in sooth,
>> Of one extreme, perhaps, can tell the truth.
> 'Tis a wise shift, and shows thou know'st thy powers,
> To leave the "North West Tales," and take to smelling ours.

With no apologies for his days on the river, Snelling revised his "Truth," and added the following lines:

> I live by hunting fur, thou say'st, so let it be,
> But tell me, Natty! Had I hunted thee,
>> Had not my time been thrown away, young sir,
>> And eke my powder? Puppies have no fur.

> Our tails? Thou own'st thee to a tail,
>> I've scanned thee o'er and o'er
> But, though I guessed the species right,
>> I was not sure before.

In his brief career on the river, Joe Snelling was an independent trader, but by the time he left for the East in 1827 the day of such free lancers was virtually over; Mendota was about to become the capital of a highly organized fur-trade region that its chief figure was to describe as "larger than the Empire of France." The trader who did most to bring about the change arrived like a young knight on horseback in 1834. Pausing to look down from the hill above the hamlet, he was struck by the picturesque beauty of the scene. "But when I descended into the amphitheatre, where the hamlet was located," he wrote later. "I was disappointed to find only a group of log huts, the most pretentious of which was the home of my fellow traveler, Mr. Bailly, in whose family I became an intimate for the next six months."

The rider was Henry Hastings Sibley, twenty-three years old, and the new chief of the American Fur Company's "Sioux Outfit." From his family he had inherited a need to pursue the western horizon; his parents had moved from Massachusetts to Ohio and then to Detroit, where his father became chief justice of the Michigan courts. Growing up on the edge of the wilderness, Sibley had studied law himself, but he couldn't close his eyes to the westering of the nation and he entered the fur trade as quickly as possible. His talent was such that after five years at

Mackinac he was offered a partnership in the Astor company.

Sibley swiftly put his mark on Mendota by quarrying limestone and erecting a handsome residence. Into his house Sibley moved a mulatto cook named Joe Robinson. He filled his library with Blackstone, Coke and Kent, with sets of Sir Walter Scott and James Fenimore Cooper, with Gibbon and Hume, with Froisart's *Chronicles* and Thier's memoirs. He used the large front room of his house as an office, where counters and shelves were piled with trading items. In his warehouse furs were sorted and packed for shipment by water to Mackinac, New York, and the markets of Europe. In his first year he noted 389,000 muskrat skins worth $44,000, in addition to 3,000 mink pelts, 3,000 deer skins, 2,000 raccoons, 1,000 each of otter and buffalo, and many beaver, martin, bear, wolf, fox, badger, wildcat, and rabbit.

Sibley carried on a fluent business correspondence with his partners in Prairie du Chien and New York. Aware though he was of the contrast in culture between himself and the average fur trader, he was, nevertheless, a champion of the men of the woods. He described them as "men of little or no education, but of remarkable energy and rare fidelity." He reported on his "hundreds of traders, clerks, and voyageurs" to whom he entrusted quantities of trade goods worth "hundreds of thousands of dollars, nay millions." He described the trader who "wended his way, in August or September, to the scene of operations, where he erected his wintering house, furnished his Indians with necessary clothing and ammunition, and dispatched them to their hunts. . . ." Sibley waited for the day when "the records of the Northwest will place the Indian trader in a proper light. . . ."

At the same time Sibley made it clear that his own standards differed in at least one respect from those of the men to whom he gave credit. One of his favorite stories was of a visit he received after his first trip of inspection along the river. He was lying in bed reading one midnight when he was suddenly surprised to see a male and female Indian standing in the room.

There was no shock to him in the Indian habit of entering without knocking. Any lack of preparedness on Sibley's part was, he said, based on his realization that his male caller was offering his good-looking young daughter as a roommate. "The poor girl . . . stood there waiting for my reply," the handsome young trader reported, noting that she had covered her head with the blanket she wore. He said that for many reasons he could not explain he had no intention of taking an Indian maiden as a wife. Mustering the little dialect he knew, Sibley turned the offer down. Not, he made haste to add, that there was "anything savouring of immorality."

Sibley did not inflict celibacy upon himself throughout the nine years he spent at Mendota before his marriage, for he had at least one daughter during those bachelor days and, in general, he found little to disturb his rapport with the natives. "There was a charm," he said, "in the wild region, inhabited only by savage beasts and still more savage man." Intellectually inclined though he was, he felt "liberated from all the trammels of society," and free to act according to his pleasure. He was serious enough about his books, and he was a favorite guest of the ladies who ruled the social life at the fort across the river. But he would not be tethered. The slim and courtly young man was a crack shot, and he often spent weeks at a time on hunting trips with his Indian friends, later recounting his uncivilized adventures for Eastern periodicals.

To the readers of the popular magazine, *Spirit of the Times,* Sibley was known under a pseudonym, "Hal—a Dakotah," and to the Sioux themselves he was Wah-se-o-man-zee, "Walker in the Pines." Standing six feet in his stockings, "I allowed my hair to grow very long," he said, "and being bearded like a pard, and dressed in Indian costume, with two enormous dogs at my heels, [strangers wondered] where such a wild man of the woods had come from." But no disguise could fully obscure the cultivated talent that described life along the Minnesota for the outdoor magazines of the day. "We insist upon it," the editor of the *Spirit of the Times* told his readers, "that no one has written upon the subject of Buffalo Hunting and Prairie Sporting generally, better than [Sibley]". He promised his audience that he would keep Sibley writing even "if we have to chase him with a sharp stick among a roving band of Sioux."

No chasing was necessary. Sibley's account of a buffalo hunt with Alexander Faribault appeared in the *Spirit of the Times* in the spring of 1846. When the entourage, with its creeking carts and spirited horses, had moved southwest of Mendota, Sibley was told by his scouts that three buffaloes were lying at rest in a depression in the prairie. "Seven of us," he said; "prepared for the chase. When within three hundred yards of them we charged them at full speed. Shortly alongside, our double-barrelled guns told with deadly effect, two of the huge beasts rolling on the ground in death, within a hundred yards of each other; the third, a fine bull, escaped from the other horsemen, who unsuccessfully discharged their weapons at him. Meanwhile the prairie was set on fire by some Indians to the windward of us . . . the flames bearing down on us, so that we had no time to secure the meat. . . . Five times we approached the raging element, and as many times were repulsed, scorched and wellnigh suffocated, until, by a desperate use of whip and spur, we leaped our horses across the line of fire, looking, as we emerged from the smoke, more like individuals from the lower regions than inhabitants of earth. Recovering from exhaustion, we went in search of the buffaloes, and descried a number on the top of a hill, bare of grass, and to which the fire had driven them. There was a very fine fat cow in the centre of the band, which I made several efforts to separate from the others. . . . She kept herself close to an old bull, who from his enormous size appeared to be the patriarch of the tribe. . . . I shot the old fellow behind the shoulder. The wound was mortal, and the bull left the herd. . . ." With the ground throbbing in the wake of the other frightened beasts, Sibley sped after his shaggy prey to administer the *coup de grâce*. "I rode carelessly along, with but one barrel of my gun loaded, when, upon nearing the buffalo, he turned as quick as lightning to charge. At this critical instant I had risen in my stirrups, and released my hold on the bridle-rein. The moment the buffalo turned, my horse, frightened out of his propriety, gave a tremendous bound sidewise, and alas! that I should tell it, threw Hal clear out of the saddle, and within ten feet of the enraged monster."

Everyone else in the party was out of sight, following the rest of the herd. "Here was a predicament," said Sibley. "Imagine your humble servant face to face with the brute, whose eyes glared through the long hair which garnished his frontlet like coals of fire, the blood streaming from his nostrils." He kept his readers waiting for the moment of truth. He described his "desperate emergency" while he made up his mind that his only chance for escape was to look his enemy in the eye. "Holding my gun ready cocked to fire if he attempted a rush, I stood firmly, although I must confess I was much disturbed, and thought my last hour had come!" For a timeless moment the tormented bull bellowed and pawed the prairie sod. "At last he turned slowly away, and I gave him a parting salute, which let out the little blood left in his body. He went a short distance and fell dead."

Too late to help, another hunter finally arrived at Sibley's side and discovered that Sibley had been hurt in his fall from his mount. "I now felt much pain in one of my feet, which had received a serious blow when I fell," he told readers of the *Spirit of the Times*. "I had to use my hunting knife to free me from sock and moccasin, and in ten minutes I was unable to walk, or even stand without support." Sibley was so seriously injured that the party turned back toward Mendota, but not without occasionally shooting a few ducks and other wild fowl for the evening's *bouillon*. After having been gone for twenty-two days, he toted up the collective bag: "16 buffalo, 3 elk, 8 raccoons, 12 wolves, 7 geese, 244 ducks, and 80 grouse, besides sundry other small snaps not worth recording."

Sibley's heart, a friend said fondly, was in the Wild West. His reputation as an expert at the art of self-defense was such that only one man in the territory, a frontier giant named Bully Wells, dared stand up against him. Roughnecks knew better than to taunt Sibley for his grand manner of living.

Among his frequent guests, however, there was one who raised the Sibley ire to the boiling point. When in 1839 the Maine boundary was in question and Congress was passing a bill authorizing a call for fifty thousand volunteers for a possible war with Nova Scotia, Sibley was host to the English novelist, Captain Frederick Marryat, who "rubbed his hands with glee when he heard the news," and disparaged the American ability to win so much as a battle. The usually temperate Sibley threatened to thrash his guest, and then went off to church. When he returned and discovered that Marryat had used his absence to try to persuade sixty Sioux to lift tomahawks in behalf of "the mother country," Sibley dismissed the author from his house and advertised in New York newspapers that Marryat was a man devoid of honor and a disgrace to England. The author of *Mr. Midshipman Easy* turned the other cheek. In his *Diary in America,* published when the Canadian border feud had been settled, he paid his compliments to the officers of Fort Snelling and regretted his parting with his "kind host, Mr. Sibley."

Playing the host was Sibley's favorite role, especially after his marriage to a gracious and beautiful girl from Baltimore. He opened his stone mansion to all "of genteel appearance;" there were times when as many as twenty guests turned his riverside house into a hotel where he provided hospitality "free of expense." An outside stairway ran up one of the stone walls of the house to a loft where all visiting Indians were welcome to sleep. The rooms below were stylishly furnished and offered the comfort of elegance to travelers as famous as Stephen A. Douglas. One grateful guest was the explorer, Joseph N. Nicollet, who stayed through the winter of 1836. "You have been so good to me, that my affection and gratitude are yours forever," he said in one of the most outspoken of bread-and-butter letters. "I need not tell you that all our regards and remembrances are perpetually turned toward the west—to St. Peter's. . . . If we take a promenade our recollections haunt us—the sight of a fine hunting dog, a double-barrelled gun, the sound of the wild cry of geese which emigrate from North to South, all this for us, seems to come from Sibley! When we drink a toast, it is to Sibley's health. . . ."

Mendota prospered with Sibley's fame. Other substantial houses were built, and the isolated village made a picturesque view from the Fort Snelling bluff. There was constant traffic of Indians, Frenchmen, half-breeds, and wanderers from the East. One winter traveler found the hamlet more striking than any other he had seen in the United States. "What must it be in spring," he cried, "when the forests put forth their young leaves, and the prairies are clothed in verdure!"

The only civilian neighbors of Mendotans in the 1830s were the Selkirk refugees who at last were evicted from the military reservation on the grounds that some were selling liquor to the Indians. They moved in a body to a spot below Mendota where a renegade French Canadian had set up a bar. Because of his disconcerting gaze, the Canadian was known as Pig's Eye, and his notoriety as a source of liquor soon caused the new settlement to be named after him; it became an appendage to Mendota when Pig's Eye residents persuaded Father Lucien Galtier to hold services on their side of the river as well as at Mendota.

To match St. Peter's chapel at the river's mouth, Father Galtier built a second log church at Pig's Eye in 1841 and named it St. Paul's. Soon he was commuting regularly between his two parishes, and the new settlement began to thrive with his help. It had help, too, from Henry Sibley when the government in 1848 made it possible for the squatters to buy legal title to their land; they chose Sibley to do the bidding for each of them. At last within the law, the community threw off the mantle inherited from Pig's Eye Parrant, and called itself St. Paul's. Not long afterward the editor of the first newspaper composed some diverting doggerel to hail the change in name:

> Below Fort Snelling, seven miles or so,
> And three above the village of Old Crow.
> Pig's Eye? Yes; Pig's Eye! That's the spot!
> A very funny name; is't not?
> Pig's Eye's the spot, to plant my city on,
> To be remembered by, when I am gone.
> Pig's Eye, converted thou shalt be, like Saul:
> Thy name henceforth shall be Saint Paul. . . .
>
> When one great city covers all
> The ground from Pig's Eye to the Falls,
> I then will claim St. Paul for mine,
> The child of 1849.
> Pig's Eye, converted, thou shalt be like Saul,
> Arise; and be, henceforth—Saint Paul!

The editor was wrong about one thing, for it was not St. Paul but its twin city, Minneapolis, that grew to surround the Falls of St. Anthony, just upriver from Fort Snelling. Henry Sibley himself was to leave Mendota for St. Paul, and to become the state's first elected governor.

10

THE PIPESTONE TRAIL

*"We are two poor men travelling to see
the Sioux and to shake hands with them. . . ."*

—GEORGE CATLIN

EORGE CATLIN, astride a horse provided by Sibley, rode into
the valley in the summer of 1836 in his long pursuit of the
Indian mystique. During the solstice heat of the previous year,
Catlin had set up his easel behind Fort Snelling and painted
with energy the games and dances of the Sioux. With a vibrant
palette he drew the likenesses of chiefs and warriors, while his
wife, Clara, conversed with the officers' wives. Having abandoned an Eastern law practice, Catlin had been sojourning in
the West since 1832 as the first of the long procession of American painters who were to commit to canvas the wild terrain
and its wild residents before both were despoiled by the westering nation.

In 1836, Catlin put Clara on a steamboat leaving the river's
mouth, and with an English friend took the valley trail toward
the pipestone quarry considered so sacred that warring tribes
honored it as neutral ground. In his pocket Catlin had letters
from Sibley to all the traders on his route. At the crossing known
as Traverse des Sioux, he forded the river and came up the

91

wooded slope to present himself at the log cabin of Louis Provençalle.

The Sioux had dubbed Provençalle with their word meaning "whitey," and the French followed suit by calling him Le Blanc. Yet the nickname had been given in irony, for Le Blanc's skin was very dark and his face was largely covered by a black beard. His manner was jovial, but he had a reputation for avarice, and there were many stories about his temper. He was said to have skinned alive a wolf he caught stealing chickens; he had set the trap that crushed the hand of one of his *voyageurs* who tried to filch a loaf of bread through a hole in Le Blanc's warehouse wall. Once when an Indian band threatened to make off with his trade goods, the old trader snatched a burning brand from his fireplace, hacked off the top of a barrel of powder with an ax, and said firmly that he would blow up himself and his cabin, along with the intruders, if they touched a single item on the counter. Not one of the Indians doubted his word, and they scattered like frightened barnyard fowl.

As a talented trader, Le Blanc had no trouble with simple arithmetic, but he had never learned to write and he kept his ledger with hieroglyphics; he drew pictures of animals to represent the kinds of pelts he was itemizing, or as symbols of the Indian trappers' names. Sometimes he conscripted a better-educated visitor to add to his pictographs the English orthography of names like Thunder Face and Whistling Wind that defeated even his primitive genius for descriptive symbols. Like most traders, he had a flock of handsome half-breed children who were treated as the aristocracy of the valley's back country, and one of his grown sons was on hand to help him welcome Catlin and his companion.

With Gallic graciousness the two Provençalles went out to meet the horsemen who had come up the valley, but their Sioux neighbors had been aroused by word of Catlin's intended visit to the sacred quarry; a delegation had gathered at Le Blanc's post to protest. Catlin, who never missed a chance to star himself in a good story, said that "a murky crowd of dark-visaged warriors filled the avenue" and made prisoners of himself and Robert Wood. The travelers were forced to listen all afternoon, he wrote, while twenty Indian speakers harangued them threateningly, and while all the Sioux took turns shaking fists in their faces.

As Catlin described the scene—in a series of letters written for a New York newspaper—a warrior named Swift Man did most of the talking:

"Brothers—We have seen always the white people, when they see anything in our country that they want, send officers to value it, and then if they can't buy it, they will get it another way." He went on. "I speak strong, my heart is strong, and I speak fast. This red pipe is given to the red men by the Great Spirit —it is part of our flesh, and therefore is great medicine."

Catlin tried to present his own case, and introduced his friend, describing him as a *Sa-ga-nosh.*

Hearing the word, the Indians cheered, for Catlin had hailed his companion as one of the English whose retreat from the valley the Sioux regretted. Some of them shook hands with Wood, and spirited out the British medals they had hidden in their garments.

"We have heard that the Red Pipe Quarry was a great curiosity," said Catlin above the babble, "and we have started to go to it, and we will not be stopped."

He wrote that he was cut off at this point by a very grim and black Indian who shook his locks fiercely, and showed hatred, brandishing his fist "within one inch of my face." The Indian cried, "We shake hands, but no white man has been to the red pipe quarry and none shall go." He held up a pipe to his arm. "You see that this pipe is part of our own flesh. The red men are a part of the red stone. If the white men take away a piece of the red pipe stone, it is a hole made in our flesh, and the blood will always run. The Great Spirit has told us the red stone is only to be used for pipes, and through them we are to smoke to him."

Catlin said he tried again to reassure the natives, but was shouted down.

"White man!" a young warrior called out. "Your words are very smooth. . . . There is no use talking any more about it—If you think best to go, try it. That's all I have to say."

As Catlin recalled the incident, tawny warriors were stopped several times by Le Blanc's son, who promised to knock down any man who didn't behave. But Le Blanc himself advised the visitors to abandon the project. Catlin dismissed the warning that these tribesmen were "disorderly and treacherous," and rode off, he said, through rearing Indian horses.

He and Wood crossed the prairie, again forded the river near its junction with the Cottonwood, and were lucky enough to escape pursuit—perhaps because of the old Sioux affection for the English. Without further incident the two men galloped up to the trading establishment of Joseph La Framboise. Here the reception was considerably different, although La Framboise said that in lieu of feather beds they would have to be content with delicacies of wild game—including buffalo tongues and beaver tails—that Catlin enjoyed listing for his readers in detail.

Their host was more than willing to escort them to the quarry, and they traveled forty or fifty miles to the "fountain of the Red Pipe, which is truly an anomaly of nature . . . a perpendicular wall of close-grained, compact quartz, of twenty-five and thirty feet in elevation . . . stratified in several distinct layers of light grey, and rose or flesh-colour quartz . . . in any and all parts of which, the Indians procure the red stone for their pipes, by digging through the soil and several slaty layers . . . to the depth of four or five feet." Catlin, enraptured by his discovery and the landscape surrounding it, further defied the Indians by taking a sample of the stone; when analyzed by a Boston chemist, it was named *catlinite*, in the painter's honor.

The honor made Henry Sibley indignant enough to write a letter of protest. He asserted that Catlin's writings were full of errors, that "people in this quarter were absolutely astounded at his misrepresentation of men and things. There is but one redeeming feature in his book, and that is his sketches of Indian faces and scenes . . . his pencil could not . . . like his pen, vary much from the truth."

For some reason, Catlin seems not to have been much interested in the native legends about the stone that had been given his name. "Having glutted our curiosity at the fountain of the red pipe," he and Wood trotted back to Fort Snelling. But two years later the quarry had another significant visitation when Lieutenant John Charles Frémont—beginning his career as a pathfinder—and the gentle explorer, Joseph Nicollet, arrived with Joseph Renville, Jr., as their guide. Young Renville told Frémont that his Indian relatives believed the quarry had a spirit of its own; it spoke in the voice of Thunder and Lightning to signal its acknowledgment of distinguished visitors.

No such phenomenon had greeted George Catlin. However, the skies darkened as the caravan led by Joseph Nicollet, with the handsome Frémont at his side, approached the ridge of the Coteau des Prairies. "Such a storm broke upon us," said the soldier in his memoirs. The vast prairie sky flashed with summer lightning; the long red stone brow was suddenly incandescent. Thunder rolled menacingly, and ended in salute. "The confirmation of the legend was pleasing to young Renville and the Sioux who accompanied us," Frémont wrote. Then the storm broke away in a glow of sunshine as the horses pawed the settled dust and the flag drifted limply from its staff at the center of the file. There was awe on the faces of the Sioux.

No single spot seemed so mystic to them. They believed that Wahegela, an Omaha wife of a Yankton Sioux, had discovered the quarry while trailing a white buffalo whose hoofs uncovered the red stone. Decades of war had followed the discovery. The Sioux claimed ownership because tribal law made a wife a member of her husband's band, and the Omaha based their claims on Wahegela's blood relationship to them. The final agreement was unavoidable. The quarry was declared neutral ground to be shared in common by all tribesmen.

In contrast to Catlin's attitude, Nicollet and Frémont went out of their way to co-operate with their Sioux companions. They provided them with gunpowder to make it easier to extract the stone. They also made note of the petroglyphs left on the quarry walls by generations of aborigines, and carved their own names with their knives. Then they turned back into the valley to be the guests of Joseph Renville, Sr., who, though the son of a Sioux woman, had become the baron of the border, the keeper of the peace in the stretching land that lay between Lac qui Parle and Canada.

As Nicollet's party crossed the river near the beautiful lake and approached Renville's log fortress, Frémont meditated on the peculiar quality of frontier hospitality. Years later, after he won his sobriquet as a trail blazer and was a general who had run for President, Frémont looked back on his days on the Minnesota and remembered Joseph Renville's welcome. He took "pleasure in emphasizing [the] great enjoyment in the change from the privations and watchful unrest to the quiet safety and profusion of plenty in such a frontier home." He added that "there is lively satisfaction on both sides [because] the advent of strangers in an isolated place brings novelty and excitement. . . ."

Joseph Renville understood this philosophy as well as any trader in the valley, and on the shores of Lac qui Parle he had built a bounteous alcazar. Inside a large stockade he had erected two houses of hewn logs and a great warehouse for his furs, his trade goods, and his overflowing supply of food. He raised sheep and cattle, and had persuaded his nomadic Yankton neighbors to plant fields of corn. His reception room was a baronial hall where a great fireplace blazed on cold days with giant logs laid vertically. Here the Yankton men came almost daily to smoke their red-stone pipes and to while away their leisure in talk. On a bench that ran along three walls, they sat among the fifty *voyageurs* whom Renville maintained as an elite guard; the trader himself habitually sat on a chair in the center of the room, his back to the fire, his feet crossed under him like a tailor's. As Sibley's house had become a traveler's haven at the river's mouth, so Renville was the anchor of hospitality near its source.

Renville was a short man with strong angular features and coarse black hair. He showed no trace of the French blood he inherited from his father, who had sent him as a youth to be taught by a priest in Montreal. But he had shrewd intelligence; he had organized the Columbia Fur Company which merged, finally, with American Fur Company interests, thus making him Sibley's close collaborator. His youthful service as an interpreter had caused Pike to commend him in his official report, and he was the author of the Sioux history that Keating included in his account of the river. He was imperious, and he knew his power. Once, having delegated his son to tell the Chippewa to retreat to their own country, he was asked why he hadn't gone himself. "I have sent my name," said Renville. "That is enough."

Peace, as symbolized by red-stone calumets, was maintained in the valley, however uneasily, by fur traders like Joseph Renville. They did not minimize the importance of the fort at the mouth of the river, but they, more than anyone else, understood the Indian character, and the Minnesota was fortunate in the caliber of its dealers in peltry. Not until the fur trade had given way to settlement was there a serious Indian threat along the river. Renville, La Framboise, and Provençalle were architects of peace, and their contribution, though misunderstood by travelers like George Catlin, was applauded by professionals like Nicollet and Frémont, who had been sent to provide the government with its first detailed map of the valley.

These traders, wary though they were of future settlement, proved themselves of real worth as young Frémont surveyed the Minnesota's tributaries and the courtly Nicollet, on clear nights, made astronomical observations in the region of myriad lakes he called "the Undine," after the legendary water sprite. Writing of his work in the valley, Nicollet said the territory was "destined at no distant day to be the happy home of an industrious and enterprising population. . . . The whole country embraced by the Lower St. Peter's and the Undine Region exceeds any land of the Mississippi above the Wisconsin river. . . ." He had forecast the demise of the fur trade, the coming of the rolling farms and the snug river towns—and the inevitable laying aside of the red stone pipe of peace.

11

STEAMBOATS 'ROUND
A THOUSAND BENDS

You've got to eat it, sleep it, hate it,
breathe it until you've got river in your
shoe soles and in your pants pockets.

—RICHARD BISSELL

S O NARROW was the river and so winding its course that for years the possibility of steamboat travel was scoffed at. The Minnesota was a watercourse for *voyageurs* who sang the ancient *chansons* of France as they paddled the serpentine curves through the wide valley. In canoes made of birch bark or carved from the trunks of cottonwoods, the effervescent French-Canadians filled the valley with the folk songs of their homeland:

> *Ah! c'est un mariage*
> *Que d'épouser le voyage.*
> *Moi, j'ettends la journé,*
> *Jour de mon arrivé.*
> *Jamais plus je n'irai*
> *Dans ces pays damnés,*
> *Pour tout n'y ennuyer.*

Every man of the crew could sing, whether he was the *gouvernail,* standing in the stern to guide the twenty-five-foot craft, or one of the *milieux,* sitting two abreast on ninety-pound bales of

99

trade goods, their red paddles flashing in the sun. Their music long outlasted the era of French domination in New France and Upper Louisiana, and regret over its passing frequently colored the reminiscences of early missionaries and old settlers. By the nineteenth century there were some *voyageur* families that had been on the river three generations—*bois brûlé* though they may have been called. If their mothers were Indians, they were described in French as "burnt-woods," because their complexions were darker. But if these Minnesota River *bois brûlés* chose the romantic trade of their fathers, if they resisted the savage call of native blood, if their legs were short and their torsos strong— and *if* they could sing—they manned the canoes that slipped along the course of the winding stream from Lake Traverse to Fort Snelling. Sweating, swearing, dark with mud, they made the necessary portages, near Carver, near Redwood Falls. Two men could carry a bark canoe, while their mates shouldered the cargo in loads varying from 180 to 270 pounds. The songs came after—as the canoe glided downstream, at the evening campfire, or over a breakfast of pork and dried peas that had cooked all night.

When the *voyageur's* canoe gave way to the keelboats, there were still songs, but they were more apt to be American. The boatmen frequently went to Prairie du Chien, and almost as frequently they brought back new tunes:

> One evening last June as I rambled
>   The green woods and valleys among,
> The mosquito's notes were melodious,
>   And so was the whip-poor-will's song.
> The frogs in the marshes were croaking,
>   The tree-toads were whistling for rain,
> And partridges round me were drumming,
>   On the banks of the Little Eau Pleine.

The Minnesota produced no keelboat characters as extravagant as the Ohio's Mike Fink, but its men were of the same breed;

they sang the same songs—like the famous "Buffalo Gals" that was a favorite from Pembina on the Red River to New Orleans on the Gulf. The Minnesota keelboats, propelled by a half-dozen (or more) men using either paddles or long stout poles, varied from twenty to fifty feet long. "Fancy a large boat of forty feet in length," a young missionary wife wrote home from Lac qui Parle in 1837. "Near the center are our sleeping accommodations nicely rolled up, on which we sit, breakfast and dine on bread, cold ham, wild fowl, etc. . . ." The cargo on this voyage, aside from the missionary family, consisted of five tons of the usual packs of cloth and trinkets being taken by the old trader Philander Prescott to his wintering post at Traverse des Sioux.

For Prescott and many others, keelboats were a vital factor in the river fur trade, and were to remain so until after 1850. That year the steamboat *Anthony Wayne*, of St. Louis, cautiously moved a few miles up the Minnesota and met a keelboat being cordelled over the rapids at Carver. "The boatmen upon 'the Rocky Mountains,' (that was her name)," wrote James Goodhue, "looked astonished and scared, and swung their hats, no more expecting to see a steamboat there than a team of walruses in harness."

Whatever surprise there may have been in that sight of the *Anthony Wayne* was due as much to Goodhue as to any other single individual. Once called "this Bombastus Furioso of the

press," Goodhue was the first newspaper editor in St. Paul, and the Minnesota Valley's greatest publicist. He saw the river as the inevitable highway to settlement. Writing in his *Minnesota Pioneer* of the four exploratory steamboat excursions in 1850, he said: "We went into this work, not as some did, for the pleasure of it, but as a necessary . . . preliminary to obtaining an appropriation from Congress, for the negotiation of the Sioux treaties."

Indian treaties and ensuing settlement seemed furthest from the minds of the passengers, as Goodhue described the first trip: "Never was a lighter hearted band of adventurers propelled by steam than the gay multitude thronging the cabin and decks of the Anthony Wayne, as she turned her bow into the mouth of the Saint Peter, to explore that rich valley in the Southwest, along which the covetous eye of the white man has long gazed with prying curiosity. . . .

"The delightful weather, the stirring music of the band, the majestic scenery, every thing, conspired to exhilarate—to say nothing of the iced brandy. The current of the river seemed sluggish, winding along through a vast alluvial intervale, like a silver eel. Uniformly about 150 feet wide, without a snag, a sawyer, a rock, a riffle, or an indenture in either bank, the river really seemed more like a work of art, a ship canal, constructed by the labor and wealth of a great state, than like a natural stream of water, draining an immense area of fertile lands. . . . Each shore was a fresh, perpendicular, crumbling bank of alluvion, being more elevated than the grounds more remote from the river, which . . . were so much depressed as to form lagoons, filled with water and tall grass, the home of numberless water-fowl; while still more remote from the river, the land rose by a gradual ascent and spread away in the rich luxuriance of a waving inclined plain, its sides crowned with small clustering groves, and a few trees scattered over the whole expanse, upon the east side of the river; while upon the west side, the same description of intervale was walled in at a distance from the river of about one mile, or often less, by a high, steep, grass-covered bluff. So crooked was the river, that we seemed all the time to be just at the end of it; but the pilot, who was certainly very skillful, contrived to wind the boat along a labyrinth of interminable twistings, apparently confident that wherever he could direct the bow of the boat, he could sweep her stern gracefully around and bring up the rear without conflicting with the bank of the river."

The pilot was an old *voyageur*, Louis Pelon. There were three hundred "well dressed persons" including seventy who had come up from St. Louis to see the wilds of Minnesota. With "a small, select band from Quincy" aboard, the passengers were moved to dance, says Goodhue's account "—an amusement which the more enlarged Christianity of the West is too liberal to frown upon as a crime. . . ." Even the steamer itself could not resist the terpsichorean mood. The *Anthony Wayne* "reluctantly turned her bow down stream, retracing the winding channel . . . at a flying pace, and *balancing* now to the shore on the right, then *swinging* to the opposite corner, then *docedo* to a swarthy forest, now it is *chassez* right, and now left and now *alamande* right and left . . . the moon is out, spreading an ocean of softened light around—now a frowning forest—now a vast jungle of grass, and now an undulating prairie, sweep along like a panorama, while countless millions of fire flies are spread everywhere . . . as if the moon and stars and all the magazines of lightning on high, had been ground up and scattered broadcast over the earth. . . . Again we reach the mouth of the river and part with our friends. . . ."

A month later, the *Yankee*, with the Sixth Regiment band from Fort Snelling aboard, pushed upriver more than one hundred and fifty miles, and Goodhue described the trip as equally gala. Just above Traverse des Sioux the passengers went ashore at what Goodhue called "Cotillion Prairie, where *all* 'danced by the light of the moon'. . . . Crossing a narrow strip of bottom land, making a speedy trail through the long grass, gentlemen,

ladies, old and young, streamed up the side of the bluff, and
from its top surveyed a lovely expanse of prairie and woodland
far in the south. The full moon was up and the music being on
the spot, several cotillion sets were formed upon the grass. . . .
But there was other music also, for which we had not bargained,
the band of musquitoes, and as those who dance must pay the
fiddler, we thought it best to adjourn before they presented all
their bills. . . ."

Among the *Yankee* party was the river's first historian, who
had read Keating's narrative and found a coincidence in the
earlier expedition's complaint that in the same stretch of river
"the mosquitoes rose all of a sudden," so tormenting the explorers
that they actually were "obliged to relinquish an unfinished supper."

Long after the valley was lined with towns the same complaint
would be raised again and again.

But Goodhue would not leave his readers with so stinging an
impression. He was the river's self-appointed public-relations man,
as well as its poet. His story of the *Yankee* trip is alive with
appreciations: "Wonderful stream! We still thread its deep,
crooked channel, measuring 8 or 9 feet deep, with no difficulty
except the too great length of the boat. . . ." He noted a deposit
of coarse, clean, sharp sand and called it the best he had ever
seen for mortar. He saw dense forests, and a vast savanna of tall
prairie grass, thousands of acres in extent. The landscape seemed
to him of unrivaled beauty, and at the junction of the Blue
Earth he found "a kind of poetic beauty unlike the rivers of
earth."

Later he wrote: "Our accounts of the exploration of these
fairy regions, were extensively, almost universally read; and
the public mind was fired with a general wish for acquisition of
the Sioux territory." He also told his readers that the various
excursions had cost him much time and a great deal of money.
But he knew as well as everyone else that the effort was the
beginning of a new era. In 1852, four steamboats made thirteen

round trips on the river, and the following year eight boats opened what was to become regular service.

Soon the keelboat men became steamboat men and *voyageurs* like Louis Pelon were marking twain from Carver Rapids to Redwood Falls. The men worked boats that plied the Mississippi as well as the canal-like Minnesota, and in the valley that once had echoed *chansons,* the missionaries and the settlers now heard drifting from the water a variation of the "Buffalo Gals" ditty, inspired by a fuel dealer's daughter whom deck hands could not resist:

> Corn-Fed Girl, see the moon shine bright,
>   Ain't you comin' out to-night?
>   Ain't you comin' out to-night?
> O, Corn-Fed Girl, ain't you walking out to-night
> With your hand laid in mine?

When farmers began homesteading along the river, the sight of the stacks smoking and the paddles churning in the bend signaled a respite after the loneliness of winter; the narrowness of the stream made it easy to form friendships with the men on deck. As the towns grew, it was customary for young and old, male and female, to listen for the deep baying of the whistle, to race to the levee, and to greet the crew with cheers to the echo. People along the Minnesota lived more intimately with their steamers than they might have on another river.

Still, the river itself did not impress some visitors. A prejudiced traveler from the St. Croix, the handsome stream that forms Wisconsin's western boundary, put down his rather uncharitable verdict in his diary: "The Minnesota River," he wrote in 1856, "is a dirty little creek."

On the other hand, Henry David Thoreau, traveling in search of health, described the stream as *the* river of Minnesota," and he underlined the article. The climate of Minnesota, about which James Goodhue wrote so ecstatically, was the attraction for Thoreau. He came at the beginning of summer, accompanied by young Horace Mann, Jr., and there was hope among his readers that he would write about the West as he had about New England. But the journey was his last, and his vivid impressions of the Minnesota River exist only in a letter addressed to his biographer, F. B. Sanborn. There are echoes of the voice that told of a week on the Concord and Merrimack:

Redwing Minnesota June 25th 1861

Mr. Sanborn,
Dear Sir,

. . .

After spending some three weeks in and about St. Paul, St. Anthony, and Minneapolis, we made an excursion in a steamer some 300 or more miles up the Minnesota (St. Peter's) River, to Redwood, or the Lower Sioux Agency, in order to see the plains & the Sioux, who were to receive their annual payment there. This is eminently *the* river of Minnesota, for she shares the Mississippi with Wisconsin, and it is of incalculable value to her. It flows through a very fertile country, destined to be famous for its wheat; but it is a remarkably winding stream, so that Redwood is only half as far from its mouth by land as by water. There was not a straight reach a mile in length as far as we went,—generally you could not see a quarter of a mile of water, & the boat was steadily turning this way or that. At the greater bends, as the Traverse des Sioux, some of the passengers were landed & walked across to be taken in on the other side. Two or three times you could have thrown a stone across the neck of the isthmus while it was from one to three miles around it. It was a very novel kind of navigation to me. The boat was perhaps the largest that had been up so high, & the water was rather low (it had been about 15 feet higher). In making a short turn, we repeatedly and designedly ran square into the steep and soft bank, taking in a cart-load of earth, this being more effectual than the rudder to fetch us about again; or the deeper water was so narrow & close to the shore, that we were obliged to run & break down at least 50 trees which overhung the water, when we did not cut them off, repeatedly losing part of our outworks, though the most exposed had been taken in. I could pluck almost any plant on the bank from the boat. We very frequently got aground and then drew ourselves along with a windlass & a cable fastened to a tree, or we swung round in the current, and completely blocked up & blockaded the river, one end of the boat resting on each shore. And yet we would haul ourselves round again with the windlass & cable in an hour or 2, though the boat was about 160 feet long & drew some 3 feet of water, or, often, water and sand. It was one consolation to know that in such a case we were all the while damming the river & so raising it. We once ran fairly on to a concealed rock, with a shock that aroused all the passengers, & rested there, & the mate went below with a lamp expecting to find a hole, but he did not. Snags & sawyers were so common that I forgot to mention them. The sound of the boat rumbling was the ordinary music. However, as long as the boiler did not burst, we knew that no serious accident was likely to happen. Yet this was a singularly navigable river, more so than the Mississippi above the Falls, & it is owing to its very crookedness. Ditch it straight, & it would not only be very swift, but soon run out. It was from 10 to 15 rods wide near the mouth & from 8 to 10 or 12 at Redwood. Though the current was swift, I did not see a 'rip' on it, & only 3 or 4 rocks. For 3 months in the year I am told that it can be navigated by small steamers about twice as far as we went, or to its source in Big Stone Lake, & a former Indian agent told me that at high water it was thought that such a steamer might pass into the Red River.

In short this river proved so very *long* and navigable, that I was reminded of the last letter or two in the Voyages of Baron la Hontan (written near the end of the 17th century, I think) in which he states that after reaching the Mississippi (by the Illinois or Wisconsin), the limit of previous exploration westward, he voyaged up it with his Indians, & at length turned up a great river coming in from the west which he called 'La Riviere Longue' & he relates various improbable things about the country & its inhabitants, so that this letter has been regarded as pure fiction—or more properly speaking a lie. But I am somewhat inclined now to reconsider the matter.

The Governor of Minnesota (Ramsey)—the superintendent of Ind. Affairs in this quarter,—& the newly appointed Ind. agent were on board; also a German band from St. Paul, a small cannon for salutes, & the money for the Indians (aye and the gamblers, it was said, who were to bring it back in another boat). There were about 100 passengers chiefly from St. Paul, and more or less recently from the N. Eastern states; also half a dozen young educated Englishmen. Chancing to speak with one who sat next to me, when the voyage was nearly half over, I found that he was a son of the Rev. Samuel May, & a classmate of yours, & had been looking for us at St. Anthony.

The last of the little settlements on the river, was New Ulm, about 100 miles this side of Redwood. It consists wholly of Germans. We left them 100 barrels of salt, which will be worth something more when the water is lowest, than at present.

Redwood is a mere locality, scarcely an Indian village—where there is a store & some houses have been built for them. We were now fairly on the great plains, and looking south, and after walking that way 3 miles, could see no tree in that horizon. The buffalo was said to be feeding within 25 or 30 miles. . . .

A regular council was held with the Indians, who had come in on their ponies; and speeches were made on both sides thro' an interpreter, quite in the described mode; the Indians, as usual, having the advantage in point of truth and earnestness, and therefore of eloquence. The most prominent chief was named Little Crow. They were quite dissatisfied with the white man's treatment of them & probably have reason to be so. This council was to be continued for 2 or 3 days—the payment to be made the 2d day—and another payment to the other bands a little higher up on the Yellow Medicine (a tributary of the Minnesota) a few days thereafter.

In the afternoon the half-naked Indians performed a dance, at the request of the Governor, for our amusement & their own benefit & then we took leave of them & of the officials who had come to treat with them.

Excuse these pencil marks but my inkstand is *unscrewable* & I can only direct my letter at the bar. I could tell you more & perhaps more interesting things, if I had time. I am considerably better than when I left home, but still far from well. . . .

Yrs truly
Henry D. Thoreau

No one has written more exactly about steamboat travel on the river. It was a capricious stream, and there were few years when it was navigable all summer long. The announcement of a timetable that might be adhered to was greeted with laughter. Nothing was more uncertain than a steamboat journey on the

Minnesota. The best of boats stopped to gather wood for fuel in riverside forests; their smokestacks frequently were demolished by overhanging bows, or their hulls punctured by snags, causing the passengers to while away hours on the banks, telling stories, hunting, or gathering wild fruit. The captains and their guests took it all in good humor. The master of the *Time and Tide,* Louis Robert, was a Frenchman long remembered for his accent and his threadbare joke: "All aboard! Time and Tide waits for no man," adding, with what a man who grew up on the river described as a sly twinkle, "and only a few minutes for a woman."

One year at the St. Paul wharf there were as many as four hundred and thirteen arrivals of steamers that had made round trips on the Minnesota. In floodtime, when the banks were brimming, there was always talk of steaming all the way to Big Stone Lake, then across the Brown's Valley divide to Lake Traverse and on up the Red River valley. Major Long's expedition had been told that the feat had been accomplished at least once in the somewhat dim past, and a party from the Selkirk colony had taken a keelboat across the divide on rollers. In the 1850's, the Minnesota's great decade, it was inevitable that the all-water journey to Canada should be tried.

"Among old settlers," said the St. Paul *Pioneer and Democrat* for May 27, 1859, "differences of opinion exist as to the probability of a boat forcing her way from Lake Traverse to Big Stone Lake. Many gentlemen thoroughly acquainted with the country assert that it can be done, if the present high water continues. . . ."

To deal with the Minnesota, the rivermen had designed boats of shallow draft. In March, 1857, the *Equator* was described as "a truly Minnesota River boat. She is owned exclusively by citizens of Minnesota, and will be kept running for the accommodation of citizens of Minnesota in the dull season as well as in the more active. There are no Pittsburgh interests in the 'Equator' to direct her from the trade. The proprietors of the 'E' will have a boat in readiness at the commencement of the low water season that will require only a heavy dew to enable her to run."

Such optimism resulted in the offering of a cash prize for the first boat to reach one river from the other. The captain of the *Wave* proposed to take her from Big Stone to Traverse for $3,000 or forfeit his boat. The *Freighter*, 137 feet long, 20 feet wide, 95 tons, and drawing only 12 inches, had a square bow "as a great advantage if it is found necessary to transport her on land between the two rivers." Her captain, John B. Davis, started for Big Stone the end of May in 1859 amid "a good deal of excitement on the levee." As the *Freighter* paddled away, she was saluted by the shrill whistles of every other boat at dockside. Davis announced that he expected to reach Traverse in eight days, and to be approaching the Canadian border in thirty.

Four days later the papers reported him "446 miles from St. Paul." His passing of the mouth of the Yellow Medicine was noted, along with the fact that only the *Frank Steele* had traversed the Minnesota so far west before. Not until fall was there an announcement of the *Freighter's* fate, although Captain Davis and his crew were seen at Mankato on July 25 in a canoe headed downriver. The *Pioneer and Democrat* published the following in November, under the heading "Another Red River Enterprise":

"The steamboat 'Freighter' is bound to consummate the object of its bold voyage last spring, and to get into the Red River in spite of a broken hull and all the rocks and rapids of the upper Minnesota. She is now lying about eight miles below the mouth of Big Stone Lake, where the Indians are said to be making a series of philosophical experiments with a view to testing the real nature of the terrible *Waken* which actuates the wonderful Fire Canoe, and as one step achieved in the direction of philosophical discovery, to have learned that steam machinery can be broken, and is positively subject to mortal injuries and physical accidents."

Some of the *Freighter's* machinery was retrieved, and the

valiant attempt to link two rivers without the help of canal and locks became a legend in the valleys of the Minnesota and the Red River. Forty years later at an old settlers' gathering, an old river hand told the story with embellishment: "The boat was sold at a sheriff's sale and was bought by J. C. Burbank of the stage company. There was a Welshman in charge of the boat, and here he stayed nearly four years away from his wife and children, with nothing to eat, only what he could hunt or fish.

"In the fall . . . we took a lot of teams, wagons and tools, under orders from Burbank, and took the boat to pieces and brought it to Georgetown. We found the boat and the little Welshman all right. His hair had over three years growth and his whiskers were long. You may be sure his clothes were not of the latest fashion or first class condition. Coffee sacks, window curtains etc. had been used to keep him covered. We divided up our clothes with him, but they were not good fits, as he was so small."

In forty years a story like this was bound to get out of hand, and the exaggerations served only to entertain. The rivermen were great raconteurs but none of them ever took a steamboat through Brown's Valley in the wettest of seasons; and a project to dig a channel to connect the rivers died aborning. Traffic on the Minnesota dwindled slowly away when the railroads began to follow the valley westward. And the settlers unwittingly frustrated the river. Cultivation of the prairies absorbed the moisture that once had drained off the ancient sod into the springs and brooks that fed the river. But in the third quarter of the nineteenth century, as a veteran of the valley summed it up, the Minnesota "carried on its swelling bosom the commerce of the great valley;" and the settler remembered "many a tale of thrilling interest . . . of those bygone days, when our sky-tinted river was navigable."

12

A LITTLE DOMAIN IN SULAND

*It was in the air. It was the talk in
the hotels, on the levee, in the social
circle, and in the village post office.*

—WILLIAM WATTS FOLWELL

OPPOSITE the mouth of the river a horde of eager emigrants had begun to gather. They came down the Ohio, up the Mississippi, across the waters of Wisconsin. They came in such numbers that, in 1849, James M. Goodhue advised the Eastern readers of his *Minnesota Pioneer* to bring along tents and bedding when they came west; there was no available shelter of any kind in either St. Paul or the rival villages of Minneapolis and St. Anthony. The opening of the lands of the Sioux to settlement had become inevitable, and Goodhue's vivid reports on his steamboat excursions, reprinted in many Eastern publications, had served as a trumpet call to Americans hungry for homesteads.

Goodhue climbed Fort Snelling's lookout tower, and the resulting lines he wrote whetted the appetites of his readers: "In the contemplation of this scene . . . one is ravished with a desire to get upon it; and to appropriate a little domain for his home. It has the look of home. How can the Sioux ever consent to part with these lands?"

Not even Goodhue cared enough about Sioux consent. The cry heard most often was: "On to Suland!" It was the year for such slogans—when "Go west, young man!" was first published in the *Terre Haute Express,* and later repeated by Horace Greeley. Millard Fillmore was in the White House, but the popular drive toward the setting sun was Jeffersonian; in Washington the government had long been committed to expansionist policies. When the Territory of Minnesota was organized in 1849, the motto written for the official seal was blunt: *Quae sursum volo videre,* "I fain would see what lies beyond." Examining the seal with its drawing of a mounted Indian pursued by an armed farmer and his plow, Mary Eastman wrote an interpretive verse:

> Give way, give way, young warrior,
>   Thou and thy steed give way—
> Rest not, though lingers on the hills
>   The red sun's parting ray.
> The rocky bluff and prairie land
>   The white man claims them now,
> The symbols of his course are here,
>   The rifle, axe, and plough.

The fur traders, who had so long been dependent upon the Indians, would rather have seen the plowshares stop on the eastern bank of the Mississippi. Yet they recognized that at last the Suland had been all but trapped out. Both game and fur animals were scarce by the middle of the nineteenth century; the buffalo had been driven to the plains of the upper Missouri and the Red River valley. The shift in wind was unmistakable. In California gold had been discovered; the settlement of the Oregon question signaled the beginning of new trains of westward-bound covered wagons. As the canny fur trader saw the end of his wilderness life, he also saw that part of the government monies paid to the tribes could be diverted to liquidate his outstanding accounts with the Indians. Even though the exorbitant prices he regularly charged for traps and blankets were based on the theory that a few Indians were not good risks, he had kept books on the credit he had given, and he now saw a chance to add to his profits. He entered enthusiastically into the clamor for treaties that would open great areas throughout the West to settlement.

The traders' moment came in the summer of 1851 when Indians all over the West were being called to council. Then the most nomadic of the Sioux rode across the flatlands of Dakota and Nebraska to gather at Horse Creek in southeastern Wyoming. Almost immediately they collided violently with the Shoshonis that trapper Jim Bridger had rounded up. The Sioux joined their allies, the Cheyennes and the Oglalas; they camped beside Arapahos, Comanches, Apaches, and Kiowas who had been summoned by Indian Agent Thomas Fitzpatrick, a seasoned trader. Some Crows came, some Assiniboins, some Arikarees, and Minnatrees. At the end of the August heat, the chiefs signed a temporary peace in the presence of Kit Carson, trader William Bent, and many others.

Northeast, at the mouth of the Minnesota, Henry Sibley had also sent out runners to gather the valley Sioux at the ford where Louis Provençalle had traded thirty years before his death. The Traverse des Sioux mission houses stood there now—white and neat in contrast to Le Blanc's abandoned log post. There was a schoolhouse for the children of the Sisseton Sioux. There were vegetable gardens and fields of wheat and corn, and two or three *bois brûlé* houses. The Indian host was Red Iron, a sub chief of Sleepy Eyes' Sisseton Sioux, who liked to farm. Sleepy Eyes himself had lived all his life at his village on nearby Swan Lake, where he had succeeded Blue Spirit as chief after representing his tribe in Washington in 1824. He was titular head of all the Sissetons from Carver to Lac Qui Parle, a thoughtful, prudent man who was opposed to selling the Suland. He had determined to wait until his western relatives arrived before sitting down to parley.

No other Sioux were camped beside Red Iron's village of twenty lodges when the *Excelsior* steamed around the bend with its bow decorated by a pair of large antlers. On board were Goodhue, Sibley, the territorial governor Alexander Ramsey, commissioner Luke Lea, and a delegation of Sioux from the river's mouth. They arrived, said Goodhue, like a boatload of immigrants, chattering in French, English, and Sioux. As the *Excelsior* nudged into shore, Little Crow's braves lined up in full-dress parade, and sang to the skies.

Peace and friendship reigned. Welcoming Indians lined the river to see the arrival, and they fell into the water in the excitement of what was for some the first glimpse of the white man's fire canoe. So confident were the treaty makers that they had left behind the Fort Snelling dragoons assigned to guard them. Mrs. Richard Chute, the lone white woman among the passengers, was never to forget how the natives made her feel at home at once, as they shyly returned her smiles. With greedy eyes they watched the barrels of pork and flour rolled out, and the herd of cattle that had been brought to feed them. Like celebrating youngsters they began to make the gathering a gala festival—a combination of rodeo, Wild West show, and frontier days' fete all rolled into one.

Le Blanc's abandoned log buildings were commandeered as kitchen and dining room, and a feast was served under the aegis of Alexis Bailly who had come up from Mendota to be camp master. Then Little Crow announced that his women were the finest lacrosse players in all of Suland, and he issued a challenge to Red Iron. Two teams immediately stripped for action. They greased their hair and adorned it with feathers, ribbons, streamers, or bands of richly worked embroidery. They put on bracelets, arm bands, and necklaces. They painted their faces and their bare bodies, decorating their torsos with suggestive designs. The white spectators, eager to make the contest more "interesting," contributed a few dollars apiece to be divided among the winners. Shrieking defiance at each other, the naked players, ran, vaulted, and swung their rackets over the turf. "The way the girls and women pick up their red legs and clatter across the prairie is curious to see," Goodhue wrote, and primly added, "At night we retired to our virtuous couches . . . sought clear slumber and found it."

Goodhue's impressions of all the activities beside the river kept his readers entertained for three weeks. He neglected nothing in the entire extravaganza, and he missed no chance to comment on feminine activities. Mrs. Chute—as the only white woman among the treaty party—was "certainly the most resolute, enthusiastic admirer of frontier life that we have ever seen . . . the most artless, fearless, confiding, enchanting woman that ever went anywhere; and her loveliness contrasts so favorably with the coarseness of those wild red women, with their dirty ears, greasy dresses and lousy heads, that there is but little danger of that romantic attachment of our young men for the black haired Sioux girls. . . ."

Young David Faribault, however, had been pursuing a romantic attachment—in person and by proxy—for more than a year, and soon the circus on the treaty grounds added to its program a public wedding; Faribault married Nancy McClure, the halfbreed daughter of a Fort Snelling officer. While blanketed Indians and their squaws sat on the ground, while the treaty party sat on benches arranged like pews, David Faribault came forward in attire that would have suited him for Westminster Abbey nuptials; his swallowtail, waistcoat, and morning trousers were impeccable. The bride, raised by her Indian grandmother, stood beside him in a long white dress and matching slippers, "trembling like a young fawn, blushing like the opening bud of a dewy peony in the glare of sunshine." Alexis Bailly, justice of the peace, adjusted his spectacles and read the Episcopal service. Surrounded by *voyageurs*, traders, and government officials, the wilderness bride was saluted with popping corks. "I have always wondered how so much champagne got so far out on the frontier," she wrote almost a half century later.

For some reason Goodhue's report did not admit that wine had flowed at the treaty site. He called it lemonade, foaming and sparkling "joyously as if it had been champagne." Then he hurried on to describe an aboriginal feast of virgins which followed the wedding dinner and, on the following day, the thunder dance, arranged by one of the chiefs to stop the series of violent storms that had been eroding the grounds. The dance, Goodhue thought, was "the most imposing exhibition, probably, that is ever seen among the Sioux." With mock thunderbirds fluttering from tall saplings the Indians danced in a circular enclosure made of brush; the dancers were followed by other braves on horseback, prancing and curveting in wild freedom until the rhythm of drum and flute became utterly frenzied. At the point of hysteria, rifles were leveled at the thunderbirds and the symbols of heaven's rage plummeted to earth.

In spite of such diversions, time dragged. The tribes came in at their leisure. More traders came—H. L. Dousman, Sibley's partner in Prairie du Chien arrived after a two-day canoe trip; so did Kenneth McKenzie, the American Fur Company's "King of the Missouri" and great expert on Blackfeet. The Minnesota Sioux made efforts to show how well their own traders had schooled them. Demonstrating their acceptance of the Great White Father's justice, one of them posted notice of a "Constable Sale," declaring that a judgment made by "Sleepy Eyes, Esq." against Iron Walking Cloud required the selling at public venue of "one otter trap, one gray stallion pony, and one coon skin" in order to pay off a just debt to the claimant, Red Eye. Perhaps to show his understanding of the white man's logic, Red Eye took occasion to announce that he was in favor of levying a tax on all canoes, keel boats and steamboats arriving at Traverse des Sioux, as a means of adding to Indian income. No one took him seriously, for the traders were loafing in the sun, hatching plans to start a white man's town on the treaty site.

Joe La Framboise, who had had two of Sleepy Eyes' daughters as wives, rode in from the Cottonwood with two hundred Sisseton. Martin McLeod went off to hurry up the buffalo bands at Lac Qui Parle and Lake Traverse. Commissioner Luke Lea listened to a petition from Sleepy Eyes, and promised the old chief that he could continue to maintain a residence on the shore of his beloved Swan Lake. Then the commissioner addressed the growing multitude, regretting the delay and assuring the tribesmen present that, whenever an agreement might be reached, he was convinced it would be "in very fact a good treaty," one that would not only ameliorate the Indians' troubles but dot "the banks of this beautiful river before us with thriving towns . . . bustling cities . . . cultivated fields, glowing firesides, and happy homes." Goodhue said the speech drew " 'hohs' of assent and approbation" from the natives.

Visions of the promised land haunted all who waited on the treaty site. The young artist, Frank Mayer (who, Goodhue said, "draws everything, from a cork of a porter bottle to a queer conclusion"), imagined civilization moving in "where now the eagle soars & the buzzard flapps his murky wing." Perhaps influenced by the work of George Catlin, Mayer had paid his own way to Traverse des Sioux in the belief that future generations would want to know what the founders of their state looked like: "What would we not give in Maryland for a picture or even a sketch made on the spot of the Landing of Leonard Calvert and his Indian treaty of 1634?" So, in 1851, Mayer compensated for the delay in the Minnesota treaty by using his pencil, comparing the figures of the Indians with classic sculpture. He wrote in his notebook that "no better 'life-school' could be conceived, the figure no more clothed than decency requires . . . the models *unconscious* of their positions, which vary from the repose of the fatigued victor to the fleet progress of the racer."

Mayer was an interested observer when a missionary brought in a big Sioux band from Lake Traverse, and when at last McLeod returned with word that the most recalcitrant buffalo hunters were on their way. With the last arrival, the total gathering included almost eight thousand. "It is no small matter," Goodhue reported, "to assemble the entire people of a vast extent of country, like this, which is inhabited by scattered bands . . . a country larger than the whole state of Pennsylvania or Virginia or New York." The bands pitched their white tepees and threw up their bark lodges "like increasing waves . . . one behind the other" so that each commanded a view of the river "sweeping in a grand, graceful curve" around the peninsula of Traverse des Sioux.

"Look," Goodhue continued; "over the brow of the second tier or prairie ridge there comes a company of Sissetons mounted on their ponies and advancing with the noise of two drums and singing one of the wildest war songs that ever sent the blood curdling over the scalp . . . now they proceed to the marquee of the commissioners, to present themselves and report their arrival and their miserable starving condition. After due ceremonies of introduction, they danced a begging dance, received presents of blankets, tobacco, etc., and retired."

The diversions were over. There were no more mock buffalo hunts with warriors disguised in skins as they created the impression of a thundering herd; no more sham battles; no more showing off by prairie Sioux pretending to be Comanches. The stars and stripes flew above the leafy bower sheltering the negotiators, and a man from the Department of the Interior raised a kite high above the trees to delight the children. But the atmosphere was not a tolerant one. The commissioners would not permit further delay to allow for the appearance of the buffalo-hunting Sissetons.

"We might have to wait long for them," said Alexander Ramsey to the dissatisfied Sleepy Eyes, "and then both they and us would suffer. By sending notice for them to turn back, they at least are prevented from suffering. . . ."

Sleepy Eyes rose to his full height before the treaty table. "Fathers," he said, "your coming and asking me for my country makes me sad; and your saying that I am not able to do anything with my country makes me still more sad. Those who are coming behind are my near relatives, and I expected to see them here. That is all I have to say. I am going to leave and that is the reason I spoke."

The aging chief got nowhere, for Ramsey immediately ordered that his band receive no more rations, and proceeded with the parley. The next day, at the insistence of his young men, Sleepy Eyes agreed to the negotiations; but he protested the amount of the purchase price. For his pains he was told by Ramsey that he was not a very good hand to manage the business of his people, and that if it had not been for wiser and more vigilant Indians the tribesmen would not have received nearly as much money.

Under the treaty terms, Sleepy Eyes and thirty-four other chiefs signed away approximately thirty million acres in Iowa and Minnesota, retaining only a twenty-mile strip as a reservation along the upper Minnesota River. Out of a $1,665,000 total long-term payment, $68,000 was to be paid annually, and $275,000 was set aside to dispose of debts incurred by the tribesmen for traders' goods. To make sure that the traders got their money, each chief was "pulled by the blanket" to a side table where he was persuaded to sign "the traders' paper." A fortnight later other chiefs at Mendota went through the same motions.

Back in St. Paul, Goodhue thumped for the ratification of the treaty by Congress. Eleven months later "the light of joy suddenly blazed" for him when the *Excelsior* paddled up from St. Louis with news that the bargain had gained governmental sanction. But another year passed before the Suland was abandoned by the tribes. The settlements along the river were about to materialize—at long last.

Traverse des Sioux itself was the first of them; within eighteen months of the opening of negotiations, the wooded spot where Le Blanc had traded alone for so many years had several stores, a union church, and "a lyceum." Soon there was a sawmill, a hotel, a livery stable, and two hundred inhabitants. The boom was on. James Goodhue had won his greatest editorial campaign. He cocked an ear along "the whole length of the fertile Minnesota, and upon the waters of the Blue Earth," reporting that "settlers have not only gone over, but have built houses and stables, and cleared lands, not dozens of settlers, or scores, or hundreds, but thousands of them. . . ."

The big, volatile man, who expressed himself so strongly in his newspaper that he once defended one of his editorials in a bowie-knife-and-pistol street fight, did not live to see the flowering of the fertile valley. In the sweltering summer of 1852 he urged St. Paul readers of the *Pioneer* to "turn out next Friday morning at 7 o'clock, with an axe or spade, or with both, to assist in opening the road into Suland . . . we can all turn out and do the work in one day if we will." This day's work was Goodhue's final contribution to the valley. He became gravely ill and the cause was laid to exposure to the intense heat of the sun during the breaking of ground for the new road. Within a month the valley's most lyric promoter was dead, aged forty-two. The "little domain" he might have appropriated was left to others.

But while the valley in general prospered, there was an irony in the fate of Traverse des Sioux. After six years as a boom town, it lost a bitter fight to be named the county seat. Hopefully erected mansions fell into disrepair as the settlers moved upriver. Foliage obscured a ghost town where a fateful treaty had been signed. Years later the Daughters of the American Revolution uprooted a nearby boulder to serve as a marker for the treaty site—"a silent reminder of that busy throng which filled these grounds. . . . ."

13

WONDERFUL
HORSELESS WAGON

*He had more of Lorenzo de' Medici in him
than would be supposed by that 70% of the
present virtuous citizenry of Minnesota who
know nothing about him, or by the 98.5% of
the general American population who have
never heard his name. . . .*

—SINCLAIR LEWIS

T HE MOST WONDERFUL event of Henderson's Fourth of July in
1859 was the trial of Joe Brown's steam wagon. "This machine was really the first automobile, and we all rode on it," a
United States Congressman said years later. "His idea was right,
as time has proven." With giant wheels and a stack belching
smoke into second-story windows, Brown's wagon attracted the
biggest crowd the newborn town had ever turned out. The great
machine was designed to haul freight and consisted of an engine
that pulled two large and massively built carts, each twenty feet
in length. It was geared to about forty horsepower, and the carts
would carry a weight of twenty apiece.

The engineer hired by Brown to build his juggernaut fired up
for the initial run on the unpaved Main Street. Henderson's men

and boys climbed aboard, and the steam wagon moved ponderously along the eighth-of-a-mile course. Hearty cheers broke from the crowd watching, for it moved—it moved to the end of the street, reversed its gears and backed down to the starting point. Again and again it traversed the course, followed by the cheering crowd that seemed, said the *Henderson Democrat*, "highly gratified with the conviction that the ponderous body possessed the power of locomotion."

Of course there were some skeptics. "There were a few among the lookers on who ventured the opinion that 'it would not work.' It would move—They could see; but 'it would not work—it could not be profitably employed.'" A week later, after some adjustments, the steam wagon was to be seen moving up the valley toward Fort Ridgley at an eight-mile-an-hour clip, and it climbed a grade of one thousand feet to the mile, turned around and descended. The *Democrat* editorialized that it was certain that machines very similar to Brown's would answer every purpose for which wagons or railroad cars were then being used, and that they would travel with facility on ordinary roads. Sad to say, the steam wagon's pilot one day tried to take his iron chariot through a swamp. The giant wheels sank deep enough to be inextricable, and years later "the first automobile" was to be found as a rusted-out monument, shot full of holes by Indians.

Joseph Renshaw Brown was not easily defeated. He had a lighter model constructed, and began to experiment with it on the table-flat lands of Nebraska, and he was still experimenting when the railroads arrived to make his trackless locomotive little more than a beginning point for the developers of steam-driven automobiles. "If I had the property Mr. Brown has lost," said a fellow pioneer, "I should be a wealthy man. These losses never discouraged him. When he failed in one thing, he turned to something else. . . ."

There were few things in the Minnesota Valley that Joe Brown had not turned his hand to. He had come to the river at the age of fourteen, a fife player and drummer boy with Lieutenant Col-

onel Henry Leavenworth. He had been one of the soldiers Josiah Snelling assigned to the construction of his citadel, and ten years later he left the army as a top sergeant to stake a claim at the mouth of the river and enter the fur trade. Never again was he outside the main current of life in the valley.

When Henry Sibley made his first trip upriver, Brown was at Lake Traverse among the wildest Sioux, running a trading post surrounded by four blockhouses and an oak palisade fitted with portholes for musketry. Here, according to the haughty English traveler George Featherstonhaugh, he lived in squalor; his food was "of the coarsest kind . . . a few broken plates placed on a filthy board, with what he called coffee and maize bread to correspond. As I swallowed this disgusting food I consoled myself by reflecting that it saved one repast out of my own stock."

It is to be doubted whether the description is any more accurate than it is kind. All his life Brown had an exceptional reputation for generosity, and there is no question that he lived to the hilt of his circumstances. He was no man to give a stranger less than his best—an inclination he proved not much later when Martin McLeod and Pierre Bottineau turned up like frozen ghosts in February, 1837.

Sitting at Brown's fire, young McLeod told of an almost incredible odyssey. Coming down from Canada, he had run into a bearded, mustachioed, saber-scarred, self-appointed general. James Dickson was enlisting an army to liberate New Mexico and conquer California. Succumbing to the talk of liberation, to Dickson's romantic concern for the Indians, the adventure-hungry McLeod joined up. Under General Dickson he was going to help make California the last refuge of the aborigines, where no white man but Dickson's elite could own an acre. The crusading expedition (Dickson carried a suit of armor) landed on the Minnesota shore of Lake Superior in October and struck out for Pembina, where gullible *bois brûlés* were to be recruited. Freezing, caught in Minnesota snow, Dickson's legion was deserted by its Sioux guides; but they finally struggled into Pembina. Here the

Hudson's Bay Company made it clear that there were to be no *bois brûlé* enlistees as long as the fur trade held power among the half-breeds. Martin McLeod gave up the "crusade," and General James Dickson, liberator of all Indians, soon vanished from the record.

Starting south with Bottineau, an Irishman, and a Pole, McLeod ran into whipping storms. The Irishman got lost and perished. The Pole was so badly frozen that McLeod and Bottineau left him in a hut and, after twenty-six days of excruciating exposure, reached Joe Brown's fort in their search for help. But when Brown sent out a relief party the man in the hut was found dead. Brown nursed his guests back to health, and in the spring McLeod went down the Minnesota and joined the fur trade with Sibley. Years later, at the Treaty of Traverse des Sioux, McLeod and Brown were instrumental in persuading the tribes to abandon their hunting grounds.

Instinctive understanding of the Indian mind was strong in Joe Brown. His influence with the Sioux had been consolidated at the end of the river when one day he joined other traders in a shooting match. The incident had the ring of classic romance. A pretty mixed-blood named Susan Frenière—daughter of a *voyageur*, granddaughter of a British colonel, stepdaughter of a Sioux warrior—had been struck by a bullet when she dashed heedlessly through the line of fire; running to the girl's aid, the former drummer boy found himself smitten for life. He paid court to the invalid, married her, and eventually built her a mansion that faced one of the most beautiful of all the river's vistas.

Among the river's frontiersmen, Brown was once called "the brainiest of them all, a sort of intellectual lion, who sported with the savage Sioux, or ruled a political caucus with equal power." Brown had had only an elementary school education and a brief apprenticeship to a printer, but he had wit and native wisdom. As a young justice of frontier peace he settled a claim dispute in a manner that the two double-dealing claimants understood. Knowing that each was guilty of attempting to cheat the other, Brown took the men a number of miles from the disputed land and decreed that they were to race to a stake that marked the claim; the man to arrive first would be awarded a clear title.

Brown's skill at handling men and making them like it caused him to be a leading figure in the organization of the Territory of Minnesota and in the selection of his friend Sibley as the man to win the support of Congress. And when he was not using his legislative skill for the benefit of the burgeoning region he was editing newspapers, laying out towns, building roads, running stagecoach lines. After Goodhue's death, Brown was editor of the *Minnesota Pioneer*, becoming in his own way at least the equal of his predecessor.

Brown combined his editorial and legislative skills. His assistant came into the *Pioneer* office at six thirty one morning and remarked that his boss was up pretty early.

"Yes, by George," said the editor, "pretty early in view of the fact that I have not been to bed. I am getting up a bill for the suppression of immorality, and I've just finished it."

Straight-backed, barrel-chested, his cool blue eyes betraying nothing, Brown went over to the new capitol, took his place in the senate, and introduced his bill with the knowledge that his colleagues recognized him as a non-drinker and a firm defender of temperance. His bill called for the elimination of many common frontier immoralities, including the serving of liquor on steamboats and the hanging of undergarments of either sex on public clothes lines.

"The Senate saw the joke," Brown's assistant said. "The bill was indefinitely postponed, but Brown carried his point." The law required every bill introduced in the legislature to be published in the *Pioneer*. Thus, said T. M. Newson, "His one night's labor had netted him just $100."

Sometime later Brown's house burned while the river was so dangerously full of ice that there was no ferry service to take him home from his office. Newson found him on the river "jump-

ing from one cake of floating ice to another at the imminent risk
of his life; now gliding down the stream; now caught in a gorge;
now struggling to gain the shore; now safe!" Newson thought he
saw a tear in Brown's eye when he himself later crossed the
river and found his employer surrounded by his family and
remnants of his household goods. "By George," said Brown, "it
was a narrow escape, but we are all here."

While he still owned the *Pioneer*, Brown platted the river
town which he named Henderson for his mother's family, and
laid out nine roads spoking out from the hub of the new community to every corner of the Minnesota region. He delegated
his son-in-law, Charles Blair, to build the first house, put up office buildings; he brought in settlers, and began to publish the
Henderson Democrat. But in 1857 he was appointed as Indian
agent and his tremendous energies were diverted to converting
the Sioux to civilization. "Experience has taught me," he wrote a
friend, "that religion among the Indians (as elsewhere) can only
be taught successfully at the tail of a plow. In other words, it
must *follow*, and never *precede* the adoption of civilized habits.
The progress of religion will be proportionate to the march of
agricultural, mechanical and educational improvement."

As an Indian agent, Brown persuaded hundreds of Sioux to cut
their hair, wear white men's clothes, and live in houses; he
helped many of them learn to farm. Yet all was not well in
Indian land. The Sioux were no more settled on the reservation
assigned to them through the treaty of Traverse des Sioux than
it began to be whispered to them that they had more land than
they needed and that they might enlarge their annuities by another sale to the government.

The agitation resulted in a trip to Washington for Joe Brown
and a Sioux delegation. The party included Red Iron, Big Eagle,
Traveling Hail, Has A War Club, Hushasha, The Thief, Tacon-
lipeiyo, Red Owl, Mankato, Wabasha, Scarlet Plume, John Other
Day, Paul Mazakutemani, Iron Walker, Stumpy Horn, Sweet
Corn, Extended Tail Feathers, and the stepfather of Mrs. Joe

Brown, Ah-Kee-Pah. While Red Iron, a proud Indian, in· sisted on wearing his blanket and putting feathers in his braided hair, the others decked themselves ridiculously in high silk hats, flowing ties, and cutaway coats.

Wherever they went in the capital they created a stir. John Other Day, with his queue tucked under his tall chapeau, his white cravat neatly tied under his chin, so charmed a white waitress in his hotel that she married him and came to live on the river. But the more significant business of the excursion resulted in the release by the Sioux of nearly a million acres on the north bank of the Minnesota for about an eighth of its recognized value. There was an ameliorating clause that allotted eighty acres apiece to heads of native families, and through this Brown later was able to count seven hundred "Farmer Indians" as useful citizens. Under his influence some of the Indians who had gone to Washington organized the "Hazelwood Republic" at the end of the river—framing a constitution, electing a president and appointing cabinet officers. It was said that what Joseph R. Brown could not do with and for the Sioux Indians could not be done. But Brown was a Democrat, and Lincoln's election and the ancient spoils system deprived him of the challenge he had found as an Indian agent. In political retirement, among the Sioux not far from Redwood Falls, he built for his mixed-blood family a stone mansion in which "to live the rest of our lives."

The pink granite edifice was three and a half stories tall and had a score of rooms. Dug into the side of a hill, overlooking the sweeping glacial valley, the mansion's entrance was on the high ground that enveloped the rear of the second story. Verandas ran the length of the house at each level. Storerooms, a kitchen and a great dining room took up the ground floor. Heavy damask curtains hanging from brass cornices and black mohair furniture imported from New York made a stately living room under a crystal chandelier. There were two pianos; one in the parlor, and one in Mrs. Brown's sitting room. On the top floor were a study and a billiard room. Here was grandeur in the wilderness where no other white family had yet come to settle. Such a house must have a name, and the Scottish surveyor who had laid out Henderson gave it one—with a humor that appealed to the former drummer boy and his French-Scottish-Indian wife. The hospitable mansion so removed from civilization was called "Farther-and-Gay Castle," as a wilderness salute to Fotheringhay, the last refuge of Mary Stuart, Queen of Scots.

Yet this house, too, was consumed by fire, and its site today is a state park. Viewed from the road at the foot of the slope, the fragmented stone walls sometimes have the look of megaliths on Wiltshire downland. From the high ground behind—where picnic tables now mark the old entrance to Farther-and-Gay —the quarried granite glows in warm sunlight, framing the shape of a house and a view that cannot be different in any real degree from the aspect Joe Brown treasured. Across the verdure of the bottom land the river is recognizable by its luxuriant leafy border; beyond, the land reaches toward a far horizon—grasslands with intermingling stands of trees. There is no feeling of impending ruin. The standing walls are a tribute to the workmanship of a man named Leonard Wohler, who quarried the granite nearby and kilned his own lime. The caprice of weather has not damaged the masonry; the gaps were made when settlers came in 1895 and carted away stones for barn foundations. That so much remains is a tribute to contemporary Minnesotans. The maintenance of such a site, as Russell Fridley, director of the Minnesota Historical Society, has said, "may suggest a world but recently vanished, yet nearly as remote to our children as that of the mound builders seemed to our grandfathers."

Joe Brown and his family had no time for such backward glances. They moved west again to the glacial bed that has since been known as Brown's Valley. For a time Brown's stagecoach lines kept him busy; he was involved in the plans to link the Minnesota with the Red River. But he never stopped tinkering with new models of his steam wagon. On the plains where there were still no railroads, and thousands of emigrants were dependent upon ox teams on the overland trail, Brown proposed to establish a regular schedule of steam wagons between Nebraska City and Denver.

Almost four decades before the first automobile was made for sale, Brown's model had brilliant red drive wheels, twelve feet in diameter and two feet across the cleated rims. Inside each big wheel was a series of meshed gear wheels on a shaft connected with the engine. The front wheels were six feet in diameter and geared to the pilot's steering wheel. The tonneau was open, covered with a bright red roof, and five feet off the ground. The Nebraska trials, said the *Scientific American,* were a "spectacular success," and the prediction was made by the magazine that the emigrant wagon trains would soon give way to steamers. Brown never did get the kinks worked out of his invention. He died while supervising the construction of his last design.

Joseph Renshaw Brown fascinated men who knew him and those who have followed his trail through history. He is a memorable character in Clyde Brion Davis' novel, *Nebraska Coast.* And he figures even more strongly in Sinclair Lewis' *The God-*

JOE AND SAM BROWN'S TRADING POST

Seeker, at the end of which the author paused to set the record straight on what was fact and what was fiction. Lewis said Brown was even more of a man than he had suggested in his novel. "If he had lived ten years longer—he died suddenly in a hotel in New York in 1870—he might have been more famous than Henry Ford and have hustled up history by forty years," Lewis wrote. "Perhaps as much as anyone he was the inventor of the automobile."

When a monument to Brown's memory was dedicated in Henderson, the Congressman who had been one of the first steam-wagon passengers said, "All traction engines and automobiles . . . are built on the same line of thought and invention; and they are in a way a far greater monument to him than this granite shaft. The condition of the roads at the time, however, was against the practical use of the steam wagon. The sloughs were not graded and the creeks were not bridged. . . . But even under these adverse circumstances his steam wagon was run. . . ." The story of Joe Brown's steam wagon has been running ever since, in the hearth-fire talk of the valley he loved.

14

BIG WOODS, BIG PASTURES

*"The land of the heart is
the land of the West."*

—G. P. MORRIS, 1851

THE MOCCASIN flower was sweet in the groves and the new grapes hung green and budding, entwined in the trees that bordered the river. Soft was the wind on the river, and soft the drowning splash of the paddle wheel of the *H. T. Yeatman* as the steamer passed Brown's Landing at Henderson. An otter barked in fear and protest, and the sound crackled in the soft May air. Spring it was, and the land was new. Sunny it was, and the sky blue over the river in tiny glimpses through the arbor of trees. A lark nicked and dived, curveting to the day's glory, reveling in its own song. The *H. T. Yeatman* parted the dark water, edging on toward a new land that was not Wales. No Snowdon in the distance, no curlew's call, no crumbling Roman marauder's castle on Teifiside.

From the deck of the *H. T. Yeatman* trails could be seen, but not one led through Welsh moorland to the cave of Twm Shon Catti, that clever thief; the trails led moccasined feet out of the *Bois Franc*, out of the Big Woods past three landings: Lower Le Sueur, Middle Le Sueur, Upper Le Sueur; past Traverse des Sioux to hunting grounds where there were elk and, maybe,

134

glowering buffalo. Soft was the land, and wilder; no quilted farms patchworked the slopes, no thatch-roofed farms and the sound of a new calf in the byre; no gray haze over the coal-tips, or the grime and sweat and the grinding hurt of "stoppages" down below in the Coronation Shaft. No more settling-up Saturday without a ha'penny with which to bless oneself, and thanks to God that at least one's children did not starve. There was a hymn to be sung—in Welsh.

Bryn Calfaria was sung, or *Calon Lan,* perhaps; and silent was Captain Sam Cabell as he listened. All the watery way from Ohio, all the long way up the Mississippi, from the shore when his passengers had disembarked to rest—for four weeks Captain Cabell had listened to hymns and to folk songs:

> "All hail to thee, Cambria, the land of my fathers,
> I would I could make thee immortal in song. . . ."

Every passenger aboard the *H. T. Yeatman* was Cambrian—one hundred and twenty-one men, women and children from Wales. Religious they were; and bearded the men; black-bonneted were the women and strong. In southern Ohio where they had tarried among other Welsh, the men had read to their wives from *Dysgedydd, Drych,* and *Cyfaill* the gushing articles written in their own language by the Reverend Richard Davies, salesman of the West. Davies was persuasive, and he could not be content with his newspaper appeals. He wrote long letters to every Welshman he knew, extolling the rich farm lands of the Minnesota Valley, telling of the new Welsh metropolis rising out of the big bend where the Blue Earth River joins the Minnesota.

South Bend was the name of the metropolis. It had been founded when Davies' friend, D. C. Evans, had joined a steamboat captain at the big turn and found J. S. Lyon, who had just arrived from Iowa in his buckskin suit and with oxen tugging a prairie schooner. In one day up had gone a log cabin for Buckskin Lyon's family, and Evans had hurried back to Wisconsin to report the news to Davies. There was a road being built to Mendota, and Buckskin had put up a sawmill. A city had risen —and Davies poured out more letters, more articles to be read by Welshmen looking for land.

In the soft spring of 1856 the *H. T. Yeatman,* 165 tons, out of Freedom, Pennsylvania, had pulled in to the Ohio landing to take aboard the Welsh party and all its baggage. The big stern-wheeler was too much for the Minnesota River even in that year's spring flood, but it managed to scrape its way in the wake of the fast-traveling *Réveille;* on May 10 it passed the bustling new community of Mankato and stopped dead in the bank of metropolitan South Bend. Surprise. Perturbation. Some sang a hymn to stop the things they thought about the Reverend Richard Davies. A hotel? It was John Griffith's log cabin. Only a few of the weary colonists could it take. Scattered wilderness shanties accommodated another handful. The remaining families spread themselves on the schoolhouse floor and rested. All the way they had traveled, and they were home at last. Next morning—Sunday—a prayer meeting was held in the open air and Sabbath school in the nearby mill.

That week the men walked the country over, looking for vacant claims, and they found the wooded sites they needed. One group discovered the bottom land they called Prairie Bach, "little prairie," and the gentle dovetailing of grass and woodland seemed to them a magnificent natural park with "recesses winding far into the forest like the avenues of a mighty labyrinth." Some settled on beautiful Minneopa Creek, others on lakes of the Undine Region where Joseph Nicollet had seen his water nymph; still others cut out farms in the Big Woods, the great hardwood forest that lay one hundred and fifty miles long and forty to fifty miles wide.

They chose sites in the brush where the timber was most convenient, building co-operatively, building from the materials at hand. While some of the men cut and notched logs, others carried and piled them, forming rectangular walls. When one side wall was higher than the other, a roof of bark was laid on slanting poles; no windows, for there was no glass; a blanket served as a door.

In a year or so these temporary shelters were replaced by plastered log cabins, built around huge fireplaces reminiscent of Wales—huge enough, one settler said, for a pair of oxen to pass through. Yet there was little else to remind the Welsh of home. Tiny, mean Anglesey fields that had been tended by grandmother while grandfather toiled in the mines were now replaced by seemingly endless acres. Hard work to clear those acres, of course; but no tribute to be paid, no "stoppages" at all.

Lucky were those who had grown up on even the tiniest Welsh farmstead; there were others who had come from the row-houses of coal towns and knew not a thing about farming. But with a scythe for hay, a cradle for grain, a plow, a grub hoe, and an ax, the collier boys broke the untilled earth. Joining in groups of a half dozen, they would hitch all their teams to one plow. The heaviest men rode the beam to keep the blade in the resistant turf, and there was, one of them reported, "much fun, much story-telling, much arguing of theological points, much noise, much quarreling, and, occasionally, a little plowing done." Fighting gophers and blackbirds, they raised corn, buckwheat, and potatoes.

Great numbers of Welsh began to migrate from Wisconsin and Pennsylvania, aiming for the river settlements that had been so glowingly portrayed that the newcomers imagined thriving towns where, when the truth was known, there stood nothing but a claim shack. Three families from the Ohio coal country followed Indian trails all one day in search of Eureka, a widely advertised city across the river from South Bend. In the dusk, when they stopped at a cabin to ask their way, a man jumped from his supper at the sound of their Welsh accents and cried, *"Fachgen, yr wyt ti ynddi pan yn y ty yma."* ("Boy, you are in Eureka when in this house.") Such incidents caused more than one pioneer to retreat.

The whole valley suffered from a disease that became known as townsite mania. At one time every possible stretch of river was marked by a boat landing. Professional gamblers and canny merchants obtained pre-emption rights, laid out towns on paper, and had hundreds of copies of maps reproduced for circulation among immigrants. Lots were sold at greatly inflated figures, and though some of these towns became thriving communities, others never existed except on paper and in the full pocketbooks of speculators.

Immigrants did not find either the valley or the townsite speculators without help. James Goodhue, while he lived, was forever huing and crying across the country. "Settlers! What do you want? Will it satisfy you to get land as good as there is in New York, or New England, where the climate is even better and the market all you please to ask?" The Minnesota territorial legislature followed the editor's lead in 1855 when it established in New York an emigration commissioner whose duty was to meet incoming ships and advertise the great Minnesota country among those who had left overcrowded European homelands. Goodhue was at least as interested in his fellow Americans whom he saw headed—mistakenly, he thought—for California: "Contrast the two regions. California is on the western verge of the continent, while Minnesota is in the very heart of it. The former is afflicted with that lingering, living death, the fever and the ague; while to the latter, the whole family of bilious ailments is unknown." And the fact was that for some time there were thousands who came to Minnesota for their health.

Such blandishments had great effect. The Minnesota country's population increased almost tenfold in the first half of the 1850's. More than eighteen thousand Germans arrived during the decade and almost twelve thousand Scandinavians. They came to the mouth of the river and streamed into the valley—to the townsites, and the rich, untilled soil. They came gladly, but not without remembered bitterness. Political and economic pressures in Germany, Scandinavia, and the British Isles had sent Europeans of all classes across the Atlantic to find shelter. Joseph O'Keefe, remembering what had brought him from Ireland to the Minnesota, said he was "indebted—for the freedom and citizenship of the great republic—to the English and the landlord-made famine of 1846-48." Just as the Welsh had risen in violence in the Chartist riots, the Irish had rebelled against the export of grain and cattle while whole families were dying of either starvation or typhus that followed Ireland's blighted potato crop of 1846. Emigrating in desperation, Irishmen found new homes not only in American cities, but on the frontier.

Some of them aimed for the Sioux country and settled in Jessenland where venturesome Tom Doheny had erected a boat dock to rival Joe Brown's neighboring village of Henderson. Doheny's brogue was there to greet newcomers when steamboats paused at the new landing, and soon there were Conollys, Donovans, Flynns, Higginses, Grimeses, McNamaras, McSweeneys, Scullys, Shaughnessys, Tierneys, Finnegans, and McKeons turning new farms into Auld Sod.

In the twentieth century, Irish grandsons keep Jessenland's town hall painted a nostalgic emerald green. "There is a saying," according to Gareth Hiebert, a fond chronicler of valley life, "that one doesn't ask a Jessenlander his nationality. If they're Irish they'll tell you; if not, you'll embarrass them." Hiebert sat talking one mid-twentieth-century day with Frank Doheny, grandson of the town's founder. "My dad," the white-haired son of Erin said, "was a year and a half old when he came here. So sick on the ocean crossing they wrapped him up twice to throw him overboard—thought he was dead." Doheny pulled on his pipe. "But my grandmother pleaded to keep him." In the Goodhue-advertised climate of the Minnesota Valley the Doheny bairn lived to be an old man, and his son took after him.

Thousands of such pioneers were convinced the Minnesota climate would have brought balm to Gilead. "Without doubt," said a letter sent from St. Peter in 1858, "this state is the most healthful part of the entire union, from east to west, from south to north. . . ." Written to the Swedish-American newspaper *Hemlandet*, the same letter described the success of the immigrant's valley homestead: "I write this for the poor man in order that he may escape poverty. One thing I want to say to you, whoever you are: If you left your native land to become a farmer, go to Minnesota! Don't delay, but pack up and be on your way."

Heeding such calls as this was Ola Värmlänning, a blond giant who became a valley folk figure—not as legendary as Paul Bunyan, but more intimately known by Scandinavian immigrants. Though the stories centered around Ola were told so often that it is impossible now to be sure how much is true, his saga was painstakingly traced by the historian, Roy Swanson. The young giant was variously reported as the son of a country parson or as the black sheep of a wealthy family that had sent him off to the New World; he was sometimes described as a victim of unrequited love. In Ola's practical jokes, however, the hero was rarely the victim. Ola was constantly taking advantage of immigrants strange to the language and customs of the Minnesota country, and his memory was cherished by many who remembered their own awkward arrivals.

Passing himself off as a man of importance, Ola frequently came into St. Paul to meet the immigrant trains. One day, as he strutted about in his visored cap, he was recognized as a fellow Scandinavian by a group of newcomers looking for work. Ola announced with a winning smile that he was an alderman, and he forthwith commandeered the picks and shovels displayed outside a hardware store and assigned the immigrants to tear up the street in preparation for paving. While his gullible countrymen caused consternation among passers-by, Ola, in sadistic humor, slipped away to watch from a distance when the police took charge of the unwitting miscreants. Ola laughed, of course; but perhaps only a Scandinavian could explain why for years afterward the valley's Swedes, Norwegians, and Danes laughed at themselves as the butt of Ola's practical jokes.

They clung to the familiar ways of their homeland. "We lived just as we had in Sweden. . . . Going to church was our only amusement." They were simple folk, bringing the Old World and new ideas to the American wilderness, or bringing deep faith and an urge for freedom. Some of them, like the Czechs who founded New Prague in 1856, lived in temporary isolation, forming a community in which they could freely speak their own language, cook their national foods, celebrate Czech holidays and follow old-country customs without arousing ridicule. Sometimes the escape was from militarism, sometimes from poverty. And equally often it could not be called escape at all—many came in the simple recognition of opportunity, bringing to the river their training and talent as lawyers or as merchants, as skilled craftsmen or as speculators ruled by acquisitive instincts.

Sometimes, in the valley, the new settlers had to deal with claim jumpers. Before the land released by the Sioux treaty had been surveyed by the government, farms were laid out in 160-acre tracts by compass; the claimant had only a squatter's right until the ponderous machinery of bureaucracy made it possible to legalize his new home. "There was no law that would protect such squatters," wrote a Norwegian who settled on the lower river. "We had to do something to protect ourselves, and so we organized for self defense, drafted our own law, and called it Clublaw, I mean to say that it was no joke to get at variance with the Club. There was no one who dared attempt to take the land from a worthy settler, and, if he did, the Club was after him."

Action was to be taken peaceably, if possible, but there were times when justice was inflicted by force. "On one occasion we saw what the Club could do," said the Norwegian minister in his memoirs. "In the middle of winter two young men came from St. Paul to jump Thompson's claim. They tore down the house that Thompson had built, moved it a couple of feet, and built it up again. There was a law that you had to live upon the land twenty-four hours before it could be pre-empted. The lads had moved into Thompson's house, with a stove and all the necessary household goods. The Club had observed what they were doing, and foregathered there in the evening, surrounded the shanty, and proceeded to tear the roof off. The young men came out, one with a loaded gun, and the other with an axe, and threatened to shoot the first man that touched their house.

"One of the club-members edged up to the one with the gun and grabbed it and pointed it up, and struck him across the arms [until] he dropped the gun. Then the other one threw his axe away. Then the rascals begged for their lives. We were not such bad Vikings. On the promise to leave and never return, we let them go."

Where there were no such protection societies, claim jumpers were often successful and were accepted into a scattered community without stigma. A future was being shaped for all, and there was more tolerance than intolerance in the valley. Among many of the newcomers there was a good deal of admiration for anyone who was adept at profit, no matter how dishonest his manipulations. In the new towns along the river the greatest wealth came not from hard work but from speculation.

A lively picture of mid-nineteenth-century boom fever is given in Edward Eggleston's novel, *The Mystery of Metropolisville*. The author says that the frontier was a country of corner lots. "Idees is in the way—don't pay no interest," one of the characters philosophizes. "I tell you, here it's nothin' but per-cent." Eggleston—who was writing *The Hoosier Schoolmaster* while he lived at Traverse des Sioux—had reason to speak with authority, for he came to the valley as a young minister in the first post-treaty rush of migration. To support himself he made soap on weekdays and sold it as he walked the river trails in search of converts. And when his growing fame as a writer took him back East, he escorted the wife he had met on the river's banks.

Other settlers went back East because the pioneer life was too

rugged to justify the valley's opportunities. Longed-for independence, prosperity, a farm of one's own—all required a will-
ingness to endure poverty and to fight the elements. A man
acquired a farm in the same spirit as a sculptor equips himself
with a block of marble—it was raw material to be shaped with
hard muscle and sharp tools. Ingenuity was necessary. On the
prairie where there were no trees, the sod itself was cut into
bricks suitable for building. Sod walls, sometimes three feet
thick, were raised and plastered with mortar of clay and buffalo
grass, and roofed with bark, slough grass, and sometimes
more sod from which the native prairie flowers somewhat in-
congruously bloomed.

The prairies through which the river ran were beautiful but
hazardous. They caught fire in summer, and in winter they
were vast expanses of emptiness that could be as threatening as
the white ice sheets of Antarctica. Young C. G. Myrick op-
timistically wrote his family in Vermont just after he had settled in Le Sueur: "There has been a good deal said about the
beauty and danger of a prairie on fire, but most of this is in the
imagination. . . . I have seen boys run more risk in running
through a pile of burning shavings. . . . The flame shoots up
more like a flash than a flame and when it passes it leaves no fire
behind nothing but ashes." Trying to prove his point, he described a fire which overtook a friend: "On he goes but faster
rushes the fire and soon overtakes him, and passes by, simply
scorching his whiskers and some hair from his horse. So much
for the poetry of a prairie on fire." The less poetic truth, however, was that the first newspapers along the river annually
reported many deaths in prairie fires, and the loss of much
stock.

It was equally true that the prairie winter could isolate the settler in blinding white danger that stretched miles toward the
white horizon at every point of the compass. A circuit-riding
minister wrote vividly of winter perils. "Should you ever travel
up the picturesque Minnesota Valley, you will find," said Alex-

ander Berghold, "four large gravestones standing near a little church. On a clear day the white marble stones can be seen at a great distance. There lie buried the three O'Neill brothers and Thomas Holden." Five boys had started with a load of wheat in quiet, mild weather that seemed ideal. Suddenly they were overtaken by a furious snowstorm, and they decided to unhitch their horses and tether them on the leeward side of their sled. They devised a shelter for themselves by putting one wagon box upside down on top the other, and closed the cracks with wheat sacks and wool blankets. The five youths crawled into their makeshift igloo and hoped that their body heat would keep them warm. Instead, they were so crowded that they had not enough air to breathe. One by one they lost consciousness, and the following morning Mike Holden found himself the only survivor. When he managed to stumble five miles to the nearest house, someone relieved him of his overcoat and discovered that it was so encrusted with snow and ice that it weighed fifty-seven pounds.

Homicidal cold, the prairie in flames—and grasshoppers. A plague of insects swarmed over the riverside farms on the heels of incoming settlers and destroyed thousands of dollars' worth of crops. The devastation was such that many of the valley homesteads were almost given up for lost. Then an enterprising Virginian stepped off a steamboat and began to visit the stricken farmers. He was Robert Blaine, in quest of ginseng, a red-berried plant that grew abundantly in the woods along the river.

Blaine represented a Philadelphia firm that had established a ready market in China for ginseng as a panacean medicine. Approaching the settlers with guile, he showed how easy it was to dig the plant from the shallow soil, and explained that because the brittle, rather translucent root was frequently forked —in the crude shape of a man—it was believed by Orientals to have the power of restoring virility to the aged and impotent. Blaine promised to buy, at six cents a pound, all the farmers dug. Skeptical at first, the valley men would sneak into the woods only on Sundays, for they feared to be the butt of their neighbor's jokes. Yet it soon became apparent that gathering ginseng was a way for a destitute farmer to make two to five dollars a day. So much "sang" was dug on the river farms that depots were set up at St. Peter and Watertown. In later years pioneers remembered ginseng as a godsend that enabled them to stay in the valley until the grasshoppers were gone and they could return again to farming. When, one summer, Blaine failed to appear on his annual buying trip, there was little disturbance. Then someone wrote to the Chinese agents and discovered that Blaine had not been quite the benefactor he had seemed. It turned out that the going price for ginseng was not six, but sixty cents a pound.

Along the river there was little ready cash from any source, and life for the settler's wife, as a result, was never easy—nor did she expect it to be so. She was a full partner in the frontier venture, capable not only of caring for her house and children, but of taking her place beside her spouse in bringing in the harvest. "The floor was just the ground," Martha Thorne said in describing her first valley home. "Over it we put a layer of wild hay and then staked a rag carpet over it. A puncheon shelf to put my trunk under, and the furniture placed, made a home that I was more than satisfied with. . . . My baby was born three weeks after we moved in. There was no doctor within a hundred miles. I got through, helped only by my sister-in-law. What do you women nowadays, with your hospitals and doctors, know of a time like this?"

When the Thornes first raised wheat, the whole family went to town to have it ground into flour. "We put the sacks in the bottom of the wagon, then our featherbeds on top of them. The children were put on these." Martha Thorne spelled her husband at driving the team, and it took them forty hours to get to the mill. "The moonlight, with the shadows of the clouds on the prairie, was magnificent. We never saw a human being," Martha said. "When we got home, we had a regular jubilation over that flour. Twenty of the neighbors came in to help eat it. They were crazy for the bread. I made three loaves of salt rising bread and they were enormous, but we never got a taste of them."

Often the frontier mother made all the clothing her men wore. She knit shoetops and sewed them to buckskin soles. She carded and spun yarn, then wove cloth. She sewed together two homespun sheets and made a mattress by inserting a filling of dried hay. She made candles of melted deer tallow. "Women in those days never had time to look at anything but work," a river wife once said. The frontier woman kept her family alive sometimes on the meagerest provisions. She ground corn in a coffee mill to make meal, and could make "coffee" out of the crusts of corn bread, or from potato chips sliced very thin and browned in the oven.

She was often a gifted homemaker, who had brought with her some special heritage to give her crude log house distinction. "In Sweden mother had woven curtains and bed coverings of red, white and blue linen—How glad we were they were the national colors here!" wrote a Carver-county woman. "Nothing could be cozier than our cabin Christmas eve. We brought solid silver knives, forks and spoons. These hung on racks. Quantities of copper and brass utensils burnished until they were like mirrors hung in a row."

Any celebration had premium value. A young wife remembered that she drove fourteen miles to attend a dance when her boy was three weeks old, and she was very proud that, though she took in every dance, she wasn't sick as a result. Dancing to the music of fiddles was a gala part of housewarmings, and harvesttime husking bees ended in the search for a red ear that entitled the finder to a kiss from any lady present. There were many in the valley—among Methodists and Lutheran sects —who were more circumspect about their entertainment. "In those early years," the Welsh historians of the Big Woods wrote, "literary societies, temperance societies, and singing schools were common in all the settlements and our pioneers made themselves useful and merry as could be in the wilderness."

Regular schooling for youngsters was at first dependent upon popular subscription; one hastily organized school charged tuition ranging from three and a half to ten dollars a year. Such fees had to be paid either by parents or by someone who was willing to sponsor another's child. In burgeoning Mankato, the school was a one-room log cabin with a large, square, iron stove in the center. Pupils sat facing the four walls at desks made of wide boards projecting into the room. More often than not the teacher was anyone who could pass a cursory examination given by the most literate person in the community. Whether the teacher was male or female, the whole responsibility for the school rested on his shoulders. "I must have fires prepared at 8 o'clock to warm well the room," a Dakota county teacher wrote in his diary, "and I must teach 6¼ hours, per day." He said he had eleven pupils, adding slyly that some of them, he was confident, came with a desire to learn. Discipline was not easy to maintain among frontier boys who preferred to be out hunting or otherwise emulating the Indians. There was one essential qualification for a successful schoolmaster in those days —good muscle.

The valley teachers also had to be qualified to meet surprise with aplomb. There was no telling when a single Indian, or a good-sized hunting party, might arrive unannounced to disrupt the classroom. The Sioux now ostensibly lived on their reservations, but they were not prohibited from wandering as long as they committed no crimes. They dropped in on mothers at home whenever they felt hungry.

"One day when we were eating dinner," a woman who lived at the river's bend recalled, "about twenty-five Indians came to the house and looked in the window. They always did that and then would walk in without knocking. They squatted down on the floor until dinner was over and then motioned for the table to be pushed back to the wall. Then they began to dance the begging dance. In their dances they pushed their feet, held close together, over the floor, and came down very heavily on their heels. There were so many of them that the house fairly rocked. Each Indian keeps up a hideous noise and that, with the beating of the tom-toms, makes a din hard to describe. The tom-tom is a dried skin drawn tightly over a hoop, and they beat on this with a stick. After they were through dancing they asked for a pail of sweetened water and some bread which they passed around and ate. This bread and sweetened water was all they asked for. It is a part of the ceremony —although they would take anything they could get."

In the earliest years the Indians and the settlers in the valley lived in apparent friendship. A frontier housewife could trade with her savage neighbors for such luxuries as maple sugar or the wild rice that the Sioux were so adept at harvesting from the saucer lakes that dotted the marshlands along the river. Sometimes, when her spouse was too busy to hunt, she bartered for game. Mrs. Robert Anderson, who was the first white woman to settle in Eden Prairie, not far from Fort Snelling, entered her cabin one day and saw a naked warrior holding her baby in his arms. "In his belt were a tobacco pouch and pipe, two rabbits with their heads drawn through, two prairie chickens hanging from it by their necks, a knife and a tomahawk." The young mother steeled herself against fear and offered her unwanted guest some bread and milk. "Ever afterward he was our friend," she said. "When he left, he gave me the rabbits and prairie chickens, and afterwards often brought me game."

The memories of those who came to the river when it was still frontier country were laden with stories of the abundant wild life. Ducks and geese would swoop down on a wheat field in spring and pull up the sprouting plants. "They came by battalions. I have seen the fields covered with them. I have seen the sun darkened by countless myriads of pigeons. In the woods nothing else could be heard." A Vermonter who arrived when he was nine years old swore that he killed a buffalo in his first season. He found a rattlesnake den and killed seventy-eight "great big fellows" in a single day. "The timber wolves were plenty and fierce," he was proud to report. "My sister was treed by a pack from nine o'clock until one. By that time we had got neighbors enough together to scatter them. I was chased, too, when near home, but as I had two bulldogs with me, they kept them from closing in on me until I could get in the house." And it was nothing to find a bear in the lean-to kitchen, raiding the pork barrel.

There were other problems. "The want of salt bothered the pioneers more than anything else," said a woman who came to the river in 1853. "Game abounded. . . . The streams were full of fish, but we could not enjoy any of these things without salt. However, our family did not suffer as much inconvenience as some others did. One family we knew had nothing to eat but po‧ tatoes and maple syrup. They poured the syrup over the potatoes and managed to get through the winter. Sometimes flour would go as high as $24 a barrel. During the summer when the water was low and in the winter when the river was frozen and the boats could not come up from St. Paul, the storekeepers could charge any price they could get."

Such stories notwithstanding, hundreds of families from New England joined those from overcrowded Europe in opening up the valley. From New Hampshire came the Singing Hutchinsons, a musical family that since 1841 had been barnstorming the nation in the cause of abolition. They had been singing their way toward Kansas where they intended to found a town and support the Free Staters' fight against slavery. In Wisconsin they were intercepted by an old friend who recalled later that he had asked them: "Why not skip all that blood and poetry, go to Minnesota, the most favored country on earth, and found a city you will always be proud of?" Three of the Hutchinsons were persuaded, and in the fall of 1855 they came down the river road in two wagons, ferried across to Carver, and picked a townsite near a grove north of the valley, naming it Hutchinson.

The singing Yankee family were practicing what they preached in the songs they wrote and performed:

> Then come along, come along,
>   Make no delay;
> Come from ev'ry nation,
> Come from ev'ry way.
> Our lands they are broad enough,
>   Don't be alarmed,
> For Uncle Sam is rich enough
> To give us all a farm.

Around their future town's first campfire, the Hutchinsons gathered with their friends. A fiddler sawed away at "The Star Spangled Banner." The barnstorming entertainers and all who could sing lifted their voices. "For the first time since the morning stars sang together," a witness wrote, "grand strains of heavenly harmony echoed through the listening groves, and finally died away on the range of encircling bluffs beyond the distant river."

> We'll cross the prairies as of old
>   The Pilgrims crossed the sea,
> And make the West, as they the East!
>   The homestead of the Free!

15

"GEMÜTLICHKEIT"
IN BROWN COUNTY

"Heimgang!" So the German people
Whisper when they hear the bell . . ."

—AUGUSTINE DUGANNE

IKE THE ECHO of thunder, revolution rumbled in lands far from the Minnesota. In the collection of kingdoms, free cities, duchies, principalities, bishoprics, electorates, and margraviates, where the common language was German, the thunder erupted. In Munich, the adventuring Lola Montez led the students in mass demonstration. In Ulm, the city where the medieval Meistersingers had lingered longest, the lower middle class cried out for more liberal government. In Bonn, the university became a battleground and Carl Schurz, the campus leader. In Stuttgart, King William granted concessions and then, as the revolution wilted, retracted them. In the wake of the rebellion's failure, two young men, destined for Minnesota Valley leadership, left for America as Carl Schurz had done.

Neither freedom of the press nor trial by jury existed in the unfederated German states, and thousands began to migrate from the crowded cities and the tired soil. From King William's Würtemburg came William Pfaender, only twenty-two. From Braun-

schweig came Frederick Beinhorn, a thirty-one-year-old cobbler. Eight years after the Revolution of 1848 they would meet in Suland.

Looking for work, Beinhorn traveled from New York to Milwaukee and then to the swampy city of Chicago. He found day labor, and with part of his wages he began to attend a night class in English. Intense and enthusiastic, he broached an idea to his classmates. Almost at once he persuaded a half-dozen fellow

Germans to join him in a search for a townsite where all could find independence and establish a heritage for their children. On August 7, 1853, when they met again at the teacher's house on West Randolph Street their number had increased to eighteen; they organized themselves as the German Land Association and agreed to accept "every person of good character." With monthly dues of ten cents for expenses, they would search for a tract with ample timber, and they stressed that it must be located on a navigable river. When the site was found, each member would have twelve lots and an extra nine-acre garden plot bordering on the town limits. Beinhorn, as the association president, was to be their leader.

Soon the membership was three hundred, and at a meeting in Chicago's Turner Hall the townsite zealots decided to sponsor a ball to raise more money for their quest. They commissioned an agent to find the fertile land they wanted. Winter passed while plans were impatiently gone over and over. They could not wait to leave. Chicago was "a miserable slough," so lacking in sanitation that hundreds that year died of cholera. The association members became even more impatient. In March, 1854, they advertised for more supporters who could pay an initiation fee of three dollars, plus an assessment of five dollars, and their membership jumped to eight hundred.

At last the agent said he was ready to lead them to the promised land, and a steamboat was chartered for the expedition. Trouble arose at a general meeting preceding the scheduled departure. The agent refused to say in what state he had found the townsite until he was paid ten cents for each member of the society. His terms were rejected. A delegation, suspecting collusion, confronted the steamboat captain and pried from him the fact that the agent had planned to abandon the colony on the sand dunes of northern Michigan.

Beinhorn must have been furious. He had grown up distrusting Hanoverian landowners, and now in America, where he counted on justice and freedom, he had been faced with duplicity that could be considered nothing but despicable. He called his members to another meeting, and tartly notified the agent that the German Land Association considered him unworthy of further trust. The irate leader rallied those who were discouraged by the Michigan fiasco. He would take a committee to explore Iowa, he said. But this was a failure too, for Beinhorn returned with the disheartening news that every desirable site had been previously claimed by others. There were more rumbles of discontent in the association. Beinhorn refused to give up and sent two men to investigate the Minnesota Valley, just evacuated by the Sioux. This time, although the report was favorable, there were members who would not go to a region so far away—so close to Indian reservations. Yet in spite of such pessimists, the association was ready at last to become a town; in September, 1854, Beinhorn sent an advance party of settlers into Suland.

One of the group recalled the journey: "After spending a few days in St. Paul and purchasing various articles . . . we journeyed up the Minnesota River in a small steamboat as far as Le Sueur. There we stopped a few days . . . waiting for members of our party who were making the trip from St. Paul by land. When they arrived we again looked over the proposed townsite but abandoned it, as it did not appeal very strongly to any of us."

Walking beside an ox-drawn wagon, the Chicago pioneers went on to the new town thriving on the Traverse des Sioux treaty site and found shelter in a frontier hotel run by a German. Winter was more than hinted in the crisp air, and there were some who felt they had been led on a wild-goose chase. Four men then volunteered to continue the search west of Mankato and the soon-to-be ghost towns of South Bend and Eureka. Townsite mania, the valley disease, already had eliminated all the desirable locations to within a few miles of the Sioux reservation. Naïvely thinking they could find food en route, the inexperienced trail blazers followed old paths until they discovered a road leading to Fort Ridgley, the outpost under construction on the edge of the Indian lands. They met a troop of soldiers hauling a cannon to Ridgley. They met a lone settler who refused them lodging. And finally in evening dark, while lightning flashes helped them to see their way, they met Joe La Framboise. The old trader, who had greeted so many strangers in the valley, took them into his house, fed them on muskrat meat, and passed around his favorite calumet. In the morning, with the sun streaming gaudily through the October leaves, he pointed downriver to an area he called Prairie Belle View. There, La Framboise said, was the finest townsite on the river.

It took the four German burghers—who had known only the outdoors of long-civilized Europe—two days to fight their way through the tangled river bottom land to the goal La Framboise had set for them. They climbed the bluff and came finally upon wide benchlike plateaus rising gradually and stretching along the valley several miles, like the tiers of an enormous amphitheater. Just beyond, they found a collection of bark lodges and tepees, apparently abandoned by the Sioux. Satisfied at last, the green trail blazers went back to gather those they had left at Traverse des Sioux, and on October 8 the party with its five women and two children settled down in the vacant Indian village.

The winter that followed has not been chronicled with as much detail as one might hope. The sound of axes rang in the woods, and a two-story log cabin was erected under the cool eye of Anathas Henle, carpenter. Three stoves were installed, and the ladies went about their baking, but there were only two barrels of flour, which was soon gone. Somebody went across the river and dickered with a half-breed for some potatoes; these were eaten up in thirteen days. John Mack said good-by to his wife and child one morning, and he and his brother Peter set off for Fort Ridgley. They got lost, of course, for wilderness instincts are not easily acquired; it was only a sixteen mile trip, but it took them a day and a half to make it. The new stone buildings of the fort had the look of prosperity; more than a dozen structures crowned the broad plateau in businesslike arrangement. There were cattle grazing near the shadow of the flagpole. But Captain Sam Woods had no food to spare. The Mack brothers brought their wagon home loaded with nothing but a head of beef and some other leavings.

Meanwhile, more settlers had arrived from Chicago and there were more mouths to feed, so John Dombach hitched up his team and headed back to St. Paul. When he returned, he found some of the colonists were so content with the Indian village site that they had begun to lay out roads through the woods, preferring the easy access of timber to the open plateau. With Dombach's load of provisions, life began to seem good. Anathas Henle was paying court to Elizabeth Fink, and Mrs. John Mack and Mrs. John Zettel were busy helping the new arrivals to adjust to the communal living. Then, on February 15, when the temperature had dropped far below freezing, a roaring fire in one of the stoves turned the chimney pipe red hot and the straw thatched roof began to blaze. One of the rafters soon burned through and chased a sleeper out of bed. In minutes the big log cabin burned to the ground.

Rather than rebuild, the colony decided to take over the flimsy lodges of the Indian village. They used some oat straw donated by La Framboise for roofing, set up a stove retrieved from the fire, and tried to keep alive as the Indians did. They nearly froze to death. For a fortnight they huddled in buffalo robes around the fire—in weather so cold that food froze to the plates when it wasn't immediately wolfed down. Mercifully, spring came in early March, and all but one had survived the ordeal.

With the rejuvenation of warm weather, the argument over the location of the townsite began anew. Elizabeth Fink kept an eye on Anathas Henle as he pointed out the advantages of the wooded area. Henry Vajen, a young Prussian who knew more about America than the others—having crossed the continent in the California gold rush—liked the looks of the creek that ran through the grove; there was water power that needed only to be dammed. On the other hand, Ludwig Meyer, who had led the quartette of trail blazers, stressed the importance of La Framboise's recommendation and cited the association bylaws that called for "a navigable river." The stalemate was finally settled in Chicago, and the decision to build on the river bluff was followed in May by the arrival of more settlers. While Henle, the Mack brothers, John Zettel and his family stuck to the claims they had made in the grove that soon was to be known as Milford, a scattering of temporary houses was thrown up on the plateau that overlooks three giant hairpin bends—perhaps the most dramatic of all the Minnesota's meanders. In short order Joe La Framboise's Prairie Belle View was rechristened New Ulm because so many of the colonists had come from the region of the ancient German city.

At last Frederick Beinhorn closed out the association's affairs in Chicago and arrived on the river. The treasury did not hold enough to pay the land-office fees for all the acreage that Beinhorn wanted for his dream colony, but he had decided to register as much as his members could afford when he bumped into a stranger from Germany strolling curiously among the new houses and surveyor's stakes. It was an encounter that had an immediate effect on New Ulm.

William Pfaender had arrived as the emissary of the Colonization Society of North America, and he had money in his pockets. He grasped at once that Beinhorn was having financial difficulties and he quickly made known his errand. His Colonization Society had for months been selling shares to Germans throughout the United States in a venture organized by the Cincinnati *Turnverein*. The Turners had come into being in Germany almost a half century earlier when Friedrich Ludwig Jahn, rebelling at the weight of the Napoleonic heel on his native land, had conceived a plan to restore his countrymen's morale through organized gymnastics. Turner societies thrived wherever there were Germans, and they spread across America in the wake of immigration. Building strength on tumbling mats and horizontal bars, Turners frequently took time out for serious debates, and the subject of pioneering was not the least of them. Settlement in the American West had been called "practical gymnastics" by the organization's newspaper, and William Pfaender's appearance on the Minnesota River had been as advance man for the colonizing program. He had searched for a townsite in Missouri, Iowa, Kansas, and Nebraska, and in St. Paul he had learned of the Chicago Germans already struggling to build a city in the valley.

Pfaender's group was more philosophic than Beinhorn's. The latter was principally interested in better homes and more independent lives. The Turners intended to bring to the prairies a community free of sectarianism where anyone could develop physically and mentally. The two leaders found little difficulty, however, in striking a bargain, and the result was the sale of the Chicago Land Association's site for approximately six thousand dollars. Though Beinhorn's stubborn German determination had been chiefly responsible for the beginning of the settlement, there might have been one more ghost town on the Minnesota had it not been for the intellect and vision that Pfaender was about to invoke. He increased the area of the site to forty-eight hundred acres, and soon a surveyor named Christian Prignitz was busy with chain and theodolite.

No other town on the river was as meticulously engineered as New Ulm; it was planned to the last detail, as Pierre Charles L'Enfant had planned Washington, D.C. Christian Prignitz, like L'Enfant had a glowing vision of his city's future. The bearded, blue-eyed young German saw rising above the river a community that one day would have from seventy-five thousand to one hundred thousand inhabitants. His design allowed no possibility of the usual speculators' subdivisions joined together in helter-skelter fashion. His city was completely platted on nearly six thousand acres of glacial bench. Framing his urban area, he placed four hundred and ninety-four four-acre rectangles for the gardens of his city dwellers—some on the deep, black bottom lands along the river, some on the glacial plateau. Young Prignitz drew no grand diagonal avenues like those of the national capital, but he laid out the distinguished parks that exist in New Ulm today, and bisected his plan with one broad, handsomely landscaped boulevard. He had no quarrels, as did L'Enfant, with his employers, and his design has survived every stage through which New Ulm has grown.

Still, the village of which Pfaender became president and Beinhorn a councilman had few houses and only a community-

HERMANN MONUMENT

owned store until Pfaender returned to Cincinnati to gather in his own pioneers. There were seventy-five who in 1857, made the journey with him on the maiden voyage of the *Frank Steele,* a steamboat built in Cincinnati especially for the Minnesota River trade. Captain William Davidson's new side-wheeler was described as "a perfect palace when compared with the old style boats," and the Cincinnati Turners were treated to the sight of enthusiastic demonstrations at every landing from St. Paul to Mankato. The river was jammed with steamers, and the *Frank Steele* was only one of eighteen boats that stopped that week in front of the great white frame building erected in St. Peter as the new state capitol.

The settlements like St. Peter that the pioneering Turners saw from the *Frank Steele's* deck were still little more than shanty towns, and the chief difference at New Ulm was the location on land high enough to escape the floods that filled the cellars of other settlers on the river. Camping out on the high plateau, the Turners joined the Chicagoans to make things hum. Beinhorn had set up the machinery for a sawmill, and soon almost a hundred frame dwellings looked down from the bluff at the steamboats squirming around the river's bends. Within days after he stepped off the *Frank Steele,* Philip Gross hung his Union Hotel shingle on a makeshift structure. Among his fellow passengers, August Schell quickly started a milling business, and so did Richard Fischer. Henry Vajen and George Jacobs opened general stores, and Henry Loheyde began to make boots and shoes. A cabinetmaker and two blacksmiths went to work, and Quirin Schaible, who had brought along his trowel from Chicago, became a busy mason.

On his Milford farm, Anathas Henle at last had settled down with Elizabeth Fink, and Pfaender, as justice of the peace, performed the marriage ceremony for Petronella Adams and William Jansen. In most of the new houses there were babies begin-

ning their lives in wilderness freedom. Half of the one thousand inhabitants lived within the city in 1857. Frederick Beinhorn opened a saloon and grocery store, and Pfaender—watching the population grow—ran a thriving farm, not far from the Henles. As long as the Sioux stayed on their upriver reservations, New Ulm prospered. *Stifttungsfest,* founder's day, was celebrated on September 2, 1857, and soon there were entertainments every Sunday in the new Turner Hall; declamations were offered, and there were dances, songfests, and sometimes debates. In 1858, the settlers in convention assembled decided to establish a newspaper that would publicize their Canaan among interested people in Germany and America.

From the lands of the Meistersingers, New Ulmers had come with the music of their native regions. They spoke in the accents of Würtemburg, Baden, Prussia, the Palatinate, Hanover, Saxony, Luxemburg, Bavaria, Austria, Swabia, Bohemia, Alsace, and Lorraine. They made music as variously. They organized choirs, and the sound of band instruments drifted over a prairie that never before had heard anything more musical than a savage drum and flute, or the sawing of a *voyageur's* fiddle.

But this *Gemütlichkeit,* when it was mixed with the beer that August Schell and John Hauenstein began to brew, stirred up trouble. There were settlers in other river towns who resented the fact that these energetic immigrants had acquired the finest townsite in the valley. Whispers went around. Some accused the Germans of being irreligious. A book published before the town was a decade old said "the Sabbaths were spent in drinking and dancing." The self-righteous author flounced her skirts in shocked indignation. "As the crowning act of their ungodliness," she said, without a glance at the libel laws, "some of the 'baser sort' paraded the streets one bright Sabbath day . . . bearing a mock figure, purporting to represent our blessed Saviour." The book asserted that Jesus Christ had been burned in effigy in New Ulm streets.

This was "unmitigated falsehood," according to William

Pfaender. All that had happened was that some celebrants had set afire a straw figure bearing the name of a former German Land Association president who had "made himself odious."

Beer and *Gemütlichkeit* were not always understandable to some of the overly pious religionists who were among the valley settlers. But to the more tolerant, the growing city became famous not only because its beer halls never closed but also because its families kept perpetual open house. "There were no cliques or clans to mar the universal hospitality evidenced on all sides in this little German city," a local historian wrote. New Ulm had become a town of *Summernachtfests*, of beer and music under the stars, of community picnics on the heights where the citizens had raised a great statue of Hermann, the Cherusci, who had fought for German independence two thousand years before. Here where two young German idealists had met, two German societies had melded to form a remarkable community. There was no alchemy. There was, instead, the natural yeast of time and progress in the wilderness, of exposure to American traditions beside the sought-for "navigable river."

16

DAYBREAK WOMAN

*The squaw who got a white husband
was in luck. . . . she had raised her
status, married into an elite,
and acquired a higher culture.*

—BERNARD DE VOTO

THE CIRCLE closed for Jane Robertson, the Daybreak Woman, at the mouth of the Yellow Medicine where she had been born in 1810. The sluggish Minnesota pulsed through her life as it did through no one else's story. It had carried her toward lower Canada, where she had spent her girlhood, and when she married, the river drew her irresistibly homeward. She was the river's daughter and her story reflected, as the river did, the change in the valley's destiny. She was known by the settlers at New Ulm, and in the lower river towns, but few if any white men understood her fully. In her person this *bois brulé,* called the Daybreak Woman by the Sioux, brought together the worlds of wilderness and civilization.

The summer that steamboats first began to bring immigrants upstream, Jane Robertson witnessed the end of the world into which she had been born. At the junction of the Yellow Medicine and the Minnesota she watched her husband, her son, and her stepfather as they supervised the construction of the Indian

164

reservation buildings that would stand as monuments—temporarily—to an ill-starred collaboration.

The blood of her Scottish ancestors ran as deeply in the Daybreak Woman as did her natal river. Her roots went back to the Firth of Clyde, and yet her grandfather knew as much about the Minnesota Valley as did she. He was an Ayrshire man named James Aryd—a first cousin of Robert Burns, he said—and he came into the Minnesota country as a Hudson's Bay Company trader toward the end of the eighteenth century. At Prairie du Chien he married a daughter of the great chief Wabasha, and as time would have it he had his own daughter Margaret, called Grey Cloud by her Sioux relatives.

Bois brulé though she was, Grey Cloud was a beauty, quickly recognized as such among the traders west of the Great Lakes. In 1805, while young Zeb Pike was parleying with the Sioux at Mendota, the bonnie Grey Cloud married Thomas Anderson, a Scots-Canadian who worked for her father. Five years later Anderson and Grey Cloud headed up the Minnesota to take over a Hudson's Bay Company post on the shores of Lake Traverse. Their daughter Jane was born before they reached their destination. The family's respite in the valley was short; war broke out in 1812 and Tom Anderson turned downriver again to enlist in the British army. With the defeat of the mother country he refused to become an American citizen as other fur traders did, and Grey Cloud herself refused to leave the land of her Sioux relatives. She was persuaded to let Anderson take the Daybreak Woman and her brother to Canada where they might be better educated.

Grey Cloud did not turn her back on life. She met Hazen Mooers when he came west from New York, and in 1818 they traveled up the river, past the site of her daughter's birth, to trade with the Indians in the Lake Traverse region.

Eighteen years later, in Canada, the Daybreak Woman began an odyssey in search of Grey Cloud. In 1838, she left her father's Canadian household as the wife of Andrew Robertson, whose nuptial promise had been to help her find her mother. In May, they sailed a Mackinaw boat across Lake Michigan, and in a bark canoe they paddled together up the Fox and down the Wisconsin to Prairie du Chien where they learned that Grey Cloud and Hazen Mooers were on the Minnesota. Dressed in calico, sitting on the deck of a flatboat, Jane, the Daybreak Woman, watched stoically as the men poled the boat around Pike's island into Henry Sibley's landing. Hazen Mooers and his wife, she was told, were now a good way upriver—past the bend where Louis Provençalle traded, past the great bend where the Blue Earth entered. The place was called Little Rock. Just the year before, Mooers had turned over his Lake Traverse outfit to Joe Brown and had moved Grey Cloud and their youngsters a hundred-odd miles downstream.

A generation had passed since the Daybreak Woman had been among her mother's people. There was a Scots burr to her English and the hint of urban habits behind her eyes, but deep within lay a memory of the twisting stream and the quiet trees that screened the water from the high valley walls as Andrew Robertson's boat inched its way against the current. In the sun-dappled water beyond the Cottonwood, she saw the ripples where a creek entered, and as her husband helped to pole the boat around a bend, she caught the first glimpse of the Little Rock trading post. Long-legged Andrew Robertson leaped ashore grasped his wife about the waist, and swung her onto the moist turf. At long last, in the August sunlight, Grey Cloud and the Daybreak Woman shyly approached each other.

The reunion was also the beginning of a lasting partnership between the Daybreak Woman's husband and Hazen Mooers. Robertson joined Mooers in trading at Little Rock Creek, and a couple of years later they abandoned the fur business together when they turned over their outpost to Joe La Framboise. The two men took Grey Cloud and the Daybreak Woman downstream and began to farm on a Mississippi island that is still named for Mooers' wife. When a son was born to the Robertsons he was named Thomas—for Grey Cloud's first husband who had reared the Daybreak Woman in the environment of her Scottish ancestors. The two families moved when Mooers and Robertson were hired to teach the Sioux how to farm, then moved again when together they were delegated to construct the buildings that would house the new Indian agencies after the signing of the Treaty of Traverse des Sioux. When Grey Cloud died, the Daybreak Woman started upriver for the last time with her stepfather, her husband and the mixed-blood son in whose intense looks there was the high color of the River Doon country.

Jane Robertson, the Daybreak Woman, watched the slender son as his father and Hazen Mooers erected fateful buildings. She was at Andrew Robertson's side when Indian Agent Joe Brown named him the first superintendent of Indian education on the Sioux reservations. When a heart attack cut Robertson down in 1859, Joe Brown had no hesitation about his successor. The job went to Jane Robertson, who was back in the valley of her birth—and back among the people of her almost-obliterated Indian heritage. It was a heritage of which she, along with hundreds of others, was to be a victim.

17

THE MAN
WHO BILKED ST. PETER

*The hair on his chest is the prairie grass
and his legs are the white pines and his
voice is now the April zephyr and now the
devastating blast of a blizzard.*

—SINCLAIR LEWIS

WHEN THE steamers drew in at the stone warehouse beside the Howes and Wainwright landing, the settlers on the decks sometimes speculated about the high white building that rose conspicuously in the center of the wide clearing that was called St. Peter. So did those who took the oxcart trail that followed the old Indian path running from the ford at Traverse des Sioux across the prairie opposite New Ulm. But the steamboat captains, who knew all there was to know about the valley, joked as they called to each other from their pilothouses. St. Peter, they said, was not above stealing from St. Paul.

The big white edifice was handsomely constructed—two stories tall, with four great chimneys jutting skyward, and fitted with an imposing council chamber. Its erection had followed a meeting, attended by territorial governor Willis A. Gorman, at which it had been resolved that if the territorial legislature,

168

"in their wisdom and sound judgment," should deem it expedi-
ent to move the capital of Minnesota from St. Paul to St. Peter
the promoters of the great white building would donate their
handiwork to the new state, along with spacious grounds "double
the area of the capitol square in St. Paul."

The St. Peter company—of which, interestingly, Governor
Gorman was the president—had been craftily organized to adorn
the river with a future metropolis as well as the seat of government. The promoters had laid claim to many acres on the southern
border of Traverse des Sioux and had cut lumber and quarried
stone for the erection of more ostentatious hotels and business
buildings than any in the other river towns. Steamboat gossip
had it that deeds to valuable St. Peter lots had been given to
several legislators to encourage their interest in the project.

The scheme was so well organized that on February 6, 1857,
citizens of St. Paul, which had been the territorial capital for
eight years, were electrified to read in the papers that a bill had
been introduced in the legislature to remove the government to
a virtually unknown place on the Minnesota River. Within a
few days the fifteen-man upper house, called the Council, voted
eight to seven in favor of the bill, and indignation meetings were
called in St. Paul and Minneapolis. Although the territorial attorney general said that it was illegal to change the location of
the capital without a popular vote, the thirty-nine-member House
of Representatives met on February 18 and endorsed the St.
Peter promoters' proposal twenty to seventeen.

All might have gone according to the dreams of the schemers
in the infant river town had it not been for Jolly Joe Rolette, the
member of the Council from Pembina, on the Canadian border.
He was the Davy Crockett of the north, perhaps better cast than
any other legislator in history for his role in the capital-fight
shenanigans. Joe Rolette was the mixed-blood son of "King" Rolette, one of Henry Sibley's Prairie du Chien partners in the fur
trade. Young Joe had been sent east to school under the sponsor-
ship of Ramsay Crooks, the American Fur Company president,

and it has been said that he made his mark on New York by consistently wearing his buckskin shirt and pants. Back in the fur trade he became Sibley's northern agent, and in 1843 he made himself important to the prosperity of St. Paul when he led the first of the annual trains of fur-laden ox carts through the Minnesota Valley.

Jolly Joe inaugurated the transportation network that became known as the Red River Trails. He loaded two-wheeled carts with buffalo hides and other peltry, rounded up some *bois brulés* as drivers and set off along an old Indian trail—up the Red River and down the Minnesota—to the St. Paul market. Soon there were long trains composed of ox carts, and two more trails across central Minnesota were opened. The crude vehicles used no axle grease, and they gave off such a chorus of creaking that they could be heard, a settler on the edge of St. Peter remembered, for a distance of six miles.

When Rolette's noisy caravan came down the valley, it could be recognized not only by the cacophony of the wheels but also by "a dense yellowish cloud" seen on the far horizon. "Gradually the cloud increased in size," an Eastern visitor wrote, "and spread away to the southward like the tail of a comet, and soon a single ox-cart could be distinguished at the head of the column, as if just emerging from the thick pall of dust. As the train approached, the outlines of the other carts, filing in long procession, could be defined; and soon the foremost came up. . . . There were some hundred and fifty carts in all—rude, wooden vehicles put together without a particle of iron—not excepting tires and linch-pins—and each drawn by a single ox, harnessed in shafts with gearing strips of raw hide. . . . Each driver had the charge of five or six carts, the animals being led by a strap tied to the cart next in front—so that, while he flourished his whip over the back of the leader, the rest were compelled to follow, *nolens volens*. . . . The heavy wheels that had never known grease kept an incessant creaking and groaning, as if speaking for the dumb oxen their unspeakable woes. A thick coat of dust covered everything, and black mud on the wheels and bellies of the cattle gave good evidence of the deep sloughs they had crossed on their route."

The *bois brulé* drivers were the constitutents who sent Jolly Joe to represent them in the legislature, and they seemed as remarkable to newcomers in the valley as did their vehicles. "That they have a story to tell you can read in their bronzed faces and the long floating *chevelure* that waves around their shoulders," *Harper's Monthly Magazine* reported in 1859. "Their dark, coarse blue coats, glittering with a savage profusion of enormous buttons of polished brass; their long, waving sashes of the brightest red, and jaunty little caps, half Tartar and half French; even their loose trowsers of English corduroy or some dark woolen stuff, if not of elk or bison skin, down to the quaint and dingy moccasins wherewith they clothe their feet, savor of the wild, wondrous and romantic. . . . No novel ever written upon the scenes of the far Western wilds and hunter life could equal the thrilling wildness and strange truth of their brief history."

The mixed-bloods who brought the trains through the valley were a gay crew who liked to laugh, to sing and dance, and who had what seemed to most observers a consistently childlike manner. Halting above the winding Minnesota at night, they arranged their carts in a great circle, with the shafts projecting outward and the tents pitched inside.

"Within the circle of their camp is heard a strange melange of languages, as diverse as their parentage," *Harper's* reporter said. "You may hear French, Gaelic, English, Cree, and Ojibwa, with all the wild accompaniment of mingled accent, soft and musical,

abrupt and guttural, in such strange, startling contrasts as flings an additional interest about the mysterious people. With their mother's blood they inherit all the native love of the wild and adventurous life . . . while to the blood of their fathers can be traced those demi-social habits . . . which they evince although entirely shut out from contact with enlightened society. . . ."

Joe Rolette himself was no slave to the rules of normal society. He habitually created so much commotion that old residents would say, "Well it's either a big fire, or else Joe Rolette's in town." He would arrive for the winter sessions of the legislature riding in a bell-festooned dog sled; and in 1857 when there was not enough snow for that, he walked the four hundred miles from his home to the capital.

Harper's took infinite pains to describe his appearance: "Short, muscular, a bullety head, the neck and chest of a young buffalo bull, small hands and feet, but with tough and knotty flexors and extensors farther up; full bearded, cap, shirt, natty neckerchief, belt, trowsers, and dandy little moccasins—so he looks to the eye. Inside of all this there is a man of character, educated in New York; but with a score of wild, adventurous years on the frontier behind him—a man of character who asserts himself always, whatever the right or wrong of the assertion."

Rolette was one of the great hosts of the Minnesota country. "Of unfailing good spirits," the magazine went on, "brimful of humour, blue three days in the year—no more and no less—sticking to his belief in a breezy, healthy way, and believing first and always in Joe Rolette; hospitable and generous beyond reckoning, and reckoning on equal unselfishness in return; giving you his best horse if you ask for it, and taking your two mules if he needs them; living for years where he might have made a fortune, and never saving a penny; a good Catholic, believing especially in absolution; a Douglas Democrat to the spinal column, and always to be counted on for good majorities in Pembina—threatening horse-ponds and nine duckings to any 'Black Republican' who dares to settle in the vicinity. . . ."

"Black Republicans," along with two or three "pumpkincider Democrats," were blamed by a St. Paul newspaper for the threatened loss of the capital to St. Peter, and Joe Rolette was one of those who had voted against the measure. As chairman of the committee on enrolled bills, he was given the proposed piece of legislation to make a fair copy, and on February 27 he left the capitol building with the original bill. The next day, in a cunning maneuver, another opponent of the bill asked for a roll call— which showed that Councillor Rolette was absent. According to the rules, the Council doors were then locked, and no members could be permitted to leave until the missing councillor was located. But Jolly Joe had disappeared, and the legislators were bound to the Council chamber until he was found.

"Alongside each member's desk," the *Pioneer and Democrat* that week reported, "was a cot bedstead on which the honorable might snatch a few hours repose when too sleepy to sit any longer in his seat. Scattered here and there through the room were baskets containing ample quantities of provisions, showing conclusively that there was no danger of the Councilors suffering from lack of food." A special police force was detailed to preserve the peace. Yet, searching high and low throughout St. Paul, the sergeant at arms reported that he was unable to find a trace of Rolette. Rumors flew around—that Joe had mushed his dog team back to Pembina; that he had gone to Prairie du Chien to visit his father's family; that he had been assassinated.

For a week the incarcerated legislators haggled. Motions were made at various times to revise the bill by striking out St. Peter and inserting the name of such other river towns as Mankato, Belle Plaine, Shakopee, even "the other side of Jordan." A member of Rolette's committee said that the removal bill could not be properly reported because there were numerous errors in the copy furnished by the secretary of the Council. And all the while the clock was ticking away—ticking toward the midnight that would end the sixty-day period beyond which the Council could not legally stay in session. Then, as the hands of the clock

on the chamber wall came together, the Honorable Joseph Rolette strode in on his short legs and stood at his seat. "Mr. President," he began. As Rolette had anticipated, the hour struck as
the gavel banged the desk. "The Council is adjourned," said the
president. "The Councillor is too late."

Jolly Joe went home without explaining his disappearance, and
Governor Gorman tried futilely to get the courts to accept a copy
of the bill which he had signed. Finally, in spite of a suit instituted by the St. Peter promoters, the legislation was declared
improperly enacted, and the river lost its chance to lap at the
shores of the state capital. The five-thousand-dollar white building, lonely on the shabby St. Peter skyline, was used as an induce-
ment to take the county seat away from Traverse des Sioux.

Joe Rolette had a moment of national fame. "Who that reads
the papers has not heard of Minnesota," *Harper's* asked, "and the
man that figured in our New York *Punch* as a runaway with the
Capitol on his shoulders?" Perhaps he wasn't as famous as Davy
Crockett, but Jolly Joe—"just off the superb horse, which he sits
as close as a Centaur, lighting a pipe, a score of wolfish train-
dogs yelping about him"—was long afterward a hero in St. Paul.
His whereabouts during the one hundred and twenty three hours
that his fellow Councillors kept themselves in continuous session
was revealed by a member of his circle. On February 28, Joe had
taken the enrolled copy of the removal bill to a banker who had
deposited it in his safe. Then Joe had climbed to Room 27 under
the eaves of the Fuller House and made himself comfortable.
At least a dozen legislators knew where he was, and the sergeant
at arms—after ranging the town in ostentatious search for the
absentee—played poker with him nightly. Joe had plenty of
wine to drink and, said one reporter, "surreptitious turkeys and
bass" to eat. One of his cronies later admitted that the St. Paul
faction had abandoned all hope of defeating the St. Peter company, and that Rolette's disappearance was designed only as a
practical joke to worry the opposition. The possibility of victory

dawned as they watched the Council clock tick on toward mandatory adjournment.

When Minnesota became a state the next year, the new western boundary put Pembina in Dakota territory, and Jolly Joe no longer arrived for sessions of the legislature garbed in a long formal coat and tie, worn over gaudily beaded leggings. "Rolette became St. Paul's mascot," said a city historian, "and there was no tribute of devotion its citizens were not willing to lay at his feet as an evidence of their gratitude." But, improvident to the end, the hero died in want in 1871. His fame survives in a full-length portrait hanging in the Minnesota Historical Society. It is curtly inscribed: "Joe Rolette, who saved the capital to St. Paul by running away with the bill to remove it to St. Peter, 1857."

18

REHEARSAL FOR DISASTER

There is a calumet for peace,
and one for war. . . .

—JACQUES MARQUETTE

EARLY IN April, 1857, panic struck the valley. The fire bell hanging in a Mankato hotel clanged loudly to gather the settlers in the log schoolhouse. Captain William Dodds dropped his interest in St. Peter's capital fight, organized a troop of forty volunteers and marched to Mankato. In South Bend the settlers took refuge at the house of John Williams and quickly threw up a wooden palisade. Welsh families from Eureka and Judson crossed the river and built a fort. Other Welshmen armed themselves, met and joined a party of Germans bearing pitchforks and scythes lashed to long poles, and on the Little Cottonwood they ran into a Sioux encampment. While the volunteer army concealed itself, three emissaries went forward to confer with the Indians. A gun went off by accident, and the volunteers, taking the shot for a signal, swept across the prairie toward the astonished savages like a cyclone, shouting and brandishing their pitchforks, scythes, and guns.

Sowing its seeds of tragedy, the Inkpaduta war was an *opéra bouffe* that could not be laughed at by its victims. It began with

176

the murder of thirty Iowa settlers and the capture of four women. The culprits were members of the band of Inkpaduta who, twenty years earlier, had been outlawed by the Sioux for the murder of a chief. In the spring of 1857, Inkpaduta, for motives that have not been made clear, struck suddenly at the settlement on Spirit Lake in Iowa, and then moved north to the site of Jackson, Minnesota, where two of the outlaws appeared at the store run by the Woods brothers, lately of Mankato. With eighty dollars in gold—loot from Spirit Lake—they bought ammunition, and then murdered the storekeepers. More than thirty Woods neighbors, gathered at one house to await the return of a messenger sent for help, were surrounded by Inkpaduta's men. When ten-year-old Willie Thomas saw a man coming down the road, he thought the expected messenger had arrived and he called to the adults inside. The besieged settlers rushed out to find an Indian in white man's clothing and faced a volley of bullets from the bushes. Young Willie fell dead, and two men and a woman were wounded before the ambushed party got back into the house and threw up a hasty barricade behind which they were pinned down until dusk. When Inkpaduta pulled out, he left seven dead and three wounded. He headed toward Dakota —pausing once to throw a woman captive into a stream where she was shot while trying to gain the shore, and allowing time for his son, Roaring Cloud, to club Mrs. Lydia Noble to death for resisting his advances.

News of the first attack in Iowa reached Charles Flandrau at the Redwood reservation, where he was Indian agent. The part-time lawyer at once headed down the Minnesota to Fort Ridgley, and the next day he was on the river road with Joe La Framboise as guide. Behind came Captain Barnard E. Bee and forty-eight enlisted men. In the aftermath of a spring snowstorm, it took the relief force a week to cover seventy air-line miles, and on the day Willie Thomas was killed they were still fifty miles away. They turned westward to follow Inkpaduta, and missed him. "The camp was there, with all its traces of plunder and rapine," Captain Bee[1] wrote in his report; "books, scissors, articles of female apparel, furs and traps." But the outlaw Indians proved to be so elusive that the pursuers at last gave up. It was Flandrau's terse comment that Bee's command had been no more fit for such a wintery march than an elephant for a ballroom.

The fiasco and the tragedies sent chills through the valley people. A special session of the legislature was convened, and the roll call had scarcely been completed before Joseph R. Brown offered a resolution requesting federal aid in tracking down Inkpaduta. But the lawmakers haggled for more than two weeks before voting approval of an appropriation of ten thousand dollars—not for the capture of the outlaw chief, but for the release of the female captives, "by purchase, stratagem, or otherwise."

Meanwhile two young Sioux brothers, out hunting, heard of Inkpaduta's whereabouts. They were Sounding Heavens and Gray Foot, who had been converted by the missionaries at the mouth of the Yellow Medicine. Traveling west on the Coteau des Prairies, the two young hunters finally caught up with Inkpaduta and his captives, and tried to bargain for the release of the women. After much dickering Mrs. Margaret Ann Marble was turned over to them, and they took her to their mother, who treated the distraught young widow with such kindness that she was loath to leave.

Mrs. Marble's rescue, however, served to give Agent Flandrau hope about Inkpaduta's other captives. He called for Indian volunteers and picked John Other Day, Paul Mazakutamani and a brave named Grass to carry on negotiations with the abductors. He bought four horses for six hundred dollars, a wagon and a

---

[1] Barnard E. Bee was later a brigadier general in the Confederate army, and was killed in the first battle of Bull Run. Shortly before his death Bee became the author of Stonewall Jackson's immortal nickname when he exhorted his men with the cry: "Look, there is Jackson standing like a stone wall. Rally behind the Virginians."

harness for one hundred and ten dollars, and one hundred and seventy-nine dollars' worth of decorative miscellany. Thus equipped, Other Day and his partners set out and after a six-day march they came across the body of Mrs. Noble. Next morning they found fourteen-year-old Abbie Gardner, the sole white survivor, in Inkpaduta's camp. John Other Day ransomed her for two horses, two kegs of powder, twenty-two yards of blue cloth, seven and a half yards of calico, and four hundred dollars' worth of trinkets, and delivered her to Flandrau. When she was sent down the river on a steamboat, the valley settlers came out to greet her, crowding the decks at each stop. Everyone was glad to see the young girl alive, but there was no satisfaction about the failure to punish her abductors.

The army, finally authorized to chase down Inkpaduta, was waiting for the spring grass to grow sufficiently to provide feed for the animals. Flandrau, meanwhile, had received a note from a Yellow Medicine trader about the outlaw's recent movements, and he requisitioned a lieutenant and fifteen soldiers from Fort Ridgley. With the addition of a dozen mounted civilians, the agent headed west, and halfway between the Redwood and the Yellow Medicine he found John Other Day sitting on a hill smoking his pipe. Some of Inkpaduta's followers were not far away, Other Day reported, but the ringleader himself had disappeared.

As dawn began to break on the following day, the outlaw camp was sighted on the Yellow Medicine. While the infantrymen filed along the river's edge and the horsemen charged from the prairie, a man and a woman dashed from one of six tepees and raced toward a ravine. The escaping Indian was shot and bayoneted and the squaw was taken prisoner. Not Inkpaduta, but his son, Roaring Cloud—the murderer of Mrs. Noble—was dead.

Any sense of accomplishment Flandrau might have had was brief. As his returning expedition passed through a Sioux encampment, assembled to await the payment of the government annuity, the captive widow of Roaring Cloud cried out from the wagon in which she was carried. Flandrau, at breakfast, was suddenly surrounded by hundreds of armed warriors. He became a virtual prisoner at his own agency, forced to release Roaring Cloud's wife and to donate two beeves for a feast of braves. When reinforcements from Fort Ridgley arrived, Flandrau left for St. Paul where he served that year as associate justice of the territorial supreme court.

Then William J. Cullen, the new northern superintendent of Indian affairs, took charge and promptly told the assembled bands that no annuities would be paid until the Sioux had brought in Inkpaduta and all his outlaws. "Our Great Father," said Chief Standing Buffalo, "has asked us to do a very hard thing . . . to go and kill men and women that do not belong to any of our bands. His agent says we shall not have our annuities until the murderers are given up to him or killed. The leaves will fall and come again before we shall see what he has for us unless we listen to his words. Our children will suffer with the cold if the goods he has are not given us." The reluctant Sioux leaders agreed to take on the punitive mission on the condition that troops accompany them, but Cullen rejected the request; the artillery men at the agency, he said, were not fitted for such an expedition, and there weren't enough infantry to spare.

The Indians became restive. A warrior showed his temper by stabbing a soldier without provocation; and when an officer demanded the surrender of the stabber, two hundred Sioux stopped him with leveled guns; their spokesman said they would deliver him the next day. The implicit threat became obvious the following noon when an armed war party moved up to the agency buildings. While the Fort Ridgley soldiers loaded their guns, three braves stepped forward and told Superintendent Cullen that the stabber would not be delivered until the annuities had been paid. Only when a young army officer dared them to act did the Indians break down. Grumbling, they delivered the culprit only to have him escape five days later with no effort made to recapture him. Witnessing this, the Sioux made their own estimate of how much respect was deserved by the Great Father and his soldiers in the valley.

Cullen, unmindful of his inability to handle a simple case of assault, continued to warn the Sioux that failure to round up Inkpaduta's outlaws meant war with the United States. He was saved from the showdown that was simmering when the opportunistic Little Crow, grandson of Le Petit Corbeau, volunteered to organize a posse. With the persuasion of liberally distributed blankets and beef, Crow signed up four warriors from each of the twenty-five bands, six half-breeds and Joe Campbell, interpreter. He left the junction of the Yellow Medicine and the Minnesota on July 22.

Six days later, he found two deserted Inkpaduta encampments, and he followed the trail northward. When he sighted his quarry on the shore of a lake, the ensuing half-hour fight was stopped by nightfall and heavy rain. "Two women and a little boy," Campbell wrote in his diary, "fell into our hands; and on the morning of the 29th we ascertained that three men were killed." In the dark, Inkpaduta, who had been a fugitive for twenty years, had disappeared. Little Crow's posse was back at the mouth of the Yellow Medicine on August 2, not even brandishing a scalp to prove the story of the battle.

In the brief investigation, several witnesses, including John Other Day, corroborated Campbell's diary account, and all efforts to bully the tribes into another try at capturing the wily Inkpaduta were unavailing. Cullen finally notified his superiors that the Indians had done all they could and, while Inkpaduta fled northward, he lined the Sioux bands up along the river and distributed their annuities. Joe Brown had written as early as July 7 that, in view of the way things were being handled, one side or the other would have to back down. As usual he was dead right—in the Inkpaduta fiasco it was not the Indians who lost face.

19

"LET THEM EAT GRASS"

*"Has not their country been made a thoroughfare
for all people who choose to pass through it, with
or without their consent? . . . Has the government provided
against the inevitable result of such a state of things?"*

—HENRY HASTINGS SIBLEY, IN CONGRESS, 1852

For FIVE years the outlaw threat did not leave the valley. On June 2, 1862, Dr. Thomas S. Williamson, a medical missionary at the junction of the Yellow Medicine and the Minnesota, sat writing a letter to Major Thomas J. Galbraith, Joe Brown's successor as Indian agent. Five Yanktonais bands, he wrote, "one of them headed by a son of Inkpaduta, have started to steal horses." He added that a couple of thousand Yanktonais were expecting to be joined by large Sioux bands from west of the Missouri and were coming to demand pay for the lands sold at the Traverse des Sioux treaty. "If they do not get it," Williamson wrote, "they will kill the Indians who dress like white people, and the white people." Williamson pointed out that the Civil War had begun and that many men had left the valley to join the Union forces. "These distant Indians hear very exaggerated reports of this, which may lead them to think the frontiers wholly unprotected," he wrote. "I think it's desirable when they come here they should see as many soldiers here as
182

they have seen in past years in time of payment. . . . I hope
you will not suffer anything which I have written in this letter
to be divulged in such a way as to cause panic in the white
settlements. . . ."

Bureaucracy moved slowly. It was three weeks before Lieutenant Timothy J. Sheehan marched into the valley with fifty
men from Fort Ripley on the upper Mississippi, stopped long
enough at Fort Ridgley to add Lieutenant Thomas Gere and
fifty more men to his command, and then on July 2—a month
after Williamson's letter—pitched camp near the Yellow Medicine. All around him on the river bluffs Sioux tepees were going
up as more and more bands came in to wait for payment of
their annuities and the distribution of provisions. Within the
week, signs of unrest were clearly to be seen in the swaggering
Indians showing off their prowess and in the demand by a party
of braves that the traders who "take all our money" be kept
from the pay table when the annuity funds arrived. On July 14,
a head count showed four thousand Santee Sioux who had a
rightful claim to the annuity, and one thousand Yanktonais
who did not. Major Galbraith maintained he wasn't worried. On
July 24, eight hundred warriors on foot and four hundred on
prancing ponies moved about the agency buildings on the pretext of hunting their ancient enemies, the Chippewa.

Three days later, Galbraith finally acted on the early June
suggestion of the missionary. He ordered Lieutenant Sheehan to
find Inkpaduta and take him and his followers as prisoners. But
Galbraith wanted no rash behavior. "While I recommend
prompt and vigorous action to bring these murderers, thieves
and villains to justice dead or alive, yet I advise prudence and
extreme caution," he wrote Sheehan. Prudence and caution did
their work, and Inkpaduta escaped again—warned by the hostile
Yanktonais in Galbraith's camp.

No sooner was Sheehan back from his abortive search for the
outlaw than he was notified by Indians in camp that they would
stage a rally on August 4. Eight hundred warriors in thunderous

splendor moved on the agency, whooping and shouting in full war paint as they completely surrounded Sheehan's detachment. The soldiers sensed at once that the make-believe of other demonstrations had ended. Suddenly, with a demon yell, a horseman wheeled and charged the door of the government warehouse, slashing it with his tomahawk. On his heels a party of braves broke open the warehouse and began to move out flour sacks. Lieutenant Gere snapped his men to the howitzer and trained the cannon on the door. "Instantly," he reported later, "the Indians fell back to either side from the line covered by the gun, and through the opening thus formed a squad of sixteen men, Sergt. S. W. Trescott at the head, and accompanied by Lieutenant Sheehan, marched straight to the government building." Galbraith and Sheehan faced each other in a heated discussion. "Now," said Gere, "came a period of excitement and uncertainty."

The chiefs and orators began to harangue their exasperated tribesmen. They said the warehouse held provisions sent to them by their Great Father in Washington. They shrieked Galbraith's name and said he knew their wives and children were starving, that last year's corn crop had been destroyed by cutworms. Everybody knew, said the orators, that it was customary to make the annuity payment at the end of June when the prairie grass was high enough for pasture. Galbraith had refused them food which was theirs, and they therefore had the right to take it. In the agent's office, however, Galbraith told Sheehan that any concession would make the Indians even more difficult to control. The twenty-five-year-old lieutenant, arguing that the Sioux were trigger-happy as well as hungry, finally persuaded the agent to make a token issue of pork and flour if the chiefs would disperse the mob and promise to appear next day at a council.

The Indians were not so easily appeased. When they realized they were not being given all they had coming to them, they refused to leave and began to make new threats. In battle order, Sheehan lined up his one hundred men, with two howitzers, in front of the warehouse. Only then did the Indians begin to leave. They made their hostility more apparent when they pulled up stakes that day and moved their tepees some miles away.

Uncertainty prevailed at the agency. Tom Gere was dispatched to get Captain John S. Marsh, the commandant at Fort Ridgley, and Galbraith sent for the missionary, Stephen Riggs, pleading: "If there is anything between the lids of the Bible that will meet this case, I wish you would use it." Riggs had little doubt on that score, and was able to talk Standing Buffalo, the Sisseton chief, into agreeing to a parley. When Gere came in with Marsh after a twenty-hour round trip, the Indians gathered on August 7, and Galbraith tried to explain again that the cash part of the annuity had not yet arrived from Washington. With great reluctance, because he would have to make two sets of records, he finally distributed the full quota of food and other goods on Standing Buffalo's assurance that all the bands would return to their villages to wait patiently for the arrival of the money. "Peace and quiet," said Stephen Riggs "now reigned at the Yellow Medicine."

At the mouth of the Redwood, twenty-five miles downriver, there were other Sioux bands waiting sulkily, but as yet they had staged no Wild West shows. Galbraith went downstream to the Redwood agency without realizing that he had made a fatal blunder. When he had issued provisions to the Upper Sioux, the famous Little Crow had been a visitor. Chief spokesman for the tribes at Redwood, Little Crow had demanded that his people also be given food, and Galbraith had assured him that this would be done. It was a promise the agent failed to keep, and Little Crow's patience was growing short.

The day was August 15, 1862. The hot prairie sun burned down on hundreds of Little Crow's people who had gathered with him in the Redwood council square. The Indians saw the great warehouse in front of them and the sheep in the fold between the agency buildings and the river. Some glanced quickly at the traders whose stores stood just behind the warehouse on the Upper Agency Road. "We have waited a long time," Little Crow said. "The money is ours, but we cannot get it. We have no food, but here are these stores, filled with food. We ask that you, the agent, make some arrangement by which we can get food from the stores, or else we may take our own way to keep ourselves from starving." Speaking clearly to the red-haired Galbraith, the chief finished his speech. "When men are hungry," growled Little Crow, "they help themselves."

The agency interpreter froze. He would not translate Crow's threat. Galbraith turned to a young minister—Dr. Williamson's son, John—who had spent his life in the valley and had played with Little Crow in childhood. "Williamson," said the agent, "you tell us what Little Crow says." Young Williamson complied.

Turning to the storekeepers, Galbraith noted that three proprietors, Louis Robert, William H. Forbes, and François Labathe, were absent. Andrew Myrick, whose store was at the bend of the road, was present, and he was clearly angry. No one had forgotten that the warriors had demanded that the traders be banished from the pay table when the annuities were distributed, and the traders had refused to extend more credit to the Indians until the money arrived from Washington. Galbraith wanted to know what the traders would do now. The clerks for Labathe, Forbes, and Robert held a brief consultation before one of them said, "Whatever Myrick does, we will do."

Apparently seething in anger, Myrick started to leave without response, but Galbraith prevented him, insisting on a statement. Speaking deliberately then, Myrick said, "So far as I am concerned, if they are hungry, let them eat grass."

Again the regular interpreter was so shocked that he refused to repeat Myrick's answer, and again the agent turned to John Williamson. There was a brief instant of stunned silence after the translation, and then the agency grounds rocked with whoops and savage gesticulations as the Indians disappeared. When they returned in the red dawn three days later they were armed.

20

THE WAR OF THE HEN'S EGGS

*"I thought there might be trouble, but
I had no idea there would be such a war."*

—BIG EAGLE

T HE AUGUST heat was still intense when a hunting party left the camp of Red Middle Voice on Rice Creek and crossed the river to wander north in search of deer. Four of the hunters —Brown Wing, Breaking Up, Killing Ghost, and Runs Against Something When Crawling—separated from the group on the edge of the Big Woods, and on Sunday, August 17, as they walked along the Pembina-Henderson trail, they came upon a hen's nest near a rail fence. It was about noon and the men were famished. In that nest they found the tinder to set ablaze the entire Minnesota Valley.

"You know how the war started," Chief Big Eagle long afterward told an interviewer, "—by the killing of some white people near Acton in Meeker County. I will tell you how this was done, as it was told me by all four young men who did the killing. . . . One of them took the eggs, when another said: 'Don't take them, for they belong to a white man and we may get into trouble.'

"The other was angry, for he was very hungry and wanted to get the eggs, and he dashed them to the ground and replied: 'You are a coward. You are afraid of the white man. You are

187

afraid to take even an egg from him, though you are half starved. Yes, you are a coward, and I will tell everybody so.'

"The other replied: 'I am not a coward. I am not afraid of the white man, and to show you that I am not I will go to the house and shoot him. Are you brave enough to go with me?'

"The one who had called him a coward said: 'Yes, I will go with you and we will see who is the braver of us two.'

"Their two companions then said: 'We will go with you, and we will be brave, too.'

"They all went to the house of the white man, but he got alarmed and went on to another house, where were some white men and women. The four Indians followed them. . . ."

The log house behind the rail fence belonged to Robinson Jones, who was the settlement postmaster and kept a small store, renting rooms and serving occasional meals to itinerant pioneers. The Indian hunters found Jones in the house with his fifteen-year-old adopted daughter, Clara Wilson, and her infant brother. Unsuspecting of the Indians' mood, Jones soon left his house to carry out a promise to join his wife at the nearby home of her son, Howard Baker. Jones and Baker, their wives, and Viranus Webster were talking beside Webster's covered wagon when the Indians came up the Baker path on Jones's heels. The four Sioux still seemed friendly, and Jones engaged them for a moment in trading for a gun. Then the three white men and the Indians began to shoot at a mark. Mrs. Webster was in the covered wagon, and the two other women had started into the Baker house. "The next thing I knew," Mrs. Baker said at a coroner's inquest the next day, "I heard the report of a gun and saw Mr. Webster fall." The white men had neglected to reload their guns after the target practice. "Another Indian aimed his gun at my husband, fired, but did not kill him," Mrs. Baker said. "He then shot the other barrel and my husband fell dead. My mother-in-law, Mrs. Jones, came to the door and another Indian shot her. She turned to run and fell; they shot her twice as she fell." Robinson Jones was shot near Webster's wagon, and Mrs.

Baker inadvertently saved herself when, in consternation, she tumbled with her child through a trapdoor to the cellar.

The Indians fled southwest immediately, pausing only long enough to shoot Clara Wilson when she appeared at the door of the Jones house. On stolen horses they galloped toward the river, and arrived, after dark, at Red Middle Voice's village. Only a few campfires were reflected in the Rice Creek waters that boiled toward the Minnesota over the turbulent granite bed, but Brown Wing, Killing Ghost, Runs Against Something When Crawling, and Breaking Up knew that what they had done could not wait to be announced. Jumping from their exhausted horses, they woke the village. "Get your guns," they cried. "There is war with the whites, and we have begun it."

The man most interested in the young men's story was Red Middle Voice who, though not a chief, had established his own band after a quarrel with his brother, the old Shakopee. He was a maverick who had considerable influence for evil. But he was also a politician, and when he heard the four murderers' story he took them downriver to the mouth of the Redwood to consult with his nephew, the new Chief Shakopee. It was obvious that United States soldiers would soon come to arrest the four hunters, and Shakopee and his uncle realized at once that the war so long debated could find no more inflammatory opening incident.

In their reasoning a final showdown with the whites had become inevitable. That very afternoon a meeting of agitators had been held at Rice Creek. Weeks earlier the unofficial organization called "the soldier's lodge" had been formed to keep the traders from the pay table, and some of the young Indians who joined the lodge were intent upon cleaning out all the white settlers. Now as the fateful Sunday drew to a close Red Middle Voice and Shakopee decided that the time had come for the soldiers' lodge to have its way. For leadership they turned to Little Crow who, though he advocated farming and lived in a house built for him by Galbraith, had more prestige among the Sioux than Red Middle Voice and many more followers than

LITTLE CROW

young Shakopee. From Rice Creek that night runners were sent to the villages of Wacouta, Wabasha, Big Eagle, Mankato, and other leaders, and through the darkness the Sioux chiefs gathered at Little Crow's white house near the Redwood agency. They found Crow in the big room on the ground floor, sleeping on strips of carpeting and a pile of blankets.

Little Crow has been described as the successor of Osceola and Black Hawk, of Tecumseh and King Philip. He was less than any of these; some even thought him less able than Red Middle Voice; but he was a persuasive speaker and he was vain about his military talent. His influence among the tribesmen was such that Agent Galbraith had hoped to make good use of him. The agent had offered to build a new brick house for Little Crow in return for the chief's promise of aid in bringing the idle Indians around to habits of industry and civilization; already Crow had started to dig the cellar. "Just three days before," Galbraith reported, "I had an interview with Little Crow, and he seemed well pleased and satisfied."

The unfortunate truth was that Little Crow was anything but satisfied, and he sat up in bed to listen warily to the story of the killings that had followed the stealing of the hen's eggs. He could not forget that the river bands had rejected him recently in the tribal election for chief speaker. He had been sulking for days, and as he sat in his bed with the agitated Indians standing around him in the darkness, his first reaction was sarcasm.

"Why do you come to me for advice?" he asked tauntingly. "Go to the man you elected speaker and let him tell you what to do."

Shrewdly the men in Little Crow's bedroom goaded him. The Sioux leaders remembered what some half-breeds had told them of the progress of the Civil War—it was only two weeks since the Union defeat at the second battle of Bull Run. To many it appeared that the Great Father was beaten. Already the Minnesota frontier had sent five thousand men south, and as many more had been asked for. To the Indians, the volunteer soldiers at Fort Ridgley compared unfavorably with the regulars they had studiously observed in other years. The river valley was all but defenseless, they said.

Perhaps at least as important in Little Crow's mind was the fact that Galbraith himself had decided to take a short leave from his post. Among his half-breed employees the agent had organized a Civil War volunteer company, called the Renville Rangers, and on the afternoon of his last talk with Little Crow he had taken his enlistees downriver to report at Fort Snelling. "The Indians now thought the whites must be pretty hard up for men to fight the South, or they would not come so far out on the frontier and take half-breeds or anything to help them," said Big Eagle. "It was believed that the men who had enlisted last had all left the state, and that before help could be sent the Indians could clean out the country, and that the Winnebagoes, and even the Chippewas, would assist the Sioux."

In Little Crow's frame house the martial mood mounted as the night wore on, and before the new day broke a strategy was worked out in council. War was declared by a chief who had been sitting in church that morning while four hotheaded braves were arguing about a nest of hen's eggs. After hearing the Episcopal sermon, Little Crow had stopped outside the agency church to shake hands with fellow parishioners who now, twelve hours later, he marked for his first victims.

21

LITTLE CROW
LEAVES THE CHURCH

"This is not our war; it is a national war."

—GOV. ALEXANDER RAMSEY TO ABRAHAM LINCOLN

THE MORNING of Aug. 18 came," wrote Mary Schwandt. "It was just such a morning as is often seen here in that month. The great red sun came up in the eastern sky, tinging all the clouds with crimson, and sending long, scarlet shafts of light up the green river valley and upon the golden bluffs on either side." The fourteen-year-old Mary that morning got ready to do a big washing.

Farther down the golden bluffs the girls who waited on tables in the Redwood government boardinghouse reacted in fright when men arriving for breakfast spoke of hearing shots in the upper part of the agency. J. C. Dickinson, who ran the boardinghouse, took no chances. He, his family, and a wagonload of girls were among the first to cross the river to safety.

There was no warning for the storekeepers on the agency road. Little Crow and his followers moved silently in the dawn and surrounded the stores, the barns, and the warehouse in the agency compound. The first target was the Myrick store, where Andrew Myrick lived with his clerks. James Lynd came downstairs and was shot dead in the doorway. Hearing the shot,

G. W. Divoll walked toward Lynd's body and was instantly killed. In his own room, Andrew Myrick guessed what was happening, dropped from a second-story window and ran for a thicket; he failed to make it. Six other traders were soon dead, and Little Crow ordered the execution of three men in charge of the barns. Only George Spencer, saved by an Indian friend, escaped the lethal attack on the stores.

In a house at the foot of a hill two miles from the agency, Nancy Faribault, her wedding at Traverse des Sioux a decade old, heard the far-off gunfire. "As the shooting increased I went to the door once or twice and looked toward the agency, for there was something unusual about it," she remembered. "My husband was out attending to the milking. All at once a Frenchman named Martelle came galloping down the road from the agency, and, seeing me in the door, he called out: 'Oh, Mrs. Faribault, the Indians are killing all the people at the agency! Run away. . . .'" David Faribault pressed his pretty wife to get her saddle, but before the horses were ready an ox-drawn wagon approached with a load of frightened men, women, and children. To speed the wagon, Faribault replaced the oxen with his horses; then he and Nancy and their eight-year-old daughter fled to the woods. They were joined in a hiding place by two children and their parents, but were soon discovered. Spared because Faribault was one of the few traders who had Indian blood, Nancy and her family turned away helplessly as the Indians slaughtered two more wagonloads of settlers. "All this," said Nancy, "took less time than one can write about it."

Upriver from the agency, Mary Schwandt was soon distracted from the sunrise. John Mooers, the son of Grey Cloud and Hazen Mooers, sent a messenger to warn Mary's employers, J. B. Reynolds and his wife, who were government schoolteachers. Reynolds put his family in a buggy, and Mary Schwandt, Mary Anderson, and Mattie Williams climbed into a wagon with Le Grand Davis, trader Francis Patoile, and a Frenchman, then headed across the prairie for New Ulm. They

were within eight miles of their destination when they were surrounded by a war party and Patoile was shot. "Mr. Davis and
we girls ran toward a slough where there was some high grass,"
said Mary. "Mr. Davis was killed. The Frenchman ran in another
direction, but was shot and killed. Mary Anderson was shot in
the back, the ball lodging near the surface of the groin or
abdomen. Some shots passed through my dress, but I was not
hit." The attackers put the girls back in the wagon and drove
off.

It was 10:00 A.M. when Jannette De Camp, wife of the agency
sawmill operator mused upon the stillness of the morning because the mill under the river bluff was shut down. Her husband had gone to St. Paul on business the day before, and she
was alone with two maids and three children. As she went to
the garden she saw an Indian stealing her husband's horses, and
the thief told her that all the white people at the agency had
been killed. Mrs. De Camp and her household fled to the top of
the hill where "the agency buildings and the traders' stores were
in flames and hundreds of shouting savages were surging about
the government warehouse, shrieking and brandishing their
weapons." Looking toward the ferry she saw a great crowd of
frantic people gathered. "It seemed incredible," she said, "that
all this had gone on without our knowledge, that not a sound
had penetrated to our place where all had been so still."

Little Crow had dispatched small parties to raid the isolated
houses across the river, and when these Indians discovered that
a heroic ferryman had been crossing and recrossing the Minnesota with load after load of refugees—refusing his own opportunity to flee—they disemboweled and decapitated him. But
the murderers were late, for by midmorning some of the ferry
passengers had struggled through to Fort Ridgley, fourteen
miles away. A half hour after the arrival of J. C. Dickinson and
his wagonload of girls, Captain John Marsh left at the head of a
relief expedition of forty-six men. He had sent a horseman to
bring back Lieutenant Tim Sheehan, who was on his way to Fort

Ripley, and Tom Gere was left to command the undermanned post on the Minnesota bluff. Marching toward Redwood, Marsh's detachment passed scores of fugitives, and many bodies of men, women, and children.

On the river road they were joined by a twelve-year-old boy who had been separated from his fleeing family. Young John Humphrey had swum the Minnesota after the ferryman's death, rowed back in a small boat and brought across his sick mother, a brother and sister, and his father, who was the agency physician. Stopping at an abandoned cabin to rest, Dr. Humphrey had sent his son to find water. "I heard the crack of a rifle," the boy remembered. "I knew we had been overtaken, and [I] ran back to the spring." After an hour or so he ventured out and was found by Captain Marsh, who escorted him to the cabin where his parents had stopped. "The murderers had set fire to it, and the smouldering ruins which had fallen into the cellar contained the mortal remains of my mother and brother and sister. . . . My father's body lay a few feet away. A bullet had pierced the center of his forehead, and the fiends had cut his throat. His axe lay near him, showing that he went outside the cabin and met them like a brave man. . . . When I came to my normal self, every living person had vanished, and I ran fast up the road to overtake the soldiers."

At Faribault's Hill, Marsh and his men took the road down to the wide bottom where hazel, willow, and tall grass grew. Here they saw their first Indians riding on the high prairie across the river. Marching back and forth at the other end of the ferry was Chief White Dog, who had been an overseer of farmer Indians and was considered civilized. He called to the young captain that he wanted a parley at the agency. Marsh had walked into an ambush. While he delayed ordering his men onto the ferry, warriors were stealthily fording the river to surround the soldiers; some of them took possession of the ferryhouse. Suddenly White Dog leaped back, firing his gun. "Look out!" shouted the interpreter, Peter Quinn. Bullets, aimed low, poured in on Marsh's men. Quinn fell dead, along with a dozen soldiers. Marsh closed ranks, but more men fell, and he ordered the survivors to break for cover. They moved into the hazel and willow brush, working their way downriver. The enemy came after them along the road, obviously aiming to catch them in the open ground ahead, and Marsh told his men to wade the river to the opposite bank. The young officer stepped into a hole halfway across and was drowned.

The new commander was Sergeant John Bishop, nineteen years old, who had been a soldier only a few months. Bishop said later, "I will never forget the look that brave officer gave us just before he sank for the last time—will never forget how dark the next hour seemed to us, as we crouched underneath the bank of the Minnesota River, and talked over and decided what next best to do." As things turned out the young sergeant was lucky, for the Sioux failed to pursue the survivors who, toward the day's close, struggled into Fort Ridgley leaving twenty-six dead. Lieutenant Tom Gere put a man on the best horse in the stable and sent him downriver with an account of the outbreak's opening. "Send reinforcements without delay," he wrote, and added, "Please hand this to Gov Ramsey *immediately.*"

Gere had had only a glimpse of the day's events. When rumors of the outbreak reached the upper agency on the Yellow Medicine, they weren't believed at first. But when the Christian Indians learned that the Wahpetons, camping nearby, had held a council to decide whether or not to join the Little Crow forces, John Other Day and Joe La Framboise, Jr., hustled their white friends into the upper agency's brick warehouse, and awaited the moment for escape. Had they heard what had happened across the river near Sacred Heart Creek, they might have moved faster. Mary Schwandt's family was attacked en masse on their new homestead. Her father and mother, two grown brothers, a brother-in-law, and her pregnant sister were killed, and twelve-year-old August Schwandt was tomahawked and left for dead; the unborn baby was cut from its mother's womb and nailed to a tree. On the road to New Ulm the children of Mrs. S. R. Henderson were snatched from her arms to be swung by their heels as their brains were bashed out in front of her eyes; she was tossed after them onto a funeral pyre of flaming bedding. Rapine and slaughter spread throughout the day along the left bank of the river.[2]

Toward the end of the morning, a band played on a New Ulm street as the townspeople gathered to hail a recruiting party innocently setting off to sign up Civil War volunteers. Traveling in three wagons, the recruiters had gone six miles on the Milford road when the Sioux howled down on them and killed three men. On the same road were the homes built by the first Germans from Chicago. The insatiable Sioux swept through the bustling community and caught Anton Messmer's family harvesting wheat. They wiped out John Zettel's family, and all seven Zellers. Before the day was over more than fifty settlers on the Milford road were dead.

Coming happily down that road on Monday morning was nine-year-old Cecilia Ochs, returning to her job of taking care of ailing Mrs. Joseph Stocker. "When about halfway I met several Indians," Cecilia remembered. "Having always been afraid of Indians I ran as fast as I could into a wheat field." The youngster arrived at her employer's house by cutting across fields, and almost immediately she began to learn what the Indians were up to. They smashed in a window and shot Mrs. Stocker. Cecilia ran for the cellar; so did Stocker; and when the Indians set the house on fire he dug their way out with a shingle. Running through woods, they found John Zettel dead "and in his arms a loaf of bread saturated with blood."

To the Sioux the butchery was simply war—war as they fought it against the Chippewa. The atrocities were perpetrated by

[2] A good many eyewitness accounts of such atrocities are now considered suspect. Dr. Jared Daniels, accompanying a burial party, declared flatly that he saw every corpse that was buried and none was mutilated in any way.

members of the soldier's lodge, by young braves who had yet to win their first eagle feather, the most precious thing in life, and they could win it as easily by slaying an infant as they could by killing in hand-to-hand combat. It was their sworn purpose to clear the valley of all whites, to reclaim the river and its bluffs and prairies from the traders whom they firmly believed had cheated them. Their annuity had not been paid, their children were hungry. They were determined to clean out the valley— and it did not matter whether it was accomplished by murder or by acts so shocking that the settlers would be frightened into exodus.

The braves ranged far that Monday in the ecstasy of slaughter. Some of them came back from the fight at the Redwood ferry carrying the knapsacks of the soldiers killed, and accosted Mary Schwandt in a house in Wacouta's village. "Mary Schwandt had fled to me for protection from their indecent assaults," Mrs. De Camp remembered. She knew some of the warriors and she asked them why they were fighting. "They replied that it was such fun to kill white men. They were such cowards that they all ran away and left their squaws to be killed, and that one Indian could kill ten white men without trying. . . . How they scoffed and jeered as they swung their rifles and tomahawks around their heads, aiming to strike as near as they could without hitting." It was, said Mary Schwandt, such "a dreadful night . . . it is a relief to avoid the subject."

Tuesday, August 19

For many in the valley Tuesday began in darkness. "On the morning of August 19th," said Charles Flandrau, "I was aroused at four o'clock. . . . I immediately started my family down the valley, gathered all the firearms I possessed, and went up to St. Peter. . . . We immediately started organizing all the men for defense." At four A.M. at Joe Brown's mansion near Sacred

Heart Creek a horseman clattered to a halt and pounded on the door. "For God's sake, hurry!" he shouted when a window was opened. "The Yanktonais have broken out and are burning the stores and killing everyone at the agency. I have barely escaped with my life!" Brown himself was on a trip to New York, but his mixed-blood wife, ten children, two grandchildren, and his white son-in-law, Charles Blair, hustled themselves into three ox-drawn lumber wagons, added a party of neighbors and headed east. Six miles down the valley they found Indians "popping out of the grass on every side," including, Joe Brown's son recalled, "the awful Cut Nose, the terrible Shakopee . . . and the impudent and saucy Do-wan-ne-yay."

As luck would have it, the bloodthirsty band included also an Indian who had been saved from freezing to death the winter before by Joe Brown's wife. While Shakopee's band howled around her, Mrs. Brown stood up in the wagon, waved her shawl and announced loudly in Sioux that she was a Sisseton and a relative of Wanata, Scarlet Plume, Sweet Corn, Ah-Kee-Pah, and the friend of Standing Buffalo, and she expected protection. The Indian whose frozen limbs she had massaged had not forgotten his gratitude, and his intervention helped to save the Browns. They went on their way until they met a young Sisseton who advised that they go direct to Little Crow. Angus and Sam Brown dressed themselves as savages, and with the Sisseton as a guide slipped through the enemy camps, found Little Crow and returned with a bodyguard sent by the war chief.

The Brown boys managed to get their family through to Little Crow's house. "When Mother entered," Sam remembered, "the chief arose from his couch and stepped up and greeted her very cordially, and then handed her a cup of cold water and told her to drink, saying that she was his prisoner now. We were all hurried upstairs and told to be quiet. The chief gave us robes and blankets and told us to lie down and go to sleep." When he returned, it was to warn the Brown family that the life of Charles Blair, the only member without a trace of Indian blood, was in great danger. The chief mixed vermilion with some animal grease and daubed Blair's face with the red paint. He gave Brown's son-in-law a new plaid blanket and a pair of red leggings, and pulled off his own moccasins and put them on Blair's feet. Then he summoned his head warrior and told him to spirit the white man through the trees to the riverbank, a few hundred yards from the house. With this help from Little Crow, Blair played Indian for seven days and finally arrived at Fort Ridgley, fifteen miles distant.

Others were also concerned about Joe Brown's family. Upriver at the Yellow Medicine agency, John Other Day stole out of the warehouse with his sixty-two white charges, including his own wife and the family of Major Galbraith. At four thirty that morning, just a half hour late, he stopped at Farther-and-Gay and found the mansion deserted. With this relief he was determined to get his Yellow Medicine refugees to safety, and he wisely avoided the dangers in the valley by heading north. Two other Christian Indians, Paul Mazakutemani and Simon Ana-wangmani, led the Stephen Riggs family and a group from the Hazelwood mission to a haven on an island in the river, while Thomas Williamson sent out ten persons from his Pajutazee mission but stubbornly hung on twenty-four hours longer himself.

During the night another caravan had started from Sacred Heart in the territory where Shakopee, Cut Nose, and Do-wan-nee-yay were running wild. Thirteen German families in eleven wagons led by Paul Kitzman had pushed halfway to Fort Ridgley when they were stopped by a small band of painted Sioux. One who had frequently eaten at the Kitzman house dismounted and came to greet Kitzman, throwing an arm around him and kissing him. "Judas-like," said Kitzman's sister, Justina Krieger, "he betrayed us with a kiss." The effusive Indian shook hands with everyone and blamed the outbreak on the Chippewa. There were Chippewa near the fort, he said, and offered to protect the German families if they returned to their homes. Backtrack-

ing most of the distance they had come, the white men gradually became suspicious, and when the Sioux suddenly demanded
all their money, Justina's husband, Frederick Krieger, slipped a
knife into her hand. "A remembrance," he said. "I think they
will kill all the men."

Krieger handed over the money he had collected from his
companions, and the caravan moved away without the Indians
following. It was not until the Germans stopped in front of the
Krieger cabin that the attack came. Shakopee, his two sidekicks,
and eleven others galloped up, surrounded the whites, and began firing. Only Frederick Krieger and two other males survived
the first volley. "The Indians then asked the women," said
Justina, "if they would go along with them, promising to save all
that would go, and threatening all who refused with instant
death." Two or three women indicated assent, and Krieger urged
Justina to join them, telling her they would probably not kill her
and that she might easily escape. "I refused," said Justina,
"preferring to die with him and the children. One of the women
who had started off with the Indians turned around, hallooed at
me to come with them, and taking a few steps towards me, was
shot dead." Five other women and two men died in the same fire.
The children, including Justina's eleven, began to slip away, and
three Indians ran after them, clubbing them with gun butts.
Justina saw a daughter die, blood gushing from her mouth. A gun
went off and Frederick Krieger slumped between the oxen. His
wife tried to jump from the wagon and was felled when seventeen buckshot pellets tore into the flesh of her back. She collapsed unconscious on the ground.

Hours later she became aware of two Indians in the darkness,
searching the corpses for valuables. One savage slashed off her
dress, cutting a four-inch gash across her abdomen. "I saw one
of these inhuman savages seize Wilhelmina Kitzman, my niece,"
Justina said, "hold her up by her foot, her head downward, her
clothes falling over her head. While holding her with one hand,
in the other he grasped a knife, with which he cut the flesh

around one of the legs, close to the body. Then, by twisting and wrenching, he broke the ligaments and bone, until the limb was entirely severed from the body. The child screamed frantically, 'Oh, God! Oh, God!' When the limb was off the child was thrown on the ground, stripped of her clothing and left to die." Justina faded into near madness. Seven children, most of them under four years, hid in the Krieger house, and died when the Indians set it on fire. In the bushes, seven of Justina's own offspring escaped. When consciousness returned to her, Justina started crawling like a wounded animal in search of safety.

A couple of hours after the savage attack on the Sacred Heart Germans, a party of raiders came up behind New Ulm and began spraying bullets into the streets. The town was composed of several brick houses and nearly two hundred frame residences, and the nine hundred citizens had been collected into the business section where barricades had hastily been thrown up. More than a hundred men had volunteered as defenders, but there were only about forty guns in town. After two hours of desultory fire, providence brought thunder and lightning and a dense rain cloud, and the attackers drifted off just as relief came from St. Peter.

Again at four o'clock on Tuesday morning red-haired Thomas Galbraith—in St. Peter on his way to Snelling—got news of Captain Marsh's death, and he turned his forty-odd Renville Rangers back toward Fort Ridgley, after arming them with Harpers Ferry muskets. Lieutenant Sheehan had returned to take command at Ridgley and, with twenty-five volunteers from among the refugees now in his charge, he had a force of one hundred and eighty armed men. "Mrs. Dunn and I," said a soldier's wife, "had asked for guns to help fight, but there were none for us." Sheehan was short on ammunition also, and he set the blacksmith to work cutting iron rods into small pieces. "Mrs. Mueller, Mrs. Dunn and I worked a large share of that day making cartridges of these," Margueret Hern recalled. "We would take a piece of paper, give it a twist, drop in some powder in one of these and give it another twist. The soldiers could fire twice as fast with these as when they loaded themselves." All the able-bodied women helped, Mrs. Hern said, and with the arrival of the Renville Rangers at 5:00 P.M. they felt secure enough to try to sleep.

Wednesday, August 20

Rounding the island at the river's mouth with the side-wheeler *Favorite*, Captain Edwin Bell, early Wednesday morning, blew his shrill whistle in a prearranged signal and Henry Sibley left his Mendota house for the boat landing. Sibley had been appointed the day before to organize an expedition against the Sioux, and he had had Bell stop the *Favorite* at Fort Snelling long enough to put aboard four companies of Civil War volunteers. Bell dropped Sibley and three of the companies at Shakopee and took the fourth as far as Carver where he was confronted, he said, with a sight he would never forget. "Men, women, and children were on the bank of the river, many in their night clothes, just as they left their beds to flee from the Indians." Fear skittered on the heels of rumors from one end of the valley to the other.

The river road was lined with galloping teams dragging wagons and carts loaded with frantic settlers and their possessions. Heads of households said through tight lips that they would abandon their homes permanently unless the government provided strong military protection immediately. At least a regiment was absolutely necessary, Charles Flandrau wrote the governor from New Ulm, to prevent the evacuation of the entire valley. The panic was cut to the measure of Little Crow's purposes. At one o'clock the chief rode onto the bluff between Fort Ridgley and the river and his warriors swarmed up out of the ravines; but Little Crow had underestimated his enemy. Howitzer fire kept the Indians at bay until dusk when, said Tim Sheehan

SIBLEY

proudly, "the gallant little garrison rested on their arms, ready for any attack."

Friday, August 22

Rain on Thursday gave both sides a chance to recuperate, and the second assault on the fort came Friday. Tim Sheehan could not see the multitude gathering because the chiefs rendezvoused on the river bottom just below the bluffs. Eight hundred Sioux rode on caparisoned ponies. Ribbons and feathers fluttered as they moved, bells jingled, war songs drifted across the valley. They dismounted about a mile from Ridgley and crawled up the ravines surrounding the collection of buildings that was called a fort. So confident was Little Crow that a string of wagons had been brought along to carry away loot, and a party of squaws was assigned to watch the horses.

Suddenly, Tom Gere remembered, the savages surrounded the fort with demoniac yells and began firing from all sides. Chief Mankato hit the garrison from the southwest and took possession of the mule barn and the sutler's store. The prairie had become alive with heads clothed in turbans made of grass to conceal the crawling warriors' movements. Watching from an upstairs window, Margueret Hern saw Sergeant John Jones wheel up his artillery loaded with shell. "At a signal these were discharged, blowing up the barn and setting the hay on fire. The air was full of legs, arms and bodies, which fell back into the flames." The Indians lobbed burning arrows at the remaining buildings, but Thursday's rain had done its work and the roofs failed to ignite.

When Little Crow tried to drive in from the northeast, Tom Gere's men poured on musket fire while J. C. Whipple, a veteran of the Mexican War who was one of the civilian refugees from Redwood, swept the grass with his twelve-pounder. Sergeant Jim McGrew threw caution aside, ran his howitzer out from the northwest corner of the fort to the rim of the ravine, and quickly cleared it of grass-adorned Indians. Still, the enemy fire was accurate enough to splinter almost every foot of timber along the top of the makeshift barricades. But Tim Sheehan's soldiers and armed civilians, outnumbered four to one, gave no quarter. Hearing Little Crow in the impassioned oratory of battle, McGrew dropped a twenty-four-pound shell at a point where a party of warriors had joined the waiting squaws west of the main body. A great stampede resulted. Chief Big Eagle admitted that "the soldiers fought so bravely we thought there were more of them than there were. . . . We thought the fort was the door to the valley as far as to St. Paul, and that if we got through the door nothing could stop us this side of the Mississippi. But the defenders of the fort were very brave and kept the door shut."

Saturday, August 23

Three times frustrated in the attempts to open that door, Little Crow found some release for his aboriginal emotion when he encountered fourteen-year-old Mary Schwandt back at his village. "I was sitting quietly and shrinkingly by a tepee," Mary wrote, "when he came along in full chief's costume and looking very grand. Suddenly he jerked his tomahawk from his belt and sprang toward me with the weapon uplifted as if he meant to cleave my head in two . . . he glared down at me so savagely, that I thought he would really kill me; but I looked up at him, without any fear or care about my fate, and gazed quietly into his face without so much as winking my tear-swollen eyes. He brandished his tomahawk over me a few times, then laughed, put it back in his belt and walked away, still laughing." [3]

The Sioux high command turned from Ridgley to New Ulm, and early on Saturday the painted army swept down the valley

[3] Some scholars believe Mary Schwandt guilty of imaginative exaggeration.

again. Using a telescope on top of the highest building in New Ulm, Charles Flandrau and his sentries, through a diamond-clear atmosphere, watched the smoke rising from the settlers' houses fired by the approaching enemy. They saw great numbers of Sioux swarming down the bluffs of the river to cut off any possible retreat to the east. "They came in a close mass," Flandrau said, "at a moderate gait, until they were within about a double rifle shot from us, when they deployed to the right and left until they covered our whole front, and then gave a blood curdling yell, and sailed down on us like the wind."

Elected to command the New Ulm defenders, Flandrau had established his first line of defense about a quarter-mile in from the rear of the settlement. His small civilian army, unprepared for the ear-piercing Sioux onslaught, fell back to the barricades, but presently found new courage. They had little to be ashamed of, according to their commander. "White men," he wisely pointed out, "fight under a great disadvantage the first time they

engage with Indians. There is something so fiendish in their yells and terrifying in their appearance . . . that it takes a good deal of time to overcome the unpleasant sensation it inspires." Flandrau's men rallied and turned the tide. He said that when the next charge came, the defenders "stood firmly, and advanced with a cheer, routing the rascals like sheep." The battle raged all day and in its course one hundred and ninety houses and other town buildings were destroyed by fire. Twenty-six citizen soldiers were killed before nightfall brought a final victory.

Downriver the red glow of the burning town reflected upon the clouds and was plainly visible in South Bend, Mankato, and St. Peter. No word of Flandrau's success had come through, and the fiery sky was interpreted as evidence of total defeat in New Ulm and the inevitability of the Sioux wiping out the valley on Sunday. Instead, Flandrau evacuated the burning town in a caravan of one hundred and fifty-three wagons. "It was a melancholy spectacle," he reported to the governor, "to see 2,000 people, who but a few days before had been prosperous and happy, reduced to utter beggary. . . ."

Nowhere was there a clear picture of all that had happened nor of the risks involved. Henry Sibley, having reached St. Peter on Friday, was met by a trusted scout who told him that all seven thousand annuity Sioux were involved in the war. Far wilder reports were being published outside the valley. The Civil War filled the newspapers, but on Monday the *New-York Daily Tribune* managed to find space on its last page for an item headed:

THE INDIAN MASSACRE IN MINNESOTA

Five Hundred Whites Massacred—Entire
Families Killed—The Sioux United for
the Prosecution of a Desperate Scheme

Typical of the exaggerations then current was the *Tribune's* assertion that a scout had reconnoitered Joe Brown's Sacred Heart mansion and found every member of the family brutally murdered. The towns of St. Peter, Henderson, and Glencoe, the paper went on, had been destroyed by fire. Shocking as such "news" must have seemed, the story was dropped. With Union forces trapped by Stonewall Jackson at Manassas Junction, and the coming holocaust at Antietam, New York readers got no more reports on the war in the Minnesota Valley. Sibley, at St. Peter, found accurate information almost equally scarce.

Though the fur trader knew Indians, he had never before organized a military expedition. It took him three days, with the help of state officials, to muster a tentative force of fourteen hundred, composed mostly of inexperienced volunteers of which some four hundred had brought along their horses. Sibley would not act precipitously, in spite of the size of his army. Because of his concern for the lives of the women and children made captive by the Indians he declined to move his soldiers until they had guns that would shoot and until he was certain of quick victory. He reasoned that only when the Sioux recognized

his army's superiority would they be persuaded to surrender
their hostages alive.

Monday, August 25

While Sibley was gathering his strength at St. Peter, Little
Crow's camp began to break up with such haste that the captives
became convinced that the army must be in hot pursuit. "I wish
it were possible for me to describe that march upward," Jannette
De Camp wrote. "Long lines of wagons, carriages, ponies with
poles trailing (as customary with the Indians); each vehicle
loaded to its utmost capacity, without regard to size or capa-
bility. . . . The long lines of cattle driven before each band,
and the horses lashed without mercy, the warriors riding outside of the cavalcade in order to prevent any escaping, all
combined to render it a scene which, once looked upon, could
never be forgotten. . . . Many of the warriors wore ladies' bon-
nets on their heads, and furs dragged downward from their legs.
Their breasts were covered with brooches and chains of value;
from their ears depended wheels from clocks and watches which
they had destroyed. The finest silks were made into shirts; beautiful shawls were used for saddle cloths and cut up for head-
dresses and waist girdles. There was no device too ridiculous
for their attire and nothing too costly for them to destroy. How
often I wished that I might have some of my own comfortable
garments to keep us from the cold. . . . All that day we were
hoping that the whites would come, as the Indians seemed in
great haste, urging on the captives with frequent threats."

Sunday, August 31—Thursday, September 3

As a week passed, the Sioux feeling of haste seemed unwar-
ranted. Sibley was cautiously organizing his forces. Joe Brown,
caught by a telegram in Chicago, had hurried back to join the

volunteer cavalry that had come to Sibley's aid and moved on to Fort Ridgley. Brown had heard the rumor that his family had been annihilated, but he didn't believe it. Commissioned a major by Sibley, he rode out of Ridgley with one hundred and sixty men to find out what Little Crow was up to and to bury bodies that for days had been rotting in the sun. He had with him Captain Joe Anderson's cavalry and an infantry company under Captain Hiram Grant. In addition, Brown's own Indian savvy was buttressed by the presence of Alexander Faribault, his son George, and Sibley's old hunting mate, the half-breed Jack Frazer, nephew of Wacouta. Jannette De Camp's husband, back from St. Paul, had volunteered for the sortie, and so had the heartsick Major Galbraith.

Sixteen bodies were found and buried on Sunday, and Brown and the two captains made their camp that night on the Minnesota bottom. The next morning Brown took a detachment and crossed the river at Redwood Ferry, went on up to the burned-out agency, and there Nathan Myrick found the body of his brother whose mouth was stuffed with grass. They found no Indians. Brown and his scouts saw signs indicating that Little Crow's village, with an immense baggage train, had headed for the Yellow Medicine about six days previously. The knowledge that the Sioux had departed was such a relief to the untried men that one of them said he and his companions "resembled a picnic party more than soldiers in an enemy's country."

They went back across the river to camp for the night and found that Captain Grant's detachment had stumbled over what remained of Justina Krieger. For twelve days she had been crawling across the prairie, and she was almost dead from hunger and loss of blood. They wrapped her in a blanket and made a bed of grass for her in one of the wagons, and then in the location Grant had selected the united command pitched camp near the deep ravine known as Birch Coulee. Wagons were parked in a semicircle and the horses picketed outside it; there were a half-dozen tents inside the crescent, but most of the men went to sleep under the wagons.

Peace reigned until just before daylight when a sentry saw what he thought was a dog or a wolf. "He fired," Grant reported primly, "and it proved to be an Indian." Indians appeared on all sides. The horses began to fall, and the men dived behind them. "It was a perfect surprise," a soldier remembered. "The day preceding gave no sign of Indians. Joe Brown, half-breed scouts, and the most experienced frontiersmen were as much astounded as if hell itself had unloaded 10,000 fiends upon our heads." After an hour's fighting in the red dawn the Sioux had been driven back to long range. But the cost was fearful. Twenty-two white men were already dead or mortally wounded; half the party had been hit, seriously or otherwise. Only one wagon remained upright. In it was Justina Krieger.

There was one young soldier who could ornament his memory of Birch Coulee with the romantic language it deserved. "But now the scene is changed," wrote James J. Eagan a quarter-century later, "and as the red early dawn, covering everything with a halo of gold, revealed to our gaze what we supposed to be 2,000 Indians surrounding us on all sides, with leaders mounted on horses caparisoned with gay colors, and themselves radiant in feathers, war paint, and all the bright and brilliant habiliments of Indian chiefs, the scene seemed unreal, as if a page from the history of the crusades had been torn from the leaves of history and the Saracen chiefs of the plains of Asia transplanted to the new world."

The more prosaic facts showed the ambushed party digging in with no time to comment on the costumes of the enemy. The soil was tough. The digging had to be done with three spades, one pick, bayonets, tin pans, or anything else with a cutting edge. The rain of Indian bullets was unceasing, but by noon the men had chipped out two hundred feet of rifle pits with dead horses helping to serve as breastworks. Few, if any, felt heroic. "To be scalped or quartered, our hearts cut out," Egan wrote, "gave us no comforting reflections. Several of the men went crazy, and jumping out to give a full view instantly met death. . . . Individual instances of bravery were many and some few of cowardice. A fine-looking man near me was unnerved; he did not shoot once, but kept crying out, 'O my God, my God!' George Turnball, first lieutenant, pulled a revolver on him, cocked it, and said if he did not stop he would blow his brains out. He stopped."

The ambushed men discovered that ordnance had issued sixty-two-caliber bullets for fifty-eight-caliber rifles, and they went to work whittling down the ammunition to the size of the guns they had been given. Meanwhile the sound of shooting had echoed against the valley walls and had been heard by the Ridgley garrison. A relief expedition was on its way as the Birch Coulee party tried to conserve the ammunition. Early in the afternoon the sound of a cannon was heard above the coulee. "We were all startled," Egan recalled. "Could the Indians have captured a howitzer? . . . We were sixteen miles from Fort Ridgley, and how could knowledge of our situation have reached the fort?" Nevertheless at about four o'clock an army detachment was sighted a couple of miles away. A few shots were fired to let the commanding officer know there were still live men in the ambush, and some of the survivors jumped to their feet and cheered. "The spirit of audacity we exhibited led to renewed fire upon us," Egan said. It developed that the relief expedition had a look at that Indian fire, and the commanding officer drew his men back while he sent for reinforcements.

At Birch Coulee there was a night of black despair before help actually arrived. Then, at daybreak, Colonel Sibley's guns were shelling the timber in the ravine. "Suddenly the boom of the canon is again heard"—James Egan remembering—"and again and nearer and clearer, until its roar, usually terrible, sounded as the sweetest harmony of heaven. Confusion seems to pervade our enemies, and they are in full flight." At eleven in the morning—thirty-one hours after the ambush—Sibley rode into the sickening scene. The dead were black and discolored from the sun's rays, and there was an intolerable stench emanating from the battleground. When Joe Brown counted the holes in one tent, he found that one hundred and forty bullets had pierced it. The one upright wagon aroused the curiosity of the rescuers. "They seemed perfectly astonished to find me alive," Justina wrote. "The blanket on which I lay wrapped in the wagon was found to have received over two hundred bullet holes during the fight." The exhausted woman was taken back to the Fort Ridgley hospital along with Joseph De Camp and the other wounded.

Far from the coulee, Jannette De Camp had heard none of the shots that had helped to cut her husband down. During the night before the ambush she and her three young sons had been led out of the Sioux encampment by the Christian Indian, Lorenzo Lawrence. Traveling at night they escaped down the river in boats that Lorenzo and his mother had hidden on Sunday. Five days later they had come to Joseph De Camp's sawmill at Redwood and Jannette had insisted upon stopping at her home to look for her husband's business records. "It was a sad sight," she wrote, "featherbeds emptied, furniture hacked to pieces. . . . But I found the books and accounts which I was after, and, taking an old satchel, I packed them in it, together with a Bible . . . and we quickly returned to the boats."

Moving with caution that Jannette found exasperating, Lorenzo and his fugitives spent all the next week on the river. "Would I find my husband and we be once more united?" Jannette asked herself. At last, in a furiously raging storm, they approached the Fort Ridgley ferry. Lorenzo took Jannette's infant in his arms and they approached the fort with the rain running in torrents down the hill. On the bluff Jannette was met by the Reverend Joshua Sweet, chaplain of the post. "I asked him if my husband were there. Tears choked his utterance as he said: 'I buried him ten days ago.'" Jannette went back to her parents' home and several weeks later gave birth to a fourth son. She returned to Fort Ridgley in 1866 as the wife of Joshua Sweet.

The Indian camp from which Jannette had escaped had been moved beyond the Yellow Medicine for strategic reasons. Little Crow's followers wanted to protect their own families and, by moving west, to involve the bands on the upper river that had not yet joined in the war. While Big Eagle and Mankato had gone downriver to ambush Joe Brown's command at the coulee, Little Crow had gone north and struck the settlements in the vicinity of the hen's egg massacre; another party of raiders had attacked the Red River country. With such quick thrusts the Sioux had hoped to frighten the valley people into a frantic exodus, and the failure to achieve this goal brought dissension over Little Crow's leadership. There was no less discord among Little Crow's enemies. Sibley's failure to score a victory in two weeks of war brought denunciation from his critics. The Birch Coulee tragedy was the result of the disastrous mistake of selecting an indefensible campsite. Sibley was not responsible for the site, but he was responsible for the delay in relief, and he was dubbed "the state undertaker."

Before the colonel abandoned Birch Coulee, he left a message on a split stick: "If Little Crow has any proposition to make to me, let him send a half-breed to me, and he shall be protected in and out of camp." Little Crow had a proposition, but it was not surrender. He sent a message on September 7 in which he named Agent Galbraith as the cause of the war; he also blamed the traders, and Andrew Myrick in particular. Any hope Sibley had that Little Crow was essentially against the massacre and might recant was blasted: "If the young braves have pushed the white man," said Crow, "I have done this myself." Then he slyly added, "I have a great many prisoners, women and children." Among the prisoners was Thomas A. Robertson, the mixed-blood son of the Daybreak Woman, who was conscripted as a translator of the Little Crow messages. Sibley sent Tom

Robertson back to tell the Sioux to turn over the prisoners under a flag of truce on the promise that the colonel would talk to Little Crow like a man. Crow stood fast. Wabasha and Taopi then made an overture of surrender, suggesting that they might bring in all the captives they could secure. But the Little Crow faction was stronger, and nobody was released. Sibley, harassed by desertions and indiscipline, finally decided that negotiation was futile, and he marched against the enemy on September 18.

Tuesday, September 23

Four days later Little Crow's vigilant scouts reported Sibley's army, sixteen hundred strong, camped near Wood Lake, not far from the Yellow Medicine, and at a council that night the Indians decided to ambush the whites on the road of the next day's march. "The morning came and an accident spoiled our plans," Big Eagle said. At seven A.M. a dozen Third Regiment enlisted men set out for the Yellow Medicine agency to bring back food from the garden in four company wagons. "They came on over the prairie . . . and if they had kept straight on would have driven right over our men as they lay in the grass," Big Eagle said. "At last they came so close that our men had to raise up and fire. This brought on the fight, of course, but not according to the way we had planned it. Little Crow saw it and felt very badly." Instead of stampeding Sibley's army while it was strung out along the road, the Indians found themselves in a pitched battle in which they were outnumbered. They fought for about two hours and then, on signal, disappeared. Such as it was, the battle was over. "It was the Waterloo for the bold and wily chieftain, Little Crow," a young soldier summed up romantically.

Unlike Wellington, Sibley let his enemy get away. He wanted those captives alive. He sent an immediate request to the hostiles for the delivery of the whites, and followed it up with a message to three friendly chiefs; then he moved on to the camp of Wabasha and Taopi and some bands who had decided to be penitent. Three days after the Battle of Wood Lake, the colonel entered the hostile encampment with drums beating and colors flying. He found that Little Crow, Red Middle Voice, Shakopee, Sleepy Eyes, and the four hunters who had started the war of the hen's eggs had vanished, along with many others.

"I conducted the poor captives to my camp, where I had prepared tents for their accommodation," Sibley reported. "There were some instances of stolidity among them, but for the most part the poor creatures, relieved of the horrible suspense in which they had been left, and some of the younger women freed from the loathsome attentions to which they had been subjected by their brutal captors, were fairly overwhelmed with joy." When the two hundred and sixty-nine prisoners of the Sioux joined the Sibley forces the bivouac was immediately named Camp Release.

Panorama

Of all the ways of telling about the outbreak in the valley the most remarkable is the method chosen by John Stevens, a sign painter who in the fall of 1862 began to make sketches of the scenes of action. By liberal use of red paint he determined to depict the tragedies of August and September so that people who did not live on the river might understand the bloodthirstiness of the savages. Stevens called his creation diaphanous painting, but there were those who saw his work who spoke of it later as a forerunner of twentieth-century motion pictures.

Stevens had added a new dimension to the painted panoramas that had been developed as popular entertainments twenty years earlier. Other artists—John Banvard, John Rawson Smith, Leon Pomarede, and Henry Lewis—had depicted Mississippi River scenes on great strips of canvas (one said to be four miles long) that unrolled before audiences in the United States and Europe.

Stevens, however, worked out what he called a wholly new style. He told the story of the massacres with colors that were described as all transparent, and were applied to thin cloth through which light shone from behind. His "moving picture" played in school houses and village halls, and went on the road housed in a long, covered sleigh that had sides of transparent canvas on which were painted striking advertisements. The ingenious vehicle was brilliantly lighted from within and was commodious enough to shelter the musicians who provided a harmonious accompaniment.

Advertising that he had "taken many of the Sketches on the spot," Stevens also had received many first-hand details from Mrs. Lavina Eastlick who lived in Mankato. Her vivid recollections of flaming cabins and plundering savages—as well as of her son's heroism—served to invest the panorama with a quality assessed by one newspaper as "a smack of truthfulness which the vivid reality calls for and which lends to it all the horribleness of atrocious murder." A decade after the outbreak the sign painter increased his effect of reality when he hired young Merton Eastlick as narrator.

Lavina Eastlick, like Justina Krieger, had survived an incredible ordeal. After she had been shot and clubbed to unconsciousness by Indians, she had managed, by crawling for days, to reach eventual safety. Her son Merton, then eleven years old, had carried his infant brother for almost sixty miles in his flight from the attackers. The wavy-haired, luxuriantly bearded Stevens was a painter of primitive talent, but his brushes charged Mrs. Eastlick's accounts with so much dramatic power that little was left to the imagination of his audience. Crude as was his drawing, the Indian devastation was felt immediately in rising smoke, blood-crazed savages, galloping horses, the spinning wheels of the wagon that Lavina Eastlick drove frantically and futilely toward escape. As a good showman, Stevens provided relief from scenes of tragedy with pleasant landscapes and portraits: Washington welcoming Lafayette, the Falls of St. Anthony, and a panel entitled "Minnesota Fruit" which showed a tree "fairly groaning under its load of infantile human specimens" while mothers held out their aprons to catch the falling babies.

In 1868, Stevens advertised his show as the "great Moral Exhibition of the Age," and cited "A Grand and Imposing Spectacle, A Bird's-Eye View of New Ulm" among the high points. He offered portraits of Henry Sibley, of John Other Day, and the brutal Cut Nose. One of his scenes showed Chief Red Iron turning over the captives to Sibley at Camp Release. Stevens felt a greater need to be entertaining than to be historically dependable. He wasn't much interested in the military trials in which three hundred and seven Indians were found guilty of rape or murder and sentenced to be hanged, nor did he try to depict the escape of Little Crow or that of the renegade Inkpaduta. But when President Lincoln commuted the sentences of all but thirty-eight savages, the sign painter had his big scene. In a colorful canvas, dominated by Civil War blue, he showed the honor guard of troops formed in a hollow square on the Mankato river front.

The event he painted has been described as America's greatest mass execution. A four-fronted scaffold had been contrived to drop the thirty-eight men at the same instant. Hundreds of valley people had gathered on December 27, 1862, to watch the macabre proceedings. The doomed Indians, marching two abreast between files of soldiers, sang as they mounted the platform. "It is winter, and wet and cold," an eyewitness wrote, "yet every street and house and hotel, door, window, and eligible spot is crowded. The poor wretches try to clasp hands, some succeeding . . . the grasp unrelaxed even in death." Joe Brown, who had come to the river as a drummer boy more than forty years before, beat the drum for the last time.

Stevens made the scene live for thousands of Minnesotans who had long believed that there could be no good Indian but a dead one. His diaphanous paintings may have done as much as anything else to keep fresh the memories of 1862. Almost sixty years

WOOD LAKE STATE MONUMENT

after the outbreak, when a Stevens panorama was presented to the Minnesota Historical Society, it was found that the revolving canvas had thirty-six panels, each six feet high and seven feet wide. Stevens had constructed a coffinlike box to contain the long spool and another for the collapsible frames on which it was mounted; there were two pedestals to hold the kerosene lamps that were used to illuminate the unwinding panorama. In 1919 and 1920 it was shown again and one of the added attractions was the appearance of Mrs. Mary Schwandt Schmidt, recalling what the outbreak had meant to her.

Effective as the sign painter's handiwork was, the panorama did not explore the aftermath of the war with the Sioux. In the spring following the mass execution, the Indians whose sentences had been commuted were sent downriver from Mankato on the *Favorite;* when they passed the Mendota bottom land, where their women and children were being held, they sang "Have Mercy Upon Us, O Jehovah," a hymn they had learned that winter from the missionaries. Within a month the *Favorite* and two other steamboats had deported almost two thousand Indians from the valley. Congress abolished all previous treaties with the Sioux, and Henry Sibley, newly appointed brigadier general, was instructed to organize an expedition to capture Little Crow and to punish the bands that had fled from justice. In June, Sibley's column, five miles in length, left camp at the mouth of the Redwood and moved upriver to jump off from Brown's Valley. Coming in behind the column, Little Crow and his son made a raid near Hutchinson to steal horses, and the outbreak's war chief was surprised in a berry patch where he was killed by a settler.

Sibley had to be content with lesser prey. His column returned to Fort Snelling in mid-September after only two minor skirmishes, but the citizen general had pushed the Sioux bands to the other side of the Missouri. Shakopee—who could engineer the slaughter of helpless women and children but could not lead a war party—had escaped Sibley's army and hid out in Canada until his capture in 1864. The return of the settlers to the valley was slow, and some of them could not bring themselves to return at all to the homes that had been despoiled by the Sioux.

News of the atrocities in the valley spread like prairie fire across all of the frontier, and Nebraska pioneers, feeling that their turn might be next, demanded troops for defense. At the same time some of the most bloodthirsty of the Minnesota Sioux attached themselves to bands that had lived for generations on the Western plains, and their boasts and grievances fomented trouble. The discontent that had begun in the Minnesota Valley was thus moved west. An army regiment wiped out a Cheyenne village at Sand Creek the summer that Shakopee was captured, and the Cheyennes then became allies of the aggressive Sioux. The next year the Cheyennes retaliated at Platte Bridge, and in 1866 the Sioux were with them when Fetterman's command was annihilated. Ten years later Custer decided to pursue a party composed of numerous tribes to the Little Big Horn. Among the Cheyennes and the many Sioux bands that then brought about Custer's end were the followers of Inkpaduta, who had been the author of the first outrages in the valley. Who killed Custer is a matter of much conjecture, but one of the most persistent of the reports asserts that he went down under the fire of two of Inkpaduta's sons.

22

HOMESTEAD VALLEY

A land of milk and honey
And water of the best
They call it Minnesota
The Beauty of the West.

—OLD SONG

PEACE SETTLED on the river in the wake of the hostile Indians' departure. Little Crow's sixteen-year-old son grew up to become the founder of the Y.M.C.A. among the Sioux; his grandson became the Reverend John W. Wakeman, pastor of the Yellow Medicine church. On November 11, 1865, as the murderous Shakopee mounted a gallows at Mendota, the first train headed west into the valley, emitting a blast from its big brass whistle; the railroads had joined the steamboats in bringing new settlers over tracks that followed the contours of the river bluffs.

The serpentine Minnesota became a more crowded westering highway. Its importance could not be underestimated, a railroad builder said, "because it was navigable and therefore a competitor for April, May, June, and July, as far up as Mankato, and a part of the time to Fort Ridgley and the Redwood and Yellow Medicine agencies." At the end of the 1860's and after, pioneers took the railroads as far as they ran, then boarded a steamboat if one was available, or fanned out from the river on stagecoach

224

lines. Even after the railroads, the life of the homesteader was isolated. "The Minnesota Valley," an articulate farm wife wrote, "had always seemed to me to reach from horizon to horizon, the river showing no partiality to either side; for hundreds of miles east and west, it had been the pride of nature-loving people."

The pride was in what the new land would yield—in an onion raised at Fort Ridgley that measured five and a half inches in diameter, in a Henderson rutabaga weighing nineteen and a half pounds. "The turnips," someone remembered, "grew so enormous on our virgin soil that we could hardly believe they were turnips. They looked more like small pumpkins inverted in the ground." The soil was rich and it nourished the seed that the newcomers brought with them. It also produced an extravagance of wild fruit that old settlers never ceased to take joy in remembering. Cranberries—"by the hundreds of bushels"—grew in the bogs. The wild grapes bending over the river made marvelous Burgundy. The Eden that lives in the memories of all nostalgic pioneers had been found.

There was a good deal more struggle than such sentimentality would indicate and some of it was publicly rewarding. As early as 1857 there stepped off a steamboat at Chaska a German named Wendelin Grimm, who had learned to farm in the rolling Tauber Valley of Franconia. He was nearly forty and he carried with him twenty pounds of alfalfa seed and enough money to acquire a good-sized farm. Grimm was determined to do what both Washington and Jefferson had failed to accomplish on their Virginia plantations. Alfalfa had never successfully been grown in the United States except in California, but stubborn Herr Grimm planted his seed in the Minnesota Valley, determined that it must survive the winter as it had beside the Tauber. Though he lost almost all of it the first winter, he had greener hay for his cattle and some new seed to plant. He kept on planting from seed that was not winter-killed, and his animals fattened. In 1863, when he drove his herd past his neighbor's place, Henry Gerdson wanted to know the secret of his success. Was he indulging his cattle by feeding them corn? "No grain at all," said Wendelin Grimm, "just everlasting clover." Other farmers asked for his seed when they discovered that Grimm's strain of alfalfa was so hardy that its roots had grown ten feet deep in the clay soil of Carver County. In 1874, the plants survived the severest winter in thirty years. Grimm's fame began to spread in the valley, yet it was the end of the century before the Department of Agriculture learned of his success. The alfalfa now known as Minnesota Grimm was brought to the aid of northern dairymen, and in 1924 the Grimm Alfalfa Growers Association erected a monument on Wendelin Grimm's homestead. "Sometimes it is given to a few to recognize and pay tribute," an editor said, "to a patient man . . . who in obscurity and perhaps in poverty has worked out great benefits to humanity. Perhaps someday our historians will tell more of the work of such men and glorify less the authors of death and devastation."

The ways of peace brought contentment to the valley homesteaders who were patient enough to withstand the inherent vicissitudes of pioneer life. Like Wendelin Grimm, they struggled not for fame but for opportunity, and they had the courage to survive repeated failures that came through no fault of their own. In the summer of 1873, grasshoppers again invaded the valley. The insect army caught the homesteaders by complete surprise. "The men came home to dinner," said a woman describing that unforgettable midday, "and the talk was all in praise of this new country and the crops. While we were talking it gradually darkened." The farmers' immediate reaction was to assume that they were in for a driving rain.

"The men hastily went out to see if anything should be brought in before the storm," the woman continued. "What a sight when we opened the door! The sky darkened by myriads of grasshoppers and no green thing could be seen." A neighbor had taken off his vest and was working in his garden. "Suddenly," he said, "my attention was attracted to the sky and I never saw a more beautiful sight. A horde of grasshoppers were alighting. Nothing more beautiful than the shimmering of the sun on their thousands of gold-bronze wings could be imagined. They took everything and then passed on leaving gardens looking as if they had been burned. When I went for that vest, they had eaten it all but the seams. It was the funniest sight—just a skeleton."

For years there seemed almost no end to the memories evoked by the mention of grasshoppers. Some said that the winged invaders made a sound like a roaring wind, or like a prairie fire. No open door or window was safe from intrusion. The insects clustered around buildings to the depth of two or three inches, swarming over shoes and eating shoe laces. Trains were delayed while grasshoppers were shovelled from the tracks. In the towns and on the farms people were filled with consternation at the total destruction of crops.

The farmers turned the soil with their plows, hoping that frost would kill the grasshopper eggs. But in June, 1874, the eggs hatched and the new plantings were completely devastated. Bounties were offered for dead hoppers; tar-covered iron plates were dragged across infested fields, hay was spread and burned to cremate the insects, ditches were dug in desperate effort to contain the scourge. The grasshoppers stayed until 1877. That spring the governor proclaimed a day of fasting and prayer. "Suddenly the next day, about noon," the historian Julius Coller wrote, "the air was filled with locusts as they rose from the ground. Higher and higher they went, glistening in the bright sun, and then they disappeared. That night the temperature fell to an unseasonably low degree; sleet and a little snow fell, and the locusts that had not joined the migration were frozen. Where the swarms migrated to, no one knows."

Fired in the holocausts of Indian savagery and in the absolute destruction of crops and livelihood, a sense of community began to govern the valley. The older downriver towns became steadily more populous after the coming of the railroads, and new towns had blossomed near the sites of the Indian agencies and on the western end of the river that now was divested of all but the most amicable Sioux. The golden, flower-strewn prairies were dotted with homesteads, and the roads to town were no longer rutted trails; a trip to the nearest riverside settlement to trade produce for supplies and to exchange gossip around the stove in the general store became routine.

The store was a place for European newcomers to acquire Americanisms, and the language of the period was full of colorful back-country idiom. It was a time when a girl who wasn't pretty was "as homely as a hedge fence"; when "one boy is half a man, two boys no man at all"; when indignation could cause a man to "beller like a bay steer." If a storekeeper said he was going to "go snucks," he meant that he would take a partner, and he might add laconically that "ye can't make a whistle out of a pig's tail." The flavor of Yankee farms was still strong in the valley colloquialism. Children cried "run Big Fraid, Little Fraid's after ye," and their parents cautioned, "Ye might as well eat the devil as drink his broth." A frontier mother might rue her offspring's behavior with a tight-lipped shake of the head, adding, "The devil's in him as big as a woodchuck"; or, "she'll do it if the devil stands tuh the door." "I'll knock him into the middle of next week," said the irate father, "he thinks he's a little god and a half." Someone else "didn't know enough to carry guts to a bear," or "didn't have the gumption of a louse"; and there was always one who was "busy as a bee in a tar bucket." Watching the foibles of the young, the river folk disparaged romance and said that "love'll go where it's sent."

The homesteaders became so linked in valley loyalties, and their knowledge of each other became so general, that they waited eagerly for gossip that might either shock or titillate them. Routine brought civilization and all its misdemeanors. As savory as any of the valley's scandals was the disappearance that helped to divert the citizens of Shakopee soon after the first invasion of grasshoppers. It came to light one autumn day when banker David How sent off a telegram to a distant town where

POWER PLANT

his young wife ostensibly was visiting. The answer coming back over the wire declared without amplification that Mrs. How was not there. Assuming that she had started for home, the banker went to meet that evening's train and was surprised when she did not step off it. As he tried to trace her movements in the two weeks she had been away, How could find no one who had seen her, and when he at last took a look at her closet he came to the conclusion that her departure was final and premeditated.

The vanished lady was twenty-nine and attractive. When she left home, she had been seen wearing a black alpaca dress, a greenish slate-colored redingote with large black velvet buttons, a light straw hat "trimmed with that new shade of green," and she carried a red leather valise and had a trunk. "We are informed by persons well acquainted with the parties," said the local newspaper, raising a properly censorious voice, "that she had no excuse for leaving home. . . . Mr. How is laboring under severe mental and bodily prostrations."

The speculations among the citizens of the riverside town were hearty and not precisely charitable. The townspeople immediately realized that one other citizen was missing. He was the prominent J. G. Butterfield, who had served with How on the town council and who several days before Mrs. How's departure had announced that he was off to Vermont to fetch his wife who was visiting relatives. "It is certain," said the Scott County *Argus,* on October 9, "Mr. Butterfield did not go to Vermont. . . . If he has really absconded he leaves [his wife and five children] in a destitute condition." The Shakopee council promptly declared Butterfield's seat vacant, and he was expelled from the fraternal organizations to which both he and How belonged.

David How stayed at home with his eight-year-old daughter and did his best to survive the ordeal. He had received a letter from his wife, and there were speculations that she admitted she had met Butterfield in Chicago, from where they had gone to New York en route to Europe. For weeks the gossip persisted. Then at the end of November, as winter locked in the valley, the entertainment ran threadbare and the townspeople reconciled themselves to learning no more from tight-mouthed David How.

A few days before Christmas, however, they again picked up the *Argus* with relish. "The notorious elopement scandal of Butterfield and Mrs. How," they read, "has received a quietus so far as the public is concerned by the return of Mrs. How to her home. . . . Her return was as unexpected to her own family as to the general public, and she entered the family circle of her own fireside as quietly as though she had just returned from a morning call. While the public was surprised, it is reported that her husband was astonished at the boldness of such a return. If she has returned penitent and bowed down with grief over her folly, it is not known in this community."

Little more was heard of Butterfield, but David and Mary

How became active again in town social functions and outwardly lived as if there had been no interruption in their domesticity. Twelve years later David gave his daughter Jennie in marriage, and after her departure the parents entertained themselves with travel. Twenty years—almost to the day—after Mary How's return, David had breakfast with his son-in-law and went back upstairs to his room. Downstairs the family heard a shot. When David How was found, he was sitting in a chair still grasping a pearl-handled revolver in one hand and a small mirror in the other. A thirty-eight caliber bullet had passed through both his temples and had lodged in the bedroom wall.

It was a tragedy no greater than many that happened in other valley towns and homesteads. What saved the story for future generations was David How's identity with the growth of the river town to which he had come almost forty years before. Squire How—as he called himself in his diary at the age of twenty-two—arrived in Shakopee on a lovely May afternoon in 1857 on the river packet *Antelope*. He came as the settlement's first druggist, and in a few years he was operating a flour mill as well as a pharmacy. As a banker with interests in Shakopee, Belle Plaine, Jordan, and New Prague he helped to finance the thriving valley farms that grew out of struggling homesteads.

Gossip was a by-product of relaxed and prosperous rural life; it helped to relieve the tedium of humdrum chores. A frontier philosophizer has said that the fierce love of freedom, the strength that came from hewing out a home, making a school and a church, "and creating a higher future for his family" ennobled the pioneer. But the nobility was always human. Along the winding Minnesota, men came to accept their success without philosophizing as they watched the disappearance of log cabins and sod houses and the mushrooming of brick and clapboard residences, the maturing of children who were natives in the valley. They were rural Victorians with rural nineteenth-century ambitions and morals. With the rest of the nation they were celebrating the centennial of American Independence, but in less than a quarter of a century the river dwellers had transformed the Suland from an aboriginal preserve to a valley of disciplined and optimistic life. The future was their promise to themselves, and from the East, from the lands of Europe, they had come to the Minnesota not only to open their part of the West but to endow the river with its own new future.

JESSE JAMES SLIPPED HERE

It was both their Gettysburg and their Waterloo.

—ROBERTUS LOVE

T HEY WERE no ordinary travelers. They were already legend- ary when they rode into the valley, and when they left it, the tales about them began to multiply. They came incognito, stop- ping at Chaska, the story goes, to sit in on a poker game with Sheriff Frederick Du Toit. They were prosperously dressed, and they stayed at good hotels, asking about farms for sale and chat- ting with bankers about investments. At St. Peter, it was remem- bered, they sat on the hotel veranda, smoking Havanas and amus- ing themselves by tossing coins to curious youngsters.

Under various names these travelers in the valley included Jesse James and his brother Frank, Cole Younger and his broth- ers Jim and Bob, Charley Pitts, Clell Miller, and Bill Chadwell, who had been in southern Minnesota before—as a horse thief. At the end of August, 1876, fresh from a fourteen-thousand- dollar train robbery in Missouri, they began to familiarize them- selves with the valley roads and the topography over which they intended to make their departure.

It was the recollection of Henry Moll, then a deputy sheriff, that they spent nine days in St. Peter. "My father and I operated a harness shop here then," Moll told the historian Win V. Work-

JESSE JAMES
& GANG

ing, "and Cole and Pitts each bought a saddle from us. They bought a horse from Arthur French at Lake Emily and another from a man named Hodges at Kasota. One day when they tied their horses in front of the *Tribune* office on Main Street, a crowd gathered to admire the animals, which were of fine stock."

While Bob Younger and Chadwell were buying horses in Mankato, Cole and Charley Pitts crossed the river to the mouth of the Watonwan and followed the tributary through Garden City, dropping in on farmers and spending a night at the Flanders House in Madelia where Colonel Thomas Vought, the proprietor, extolled the land that might be bought in the nearby Lake Hanska area. The strangers were treated as prosperous businessmen. Five of them appeared in Mankato on Saturday, September 2, causing a good deal of stir among horse fanciers. They were all dressed in linen dusters, the fashionable travelers' garb of the day, and there was at first no hint that the voluminous costumes served the additional purpose of hiding sidearms. They dropped in at the First National Bank to change a fifty-dollar bill and then made a few purchases before separating to register at different hotels. Sunday they rendezvoused at Jack O'Neill's, a gamblers' hangout on the other side of the river, and were unaware that a Mankato citizen claimed to have recognized Jesse.

The Mankato police watched them until midnight and then went home to bed. At noon, riding through town in twos and threes, the strangers found a group of men gathered on the sidewalk outside the bank. When one of the group gestured toward the approaching horses, the riders decided to take no chances. They turned away, to return several hours later. Finding the same group again (actually idle citizens watching a building being constructed across the street), the legendary Jameses and Youngers abandoned Mankato as a target for armed assault.

They rode east through the Undine region and spent Monday night in the village of Janesville. On Tuesday they turned north into the lake country and stopped in the unpromising hamlet of Cordova. On Wednesday they began to focus on a new target, and they divided to make use of Millersburg and Cannon City as jumping off points for the morrow; both places were within an eleven-mile radius of Northfield, a one-bank town the band had cased in preliminary surveys. Jesse James had Bill Chadwell's experienced word as a horse thief that the Northfield haul would be a good one.

The Northfield raid was the only real blunder in Jesse's career. Within seven minutes the would-be bank robbers had met defeat. The suspicions of a vacationing medical student and a hardware man were immediately aroused, and a half-dozen Northfield businessmen were soon involved in a street fight. Inside the bank, Frank James had killed the assistant cashier, but the townsmen had shot both Clell Miller and Bill Chadwell dead, and Jim and Bob Younger were badly wounded. Riding abreast, the survivors hightailed it down the Dundas road, with Bob and Cole Younger sharing a mount. The news leaped after them over the telegraph wires. Sheriffs, police chiefs, and detectives throughout southern Minnesota were notified, and volunteer law enforcers were called for. Before evening on Thursday two hundred men were chasing the famous gang, and on Friday there were five hundred.

Picket lines were thrown out to cut off every possible escape route, but the hastily enlisted vigilantes were sorely lacking in experience. Not long after the Northfield fight, a party of pickets went into a village restaurant and thoughtlessly left their guns stacked outside. While they were eating, Jesse and his gang whipped into town, saw the abandoned artillery, and with typical bravado stopped long enough to water their horses before they rushed on. Moving westward in drizzling rain, they outwitted three pickets on Friday and forded the Little Cannon River. Confusion broke out among the pursuers. Telegrams clicked back and forth. The railroads were impressed to shuttle posse members from one position to another. More pickets were posted on all the roads and trails, but the Northfield raiders were loose in the Big Woods where there were numberless sloughs and the rain-drenched ground was so boggy that the trace of fleeing horses was soon lost.

Jesse and his men had appropriated new mounts as pastures offered them, but by dark on Friday they were still in swampy country and they spent that rainy night in an uncomfortable shelter made by spreading their horse blankets over bushes. Dawn convinced them that they would never get out of the sloughs on horseback and they abandoned their mounts to set off on foot. They found an island of dry land in the swamp, decided to rest during the day and travel at night. Sunday morning they heard the church bell at Marysburg. They worked their soggy way around the hamlet, and at last, on Monday, found a deserted farmhouse near Mankato. In five days they had covered only fifty miles, yet they had evaded the pursuers without having a single shot fired at them.

Famished, they commandeered themselves breakfast on Tuesday at the house of a German settler, and went back to their deserted farmhouse. On Wednesday they found Thomas Dunning in the woods and made him a prisoner. After binding him and extorting information from him, they debated about killing him; Jesse was outvoted when they let Dunning go on his fear-stricken promise that he would breathe nothing to anyone. Dunning, of course, changed his mind and raced to tell Henry Schaubut, the Mankato banker who owned the farm. The outlaws, however, had learned from Dunning that the posse fever had cooled, and they decided to sneak through Mankato. They were passing Boegan's lumber mill when an ear-splitting whistle broke the night. Had Dunning lied when he said the manhunt had been all but abandoned? The whistle sounded to the outlaws like a signal to arouse the entire countryside. They began to run, and it was moments later before they realized that the whistle was regularly blown for the midnight shift.

Years later Frank Franciscus, a Mankato newspaperman interviewed Cole Younger: "Cole said they followed the old St. Paul and Sioux City right of way through Mankato. The road ran along Fourth Street and crossed the Van Brunt slough between Mankato proper and West Mankato on Van Brunt Street. There was a trestle over the slough and Cole told me they encountered members of a posse on the trestle. He said he asked them what they were doing and they explained that they were looking for the Youngers."

The pickets on the bridge got no inkling that their quarry was slipping past them, but when Tom Dunning told the news to his employer, the manhunt was reorganized under E. M. Pope, a Civil War general, and the number of pursuers of the six wanted robbers was increased to almost a thousand. The Jameses and the Youngers had been on the loose for a week since their defeat at Northfield. To make better time they decided to split, the two James brothers taking one route, the Youngers and Charley Pitts another. Frank and Jesse found a horse and that night near Lake Crystal were challenged by an alert sentinel. When the sentinel fired, the horse threw his riders and the Jameses escaped in the dark, but Jesse's hat was left behind. There was a smoking bullet hole in it.

With the general in command the river towns had taken on the aspects of war. In Madelia, on the peaceful Watonwan River another Civil War veteran, Colonel Tom Vought, had swung into action as soon as he had heard about the Northfield raid. He remembered the white linen dusters of the two men shopping for land and immediately realized who his guests had been. He remembered too that Cole had expressed particular interest in a bridge between the two lakes, and Vought stood guard at the bridge for a couple of nights, chatting with Oscar Sorbel, a seventeen-year-old farm boy who lived nearby. Vought charged Oscar to be on the lookout for men meeting the description of the two who had stopped at his hotel and to bring word to him in town.

The Younger brothers and Charley Pitts, meanwhile, had been

making slow and painful progress. Jim, whose jaw had been shat-
tered by a Northfield bullet, was getting near the breaking point;
Bob's elbow had been crushed, and the men had dared not find
a doctor. Cole had to cut himself a staff to keep going. They
dragged themselves across the valley swamps, and on September
21 they passed the Sorbel farm where Oscar and his father
were milking. Cole and his brothers said good morning, and
Oscar scanned the heavy six-foot figure that Colonel Vought had
described. "There goes the robbers," he told his father. Oscar
was scoffed at, but he wouldn't be dissuaded. He jumped on a
horse and became the valley's Paul Revere as he raced toward
Madelia shouting, "Look out! The robbers are about!"

The two weeks that had passed since the Northfield battle
caused people to think that all the band must surely have escaped, and no one would believe Oscar Sorbel. But boys like Oscar could make themselves experts on outlaws by reading the
scores of dime novels that had been written about the James and
Younger families. Just the year before there had been published
*The Guerrillas of the West; or the Life, Character and Daring
Exploits of the Younger Brothers.* Such books told of the border
warfare, in which both Youngers and Jameses had fought with
Captain William Quantrill, as well as of their days of outlawry.
The bandits running loose in the Minnesota Valley were famous
even then from coast to coast. Any boy like Oscar Sorbel could
guess that Cole and his brothers were brazen enough to walk
down a road in broad daylight. Oscar booted his old farm horse
toward Madelia and just as he came in sight of the town his
doughty mount fell down. Oscar picked himself out of the mud,
threw himself back on the horse, and made for the Flanders
House.

"I saw 'em, Colonel! The robbers!"

As Tom Vought began to question the boy, Sheriff James
Glispin came up. Oscar's description seemed to make sense, and
the two men, joined by three others, got their guns, sent off the
news on the telegraph, and rode for the Sorbel farm. They dis-

covered that the Younger party had cut away from the Watonwan to cross the Hanska Slough, the wild morass that adjoins Lake
Hanska. Perhaps they were heading for the Cottonwood which
would lead them to the Coteau des Prairies and an escape
through Dakota.

Pushing their horses through the slough, the posse got a look
at the fugitives and the sheriff ordered his quarry to halt. Cole
and his men ran. Before they were seen again they were back on
the other side of Lake Hanska, heading up the Watonwan. A
posse member fired at long range and smashed Cole's walking
stick. The outlaws scrambled toward some horses in a farm
corral, but were cut off by the sheriff. When bullets began to fly,
the fugitives managed to get down to the river near another
farm. Boldly, they used a ruse that had worked before; they
identified themselves as an advance group of peace officers and
demanded the farmer's horses. They were foiled when the farmer
ran his team off in the opposite direction. The Youngers started
for the farmer's granary as a likely place to make a stand, but
were diverted when they saw more horses in the woods. When
the rush they made for the animals was stopped by bullets, the
exhausted outlaws took refuge in the brush of the river bottom.
They had boxed themselves in between bluff and river, in five
acres of willows, box elders, wild plums, and a tangle of grape
vines.

Reinforcements had arrived to join the posse, and they were
picketed to cut off any escape. The sheriff lined up seven men
eight feet apart and they moved cautiously toward the river,
then turned and advanced about fifty yards through the brush.
Thirty feet ahead they found their quarry almost concealed in a
thicket of vine-covered willows and plum trees. A bullet sang in
from the ambushed robbers. The posse fired. Charley Pitts rolled
over, dead. Three of the posse were grazed as the Youngers returned the fire, but the pursuers' aim was more accurate. Cole
was down, so was Jim. When the sheriff called for surrender,

Bob struggled to his feet. "I surrender," he said. "They are all down but me." An over-wary picket on the bluff fired and Bob was wounded for the fourth time. When the posse went in, they were astonished; Cole had been hit eleven times, Jim five, and Pitts' body had five holes in it.

When the Youngers were under heavy guard, Banker Schaubut arrived from Mankato, and Cole asked him about the fate of Jesse and Frank James. Nobody knew; but the banker, indignant that his bank had been the original target of the gang, began to lecture Cole. Cole looked at him.

"Would you like to know the difference between what you do and what I do?" the captive asked.

An eyewitness said Schaubut showed interest.

"It's very simple," said the outlaw who was the hero of dime novels. "You rob the poor and I rob the rich."

Cole never again mentioned the James boys, and when he was asked why he and the band had come all the way from Missouri to rob a bank in Mankato, he was ready with an answer. It pleased him to say he had been told that seventy-five thousand dollars had been deposited in the Mankato institution by the controversial General Benjamin Franklin Butler, whose treatment of Southern women had been so shocking that he had been removed from command of Union forces in New Orleans. The invasion of the Minnesota Valley, Cole insinuated, was an act of revenge. Cole seemed to think that if he played the role of a chivalrous Confederate veteran—and denied involvement with the more notorious James boys—he might get a lighter sentence. But after he had served a quarter-century in the Minnesota penitentiary, and long after Jesse's assassination, he joined Frank in a Wild West show. He learned then that the fleeing Jameses had been lucky with horses and had cut across the valley to the Pipestone Quarry, turning south through Dakota to escape the Minnesota vigilantes.

The raid of the Missouri gunmen became enshrined in folklore, and new chapters about the Minnesota robbery attempts were added to already published books about them. One song was called "Cole Younger" and it had two stanzas that were a sort of hero worshiper's lament:

> We started out for Texas, that good old Lone Star state,
> And on Nebraska's prairies the James boys we did meet.
> With our guns, knives and pistols, we all sat down to play,
> With a bottle of good old whisky, boys, to pass the time away.
>
> We saddled up our horses and northward we did go,
> To the God-forsaken country, salled Minnea-sot-e-o.
> I had my eye on the 'Kato bank, when Brother Bob did say:
> "Cole, if you undertake this job, you'll always curse the day."

As the years passed, more and more stories about the manhunt were told in the river towns. A Shakopee druggist liked to remember that about two o'clock one night before the raid he had been roused to supply spirits of niter for a sick horse. "It was dark and I could not see the men clearly, but we have always thought they were the James-Younger gang and that they were camped near the Bloomington bridge." Another Shakopee story has it that John Dean, the local farrier, was paid to shoe the gang's horses backwards. He followed the instructions because he thought the customers were Eastern dudes staying at fashionable Lake Minnetonka. Some of the yarns were more realistic. In St. Peter, Henry Moll told Win Working: "Next we heard, they had been surrounded at Minneopa and then came the news that they were seen at Madelia. I had ten government guns and rounded up nine men to go with me, planning to take the noon train to Madelia. But we missed the train and didn't leave until seven o'clock that evening and the men had been taken when we arrived." According to another historian, "The robber hunt was the great joke of the season."

It provided material for fine, imaginative stories, however, and in Northfield, the town where the gang spent only seven min-

utes at work, the citizens have been celebrating Jesse James Day
for years. They have no heritage of famous patriots as overnight
guests, but some of them like to say that Jesse James slipped
here.

24

VIKING VISITORS?

What so truly suits with honor and honesty
as the discovering things unknown?

—CAPTAIN JOHN SMITH

W E PADDLED on, raging at the heat and flies, until we came to the little Pomme de Terre, or Potato River, clear as crystal, flowing into the muddy Minnesota. We peeled off our clothes and plunged in." Thus two young high-school graduates, in 1930, paused in an effort to prove that it was possible to travel, entirely by water, from ocean to ocean, straight through the heart of the continent. Their school principal had pronounced their project the nearest thing he knew to the Lewis and Clark expedition. From Minneapolis they had pointed their canoe, the *Sans Souci*, into the Minnesota, past Fort Snelling and on over the Carver Rapids. In six days they had reached Mankato and soon were in New Ulm where the last steamboat had turned downriver in 1874. Every place they stopped people read the words "Minneapolis to Hudson Bay" painted on the canoe, and scoffed openly or laughed covertly. The boys refused to be discouraged. They stopped at Fort Ridgley to relive the battles of the Sioux outbreak: "The view of the Minnesota Valley was inspiring from the hill on which the fort stood, but we were startled when we saw how much the river ahead twisted and

244

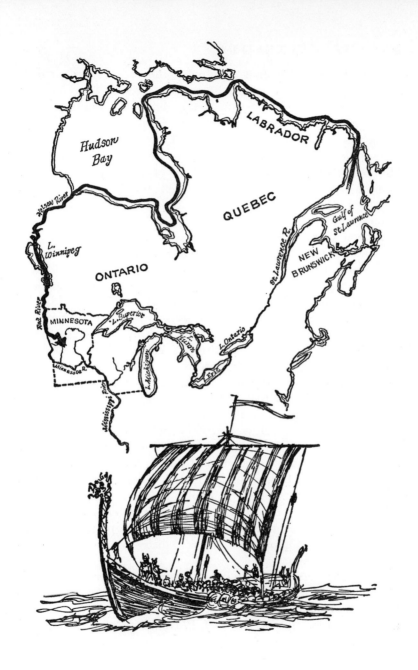

turned." Indeed, they had no idea of the ordeal they were to subject themselves to when, after three weeks, they left the peaceful Minnesota and followed the Red River north to Lake Winnipeg, thence through the wilds of Canada to York Factory.

The boys were Walter Port and Eric Sevareid, who later was to become famous as a political commentator. Growing up in Minnesota, they had heard the story of the Kensington rune stone, a controversial slab of laminated granite upon which is engraved a prayer for help purportedly left by Vikings seeking a water route through the American heartland. The rune stone had been unearthed not far from the upper reaches of the Pomme de Terre, the tributary that might have taken the Norsemen south to the Minnesota and ultimately to the Gulf of Mexico. Sevareid and his friend, having the advantage of modern maps and the knowledge that one short portage would take them into the northward flowing waters of the Red River valley, did not leave the Minnesota at the mouth of the Pomme de Terre, but followed it all the way to Brown's Valley. There a good Samaritan, in return for two cigars, hauled their canoe from one stream to the other. After four months of harrowing adventures, the boys proved—not that Vikings had actually come to Minnesota—but that, had they come, they could have followed the Minnesota River in an all-water round trip from Vinland.

Because the Minnesota seemed the obvious water route for any Norsemen headed south from Canada, the stone found near one of the river's tributaries fascinated valley people for years. Scandinavian settlers made a hobby of runic inscriptions and schoolteachers in some of the river towns entered the debates carried on among those writing letters to newspapers; the authenticity of the Kensington archaeological discovery was long a matter for argument.

The controversy began with a letter written on New Year's Day, 1899, by a Kensington real estate and insurance man to the *Svenska-Amerikanska Posten* in Minneapolis. "I enclose you a copy of an inscription," wrote J. P. Hedberg, "on a stone found

about 2 miles from Kensington by a O. Ohmann he found it under a tree when grubbing—he wanted I should go out and look
at it and I told him to haul it in when he came (not thinking
much of it) he did so and this is an excest copy of it. . . . you
perhaps have means to find out what it is—it appears to be old
Greek letters."

The publisher of the Swedish newspaper turned for help to
the University of Minnesota and within a few weeks Scandinavian readers in the valley and others throughout the Midwest
were excited by the report of a fourteenth-century Norse expedition that appeared to have traveled as far as Minnesota. What
Hedberg had guessed might be old Greek letters were runes,
the characters of the ancient Norse alphabets.

Freely translated the inscription said: "8 Goths and 22 Norwegians on an exploration journey from Vinland westward. We
had our camp by 2 rocky islets one day's journey north of this
stone. We were out fishing one day. When we came home we
found 10 men red with blood and dead. AVM save us from
evil. We have 10 men by the sea to look after our ships, 14 days'
journey from this island. Year 1362."

The scholar who made the translation was cautious and said
that he did not know whether to rank the discovery with the
Rosetta stone found on the Nile or with the bogus Cardiff
Giant that made so much money for Phineas Barnum. Not long
afterward his caution seemed justified when the inscription was
declared by three Oslo University experts to be a forgery perpetrated by a Swede with an amateurish understanding of
runic characters. The stone itself was ejected from the limelight
and for nine years rested face down in Olof Ohman's farmyard.
Then a student named Hjalmar Rued Holand visited Scandinavian settlements in the valley and in the course of his research
encountered Ohman and his story. Holand took the rune stone
home with him as a souvenir and began a defense of its authenticity that has lasted for more than half a century.

Holand did everything he could to prove that Ohman was not

the author of a hoax. He noted that the runic inscription told of a campsite near two "rocky islets" north of the stone and, undismayed by the hundreds of Minnesota lakes that contain such skerries, he began his search. On a Sunday afternoon in 1919, after much previous exploration, he climbed a hill beside Cormorant Lake, eighty-one miles north of Ohman's farm, and saw two skerries. The beach below the hill seemed to him an ideal place for a mooring site and, sure enough, there he found three large stones, each with a hole drilled in it. As the result of further research in rocky Norwegian fjords, Holand asserted that it had been ancient practice to make a boulder serve as a pier by drilling a hole to fit an iron pin with an attached ring. Thus could dragon ships conveniently tie up no matter where their crews might choose to roam.

Holand had no difficulty in imagining Viking ships in American waters. He saw a vessel perhaps seventy feet long, with richly carved prow and sternpost, roving interior streams long before the advent of Columbus; there was no reason why helmed and armored Norsemen who had pillaged most of the known world should not have ventured into the unknown world. Gradually he developed an itinerary for his Kensington Vikings. He delved into history and investigated the legendary Paul Knutson expedition sent to keep Christianity from perishing in the Scandinavian colonies. As Holand worked it out, the Paul Knutson assignment was accomplished between 1355 and 1364, with the Vikings prowling the coasts of Vinland in search of apostates who had moved ever westward to find better subsistence. Holand's route takes the expedition north from the Gulf of St. Lawrence, around Labrador to Hudson Bay, and traces the shores of the bay to the Nelson River. "To him," Holand says of Paul Knutson, "as to other people of his times this new land was a large island, and somewhere on the shore of this island these apostates whom he was seeking must be found unless God had struck them down in their iniquity. The thing to do therefore was to follow the shore until he found them. . . . Paul Knutson would have been right in reasoning that by ascending the Nelson he could find another river that would carry him back to Vinland."

Holand assumed first that the Paul Knutson party found its way in a southerly route across northern Canada to Lake Winnipeg and then pushed up the Red River on the Minnesota border. "On reaching the Buffalo River, which joins the Red a few miles north of Fargo," Holand wrote, "They ascended the Buffalo because their intention was to return to their headquarters in Vinland, far to the southeast, and the channel of the Buffalo leads southeastward. About two miles east of Hawley there was formerly a lake, and on the south side of it is a mooring stone." Boulders containing drilled holes have served Holand well. As defender of the Kensington inscription he has maintained that the Vikings followed the Buffalo to its most southerly source, made a portage of a thousand feet to Nelson Lake, and drilled another hole in a boulder to mark their campsite. Soon they were at Cormorant Lake where they were attacked by Indians, as described by the runes. Citing other drilled boulders, Holand took the fourteenth-century travelers thirty miles along the Pelican River until, unfortunately, that stream turned west. "But to the east," said Holand, "was a string of small lakes which led them to the upper reaches of the Pomme de Terre River." A few more mooring stones and the pre-Columbian Vikings, led by their intrepid twentieth-century guide, "would reach the former lake at Ohman's farm, where they left a mooring stone as well as their inscription on the island."

Other investigators have found rocks all over Minnesota that have been drilled in a manner similar to those identified as mooring stones, and there is general agreement that such holes have been made either by surveyors as section marks or for the purpose of splitting rocks by blasting. Holand, however, as scholars have pointed out, accepts only the stones that conform to the route that he himself has chosen for Captain Paul Knutson. Along the Minnesota River, Holand's arbitrariness strikes many people as ridiculous. Why should the Vikings not have learned of the route taken by Eric Sevareid and Walter Port? Had the Norsemen been able to conquer the torrential streams south of Hudson Bay, they would certainly, so the valley partisans think, have discovered from the natives the easy connection between the Red River and the Minnesota and have continued their comfortable way to the Mississippi, the Gulf of Mexico and thence north along the Atlantic coast to Vinland. Still, Holand claims to have found fourteen "Viking" implements along his route, including battle axes and a sword that at least one expert thinks may be medieval.

Although the Kensington rune stone was once displayed at the Smithsonian Institution, there has been no official decision as to its authenticity from that venerable museum, and there is still debate among runologists, archaeologists, and historians. In Douglas County, however, the honor of the stone is well established. A gigantic, eighteen-ton reproduction has been erected by the Kiwanis Club in "Runestone Memorial Park" at Alexandria, the county seat not far from Kensington. The controversial slab itself is now enshrined in a specially designed building, and hundreds annually come to stare at the runic mystery. Among the river dwellers there are many who think that it does not matter if the runes were carved by a Scandinavian immigrant named Ohman in the 1890's. They see the story of the stone as an amusing episode of frontier life, and some of them think that the stone should be viewed today not as an ancient Viking petroglyph, but as a memorial to the ingenious humor of pioneer settlers and to the good sportsmanship of their descendants.

25

SON OF THE MINNESOTA

Launch'd o'er the prairies wide,
 across the lakes,
To the free skies unpent and glad
 and strong.

—WALT WHITMAN

IN THE MIDDLE of the nineteenth century, glowing articles about the Middle West appeared in the *Jönkoppings Tidning,* a newspaper published in the Swedish province of Småland, and something called "America fever" began to infest the Scandinavian peninsula. In the village of Reftele, a young man named Gustav Johnson caught the disease and soon he had crossed the Atlantic and made his way to St. Paul. Perhaps as impoverished as any of the immigrants who streamed into the Minnesota Valley were Gustav and the friends who started up-river with him in 1855. Unable to afford the cost of steamboat tickets to Traverse des Sioux, they bought some lumber and built a rowboat, loaded it with a barrel of flour and some salt pork, then spent ten days rowing upstream to the river bend where there already was the beginning of a Scandinavian colony.

Gustav found land near St. Peter and at Traverse des Sioux he met a girl who had been born not far from his own Swedish home. Though the marriage that followed began on Gustav's eighty-acre valley homestead, the Sioux uprising chased the Johnson family into St. Peter and Gustav, like many others, decided to give up farming. The move to the river town proved to be his undoing; though he was a good blacksmith, Gustav was soon spending more energy drinking with his clients than he spent at the forge. Twice he abandoned his family for months at a time and finally, when he could not be ignored as the town's worst drunk, he was committed to the poor house. His wife had long since been forced to take in washing to keep the family alive.

The mantle of man of the family had fallen to a thin young son named John Albert whose morning rounds delivering laundry made him habitually late for school. Carrying his loads through the unpaved streets of the river town, John Albert Johnson grew up along with the community. He shared the citizens' excitement when a twenty-five-thousand-dollar wagon bridge replaced the ferry across the river. When he was eleven, he watched the building of a block-long three-story brick hotel; it had sixteen chimneys. His rounds took him off the main street, past the furniture factory, the foundry, the flour and feed mills, breweries, H. C. Miller's cigar factory, the coopers and the wagonmakers.

In overalls, hickory shirt, and battered straw hat, John Albert Johnson looked little different from other children of struggling immigrant families. But a teacher from New England, who had felt impelled to reprimand him for his lack of punctuality, found in the boy that rare treasure, a pupil eager to learn. Realizing that the Johnson family spoke only Swedish at home, the teacher devoted her after-school hours to helping the boy improve his English. The bustling town had developed a sense of pride in the things of culture. In Johnson's school was a small girl whose musical talent was so encouraged that she later became an internationally known Wagnerian soprano. The townspeople had helped to raise the money for a college that opened in 1876. And young John Albert Johnson became such an avid reader that a banker who found him devouring a lurid juvenile

gave him a subscription to the library on the promise that he
would be more discriminate in his tastes.

The youngster matured in the same way as many others in the
valley. He knew all the boats that steamed into the St. Peter
docks; he heard the cries go up when the packet *Mankato* sank
just below the new bridge in the spring of 1871. He watched the
laying of the railroad tracks that soon made the steamboats out-
moded. Alert to everything, he heard the talk about the Grasshopper Relief Association organized by the Norwegian Lutherans
and the ten thousand dollars and the wagon loads of wheat that
were distributed to the destitute. With the town's prosperity
diminished in the seventies by the insect plague, he quit school
at thirteen to help his mother and got a full-time job at ten
dollars a week in a general store. When three years of grasshoppers forced his employer out of business, the maturing youngster went to work for a druggist.

The town progressed in spite of setbacks, and so did John
Albert Johnson. His appetite for reading took the place of formal
education and his energy and friendliness brought him more and
more opportunities. To persuade him to stay permanently in St.
Peter a covey of businessmen advanced the money that bought
Johnson a partnership in the St. Peter *Herald* and the title of
editor.

Twenty-six years old when he assumed his new role, John
Albert Johnson continued his education while he edited the
Herald and threw himself into community projects. "John knew
everybody in the village and the surrounding country," his biographer said, "could sympathize with the village loafer, advise the
mayor, play a game of cards in a dull hour, organized a baseball
nine, play a very good game himself, infuse life into a social
club, write gossipy reports of local news, and produce a learned
editorial now and then."

A new turn to his career was soon inevitable. He had become
widely known through the valley and, as president of the state

editorial association, was highly respected among his peers. When he was thirty-seven, he was elected as a Democrat to the state senate. Although his opponents had dragged out the sordid story of his father's failure, Scandinavians in Bernadotte, Norseland, New Sweden, Granby, Traverse, West Newton and North Mankato rejected the smear. The immigrant vote in the valley and elsewhere was to become the foundation of a popularity that kept Johnson's name alive for generations after his death. He was the son of immigrants and he did not underestimate their kind.

The valley people liked to tell a story about a Swede named Ole who switched his vote from the Republican, Knute Nelson, to John Albert Johnson:

"You must think Johnson's a great man," one of Ole's friends said.

"Ya, I do."

"Is he as great as Knute Nelson?"

"Ya, much greater."

"Is he greater than Roosevelt?"

"Ya, bigger."

"Is he bigger than God?"

"Well, Johnson's a young man yet."

John Albert Johnson was the state's first native-born governor, and when he was elected in 1904 special trains brought ten thousand people down the valley to St. Peter to help him celebrate. Two years later he was re-elected in what was considered in a normally Republican state a phenomenal victory. The rest of the nation soon took note, and a White House boom began for the uneducated boy from the banks of the Minnesota. It was the era of William Jennings Bryan, but there were some Democrats who thought that the Great Commoner's two defeats in previous presidential campaigns were enough. Some newspapermen of the day were more realistic. Toward the end of 1907, the famous Gridiron Club in Washington gave its annual dinner and, as usual, jauntily roasted men in the public eye. To the tune of

"Poor John" the Minnesota governor was raked over the coals in a long-winded parody that underscored Bryan's domination of his party:

> Bryan put him through a cross-examination;
> Johnson said he would like the nomination;
> Then Bryan shook his head:
> "Want it myself," he said.
> Poor John! Poor John!

Newspapers in New York and throughout the country fostered Johnson's candidacy, but to no avail. The Democrats chose Bryan again, and the Minnesota governor announced his retirement from public office. He had not reckoned with those who wanted him to continue as governor, however; he was nominated for a third term by acclamation that was little short of hysterical. It made his wife furious, for she worried about her husband's health and wanted him to have the peace and quiet of their home on the river bluff.

When finally he came back to St. Peter after his re-election, the river town burst into pageantry. There were parades and the blaring of bands as the valley people gave themselves a holiday. Trains ground into the station bedecked with banners anticipating Johnson's candidacy for the White House in 1912. Every school child and college student waited on the platform to greet him. "And so once more St. Peter celebrates the victory of her favorite and faithful son," wrote his biographer. "November 12, 1908, every steam whistle in the town is blowing, bells are ringing and cannon fire a salute of thirteen guns, crowds cheer— a tall, over-coated man steps from the train and, three times governor, John Johnson returns to his own people. Among those who welcome him is the little girl with whom he went to school, now Madame Olive Fremstad [of the Metropolitan Opera]. They talk over the old days; and their talk ranges from Gibb Patch's cornfield to the capitol at Washington and from the school days in old St. Peter to the conquests of the prima donna."

It was the river's only presidential rally. Within a year, John Albert Johnson, son of the inebriate immigrant who built himself a boat to row upriver, died after an operation at the age of forty-eight. His death filled the hearts of the river folk with genuine mourning. It was said that fifty thousand persons passed his bier in a sad procession of farewell. Tributes poured in to his widow, and Andrew Carnegie wrote: "We can comfort ourselves by the thought that up to the day of his death his record resembled that of Lincoln . . . a man of the people who went to the hearts of the people." In the lifetime of John Albert Johnson the valley had changed from wilderness to a region of pastoral culture. It had come of age.

26

NON-KENTUCKY THOROUGHBRED

Good horses make short miles.

—GEORGE HERBERT

IN THE EARLY years of the twentieth century thousands of people found their way to a horse-lover's mecca on the river flats. The architecture that drew them was at least as flamboyant as that of any Oriental mosque, and the sun sent splinters of dancing light into the valley, reflected from the silvery onion-shaped dome of the palace of Dan Patch. No human inhabitant along the river was ever as famous as the pacer who for fourteen years cropped the bluegrass of M. W. Savage's farm.

Happily spending the money he so easily made through his International Stock Food Company, Will Savage bought Dan Patch in the winter of 1902, when the big stallion was six years old. The price was $60,000—more than twice as much as had been paid for any pacer before him—and it was only one of the indications of the value Savage placed on his horse. The river farm that became Dan Patch's home covered more than seven hundred acres and included two race tracks, one a mile in circumference, the other an enclosed half-mile with more than twelve hundred windows in its walls. Directly across the river on an overlooking bluff was Savage's big house. "I can sit on my front porch," he was quoted as saying, "and time every horse being worked on the track a mile away."

For Dan Patch and his stable mates Savage built an octagonal barn with six long wings jutting obliquely outward. Under the glittering bulbous dome that rose more than one hundred feet was a spring-fed water tank discharging five thousand barrels daily; the octagon enclosed a cooling ring eighty feet in diameter. Each of the wings contained commodious stalls with steam heat and modern plumbing. Dan's quarters were twenty feet square and decorated with monogrammed blankets and great photographs of racing scenes.

The riverside showplace in which Dan Patch lived was a characteristic example of Will Savage's flair for exploitation. His rise from an Iowa druggist to millionaire Minneapolis manufacturer was the result of his ability to coin a phrase: he had built a world market among stockbreeders with the simple words *Three Feeds for One Cent.* An advertising periodical called him one of the greatest advertising men of all time, and his showmanship earned him the soubriquet "a second Barnum." Dan Patch's name became a household word. Savage once got more than two hundred thousand requests for a reproduction of Dan's portrait. There were cigars and tobacco named for him. Sleds, coaster wagons, and even washing machines made claims to speed by establishing themselves as namesakes of the stallion who lived in luxury on the grass lands a few miles upriver from Fort Snelling. The railroad that ran nearby was called the "Dan Patch Line," and the nearest town, once Hamilton, was rechristened Savage in honor of the man whose horse brought so much fame to the valley. A half century after the stallion's last race, the town still kept freshly painted the inscription on its water tower: "The Home of Dan Patch."

Dan Patch seemed almost human to the river folk. In an era before the automobile had become a yardstick of status, the breeding, rearing, and ownership of horses were common to all classes, and the light-harness racing steeds seemed closely related to everyday life—far more so than the exotic animals of the thoroughbred turf. But Will Savage's pacer was even more dis-

DAN PATCH

tinguished because of his high intelligence and his ability to communicate with crowds and with visitors. No day passed but what dozens of people turned off the river road into the wide graveled lane that led to Dan Patch's mosque, and frequently they found Savage, as one of them remembered, "talking to Dan Patch as if he were a person."

When Dan had arrived on the farm that soon was to bear his name, he had equaled the record for the mile, but his great career had hardly begun. Savage had recognized the pacer's ability to inspire immense loyalty from racing fans, and he instituted Dan Patch Day as a fixture in the programs of state fairs throughout the country. "There was something about Dan that 'got' a crowd," *The Horse Review* reported. "He had a visible air of greatness. . . . When the stand was roaring an ovation to him . . . he would turn his head and gaze into it with an air . . . almost like that of a star of the dramatic stage." With the crowd roaring at the Minnesota State Fair in 1908 Dan—

pacing the mile in 1:55—set a record that was to go unbroken for three decades.

From 1908 on, the pacer's name and his record-breaking time were emblazoned on a pennant that waved in the valley sky above the glittering cupola of Will Savage's grandiose barn. When the horse went traveling, he was ensconced in a private car, of course, and he was usually accompanied by as many as fourteen attendants. When he retired from the track, his master's indulgences were as great as ever, and Dan Patch spent the last seven years of his life with no other responsibility than keeping an eye on the talented colts he had sired.

On July 4, 1916, both Savage and his horse became ill. Dan's heart had been overworked by his years of exerting his tremendous will to win. When he collapsed, he lay still for ten seconds; then, the onlookers said, he stretched his head forward proudly and his ears went flat as they did in his dash for the finish line. In his delirium he went to pacing. His legs moved faster and faster in perfect rhythm; gradually the movement slowed, and the talented animal that valley people called "the world's most famous race horse" came to his final halt. In the hospital Will Savage heard the news and suffered shock. Thirty-two hours

later he too was dead. Man and horse had funerals at the same hour, and Dan Patch was buried under a tree beside the river.

The valley mourned the coincidental deaths. There were many tributes to both the pacer and his owner. As execrable as any were some lines entitled "The Minnesota 'Savage'," written in parody of Longfellow:

> You who did the planning, thinking,
> You who made my pathway easy;
> Had my stalls all hung in satin:
> 'In the land of Sky Blue Water.'
> When you whispered, I obeyed you;
> Did my best for you, my master;
> Now I'm waiting, master, waiting,
> In the Happy Hunting Ground.

27

LAC QUI PARLE—TALKING WATER

*. . . many upward days' voyaging were unraveled
in this rapid downward passage.*

—HENRY DAVID THOREAU

WE CIRCLED around Big Stone Lake and went through Joe Brown's last town—the village that had changed its name to Brown's Valley after the great adventurer died in 1870. It seemed fitting that there was still the look of a frontier here; the sun burned into a wide main street that had space enough for a full-dress Indian stampede; in the nearby park was Joe Brown's trading post, much the way he had seen it last. We swung south through Dakota prairie transformed into stubbly fields and watched the telephone wires stretching endlessly west to disappear in the horizon. To the east the flatland broke in scrub woods, and we took a back road that led down near the shore of Big Stone and saw the signs of cottagers and bait vendors. The hot afternoon cooled in the long shadows as we came through Big Stone City (where the Indian Lorenzo Lawrence had been a white man's constable) and went down the hill into Ortonville.

Here, in this long, lovely lake is the river's beginning. Not far downstream is where the steamer *Freighter* mired and rotted away after Captain Davis' attempt to ride the floodwaters from the Minnesota to the Red. Not even the Army engineers could agree in 1894 on the feasibility of a canal to link the two rivers; navigation on the upper Minnesota ended in the 1870's. Occasionally now a canoe floats in the shadows of the gigantic granite outcroppings, and once in a great while someone—adventurously dreaming of days when the rain-soaked prairie fed the river with a thousand tiny rivulets—has paddled the winding river's odyssey from Ortonville to Zeb Pike's island at the mouth. Clyde and Shirley Ryberg made such a trip in the 1950's, and so did Dick Gahler and Roger John. Logging his voyage, Gahler reflected on his first day: "The trees that grew on each side of the river met at their tops over our heads, enclosing the river like it was in a long, endless greenhouse."

From the bluffs, high and flat in the prairie sun, there are moments when there is no river to see; the serpentine hint of water is obscured by the bower of leaves. A traveler must come down onto the bottomlands and pause at an aging bridge to catch the earthy smells and the shade made limpid by the slow-moving stream. It is a barefoot boy's river in its beginning stretches, a long shallow pool lazing in its bends, unmindful of any dictum that rivers must roll meaningfully toward the sea. Through miles of hairpin turns it makes its uncertain way out of Big Stone toward Odessa and towering bedrock islands. Here where the River Warren once filled the valley that is more than four miles wide, the Minnesota submits to man's control and widens into Marsh Lake, trickles through locks before it again comes into its own in Lac qui Parle.

"We spent half a day in the vicinity of Lac qui parle," wrote William Keating in 1823; "our tents were pitched on an eminence . . . commanding an extensive prospect, adorned with this beautiful sheet of water. . . . Above the lake . . . gentle slopes blend gradually the prairie and the valley of the river."

My wife, Judith, and I had the same view more than a century and a quarter later—and from our vantage point we saw no slopes scarred by bulldozers, nor even the glint of asphalt shingles in the thick foliage that might have hidden a lakeside cottage. Except for the dam at the foot of the lake it is possible to see Lac qui Parle today just as Joseph Renville saw it when he built his fortress. We climbed a hill to a restored mission, raised up with new logs on the foundations unearthed by archaeologists. Not much more than a hundred years had passed since Williamsons and Hopkinses and Ponds had labored here to Christianize the Sioux, but in a land as newly opened as this almost any yesterday seems ancient. We followed an old path down the back side of the hill toward the spring. "I kept house in a little room on the second floor of a log house," a missionary wife wrote. "Dr. Williamson and his family lived on the lower floor." There was no facsimile of that house, but the spring was there, and a carload of tourists from Omaha giggled and looked uneasily down the steep path to a cranny where the water bubbled. "Mrs. Riggs and I walked the rest of the journey," the missionary wife remembered of her trip to Lac qui Parle, "she carrying her fifteen months old baby. This was July 4, 1843. My first baby was born the following September." In 1960, the touring wives had not heart enough for the short climb that might have snagged their nylons.

Standing in the restored mission house the memories of the old frontier blot out the hum of traffic that comes distantly through the obscuring trees. "In 1843 in Lac Qui Parle, we had a cow. We paid thirty dollars to the Red River men for her. . . . Our flour was sent to us from way down the Mississippi. When we got it, it had been wet and was so mouldy that we had to chop it out with an ax. . . . One day as I was sitting alone at my table writing, the door of my room opened and a hideously painted Indian came in. . . . I determined that I would try not to let him know how frightened I was. I sat still at my table and kept on with my writing and in a short time he went downstairs again. This Indian was the famous Little Crow, the leader of the outbreak of 1862."

Mrs. Gideon Pond—she who, in her ninetieth year, remem-

bered Lac qui Parle so vividly—had a gift for happiness that
sustained her through her long life on the river. As we went
downriver we were passing long dead campfires where she with
"great solicitude and care" had baked bread in a Dutch oven,
using home-made yeast soaked in river water. The river had
served such pioneers for almost limitless purposes, but in the
twentieth century it flowed beside us in indolence as we went
on to Joe Brown's Farther-and-Gay Castle. I looked at that view
and held it in my mind. A man who knew every inch of the
river had framed this segment for himself. It was this horizon,
cresting the rolling valley, that seemed to be the sum of all
Brown's westering ways. I took a last look at the warm glow of
the pink stones that had thrust his mansion into the prairie sky,
and then we went down into the rich bottom land, crossing the
sleeping river, and climbed the opposite bluffs to go into Delhi.
We turned east for a mile and drove to the farm where Robert
Starr had been born forty years before. He lived in the house of
his birth with his blonde wife Ethel and their children, and when
he met us at the door, he would have it no other way than that we
join him in the day's noon meal of bullheads from the river.

We were not the only unexpected guests. The weather was
going into fall and the crops were in and it was a day a man
could leave his farm. A young couple from a neighboring place
had been persuaded to share the fish, and we all talked of the
river's history. There are some who can be led to speak of
their history and you can almost make them like it. These were
not such people. This was talk that had been carried on from
one day to another, that needed no visitors from downriver to
surface it with enthusiasm. In these reaches of the river west of
New Ulm the Sioux had helped the settlers to weave a unique
web of blood-and-guts history a century earlier. The warp and
woof of that saga are far from forgotten. People like Bob Starr
live on the terrain of war, and they speculate about the events
of summer's end in 1862 with the addiction of long habit. Not
because they had heroes among their ancestors; those people

are gone. Along the Upper Minnesota history lies on the land—not in local genealogies and attic trunks of letters or in Grandpa's statue in the park. A man like Bob Starr had a father who came north out of Iowa after the region was cleared of Indians, and a boy grew up on the river reading what had happened; he followed the trails that took Little Crow's howling battalion down to Fort Ridgley and he could figure pretty close where all the houses stood that had gone up in flames. A boy on the banks of the Minnesota didn't need television or John Wayne or a Walt Disney Davy Crockett because he only had to squint his eyes a bit to see the Sioux whooping through the valley, burning and pillaging and smashing the brains of frightened infants. He saw it all happen against tumbling bluffs that hadn't changed a bit in a handful of decades, against rolling fields still unurbanized.

Bob Starr could not resist seeing it all again, and he turned to his wife (like a youngster who knows he's playing hooky) and said he guessed he wasn't needed that afternoon to paint the milkshed, the boys could do it alone. He could tell us where to look, but it wouldn't be any trouble for him to help us find our way. He guided us over the river road to the farm on which Mary Schwandt's family had been annihilated, then on to the ambush at Birch Coulee. Back in 1894 there was a good-sized rumpus about the granite column that points cloudward from the bluff to keep alive the memory of those thirty-odd hours under Indian fire. The memorial commissioners, it seems, took it upon themselves to have the monument erected a mile and three-quarters south of the battleground, and when the protests started pouring in, the commissioners said that the coulee site was too inaccessible for travelers, that anyhow the man who owned the land wanted too much money, and that, inasmuch as the Sioux had crossed the bluff in their retreat from the ambush, the chosen site might just as well be considered part of the battleground. That was only the beginning. When the forty-six-foot pillar was dedicated on September 3 that year, distinguished speakers quarreled acrimoniously over who had been actually in command during the siege. Joe Brown had been dead for a quarter of a century, but Captain Hiram Grant was present at the dedication and, for whatever reasons, he wanted to have full credit for the unfortunate affair. "So help me God," Grant sputtered at the gathered multitude, "Major Brown did not give me an order."

Joe Brown's son said Hiram Grant hadn't even been mustered in at the time of the attack, so how could he be in command of anything? The bickering continued for a year, but even though the legislature finally ruled that the monument must be moved to the coulee and that the inscription must state that Grant's command had been subordinate to that of Brown's, nothing was ever done about it. The original monument still stands on the bluff, and not far away is another, a less contentious marker that pays undisputed tribute to John Other Day, Lorenzo Lawrence, and several other Sioux who saved the lives of white men during the outbreak.

Bob Starr talked all the way as we crossed the river to the Lower Sioux Indian Community southwest of Morton. Near the site of the old agency buildings, where the outbreak had begun, there is now a handsome church on the edge of a peaceful square of green grass that is kept in velvety trim. An Indian in overalls sat impassively on the steps of one of the white frame houses. In the school there was nothing to distinguish the work on display from that of children in any other school. Around the village green are almost eighteen hundred acres of sandy farms, some of which produce good crops of corn, rye, and small grain in years of sufficient rainfall. A state report says: "Probably a higher percentage of Indians are self supporting through agriculture in this community than in any other in the state." This does not mean that these few Sioux have found total peace beside the river their ancestors once possessed. Few of their white neighbors are willing to treat them as equals and their daughters are easy prey for cocky Saturday-night loiterers.

Starr wanted to show us Rice Creek where a far more mili
tant group of Sioux had gathered beside one of the Minnesota'
most lyric tributaries. We drove down a farmer's lane beside a
cornfield and then the car made a wild pilgrimage across the
stony pasture to find the stream foaming noisily over a slippery
granite ledge before it dropped gradually into a tamer course
that runs through deep woods to the river. When you see Rice
Creek in twilight, you can join the youngsters whose imagina-
tions people the valley with the outbreak's lurid cast of characters. "The encampment," Jannette De Camp had said, "was like
a city. . . . While we were at Rice Creek they held a council.
. . . How vividly I remember the time when a medicine man
came to doctor our wounded friend. . . . We were all thrust
out of the tent and sat huddled together for warmth till nearly
midnight, when the evil spirit, having been ejected from the
sick man and shot at as it departed, we were allowed to return."
There has been no city of tepees here for a hundred years, and
the glades beside Rice Creek are famous now as picnic grounds.

The history is not all gore and holler and visionary healing.
Starr took us to Gold Mine Lake, a favorite swimming hole just
a few yards from the river bluff. The story here has the music of
a lively fiddle, the throaty beckoning of girls in the night, a hotel
with carnal overtones, the chug and spit of a hoisting engine,
and the glint of gold. A small glint, maybe, but no matter.
Though nothing remains but a water-filled shaft, the terrain between the lake and the river was alive with activity in 1894.
Samples of ore had been dug out and assayed at ninety-four
dollars a ton, it was said. "Probably the richest find," the Redwood *Gazette* reported, "Is the one on the Schroeder farm."
Schroeder got three thousand dollars for a fourteen-acre tri-
angle and the boom was on. The new owners began to sell
stock. A town called Springville grew up overnight. The Gold
Mine Hotel—twenty-four by forty-eight feet—was crowded with
roistering miners, and dancing girls were transported from Minneapolis to Morton by train, then by stagecoach to the boom town.

"Two or three hundred people visited the property last Sunday," the *Gazette* told its readers; "it has already commenced to be a good harvest for the livery men, and soon it will benefit the other interests of the city."

The steel cable creaked over the windlass in the one-hundred-and-sixteen-foot shaft, bringing up buckets of quartz which the miners then pushed over a narrow-gauge railway to a crusher on the riverbank. No one seemed daunted by the opinion of University of Minnesota analysts that "there is nothing, absolutely nothing in the line of gold in paying quantities in Redwood County . . . and investment there is pure folly." Work continued for a year and dancing miners rocked the Gold Mine Hotel on Saturday nights. Then the perpetrator of the Minnesota Gold Mining and Refining Company mysteriously disappeared. For another year an effort was made to retrieve the investors' money, but the ore that had been touted—in one wild announcement—as being worth as much as $2,940 a ton was reported by the *Gazette* in June, 1896, at the negligible value of a dollar and a half a ton. Work stopped, and at last the question of gold in the valley in paying quantities was settled.

The Redwood stretch of the river is better than a gold mine for the kind of stories that the valley people like to collect. Not long ago the county historical society moved the abandoned railroad depot from North Redwood to the Redwood fair grounds and took steps to turn it into a museum. A few telephone and power lines were cut, and the awkward frame building moved along the river road like a juggernaut, the local history buffs following it curiously. It was being moved as a shrine to mark the birthplace of Sears, Roebuck and Company,[4] not because the river folk have more salaams than the average for the mail-order business, but because a youngster named Dick Sears was the first telegrapher and the depot agent. In 1886, when the young agent received a shipment of watches addressed to a Redwood Falls merchant, he was told the merchant had not

[4] The carefully treasured building burned in August 1961.

ordered them. Seeing a chance to make some extra money, Sears set out to market the watches himself. He telegraphed other agents up and down the valley and netted five hundred dollars by delivering watches by mail. He didn't ask his customers to pay in advance and soon discovered that people liked the idea of being trusted. He capitalized on his new approach to merchandising through advertisements headed "Send No Money," and soon he gave up his job to start a mail-order house aimed at rural customers. It is not a bad kind of thing to have happened in the valley, the river dwellers say.

Along the Minnesota people have a way of making the past a part of the present. At New Ulm the descendants of those who came from the lands of the Meistersingers have bent the music of the pioneers into new and profitable shapes. There are professional orchestras that claim other valley towns as home, but New Ulm, on the city's hundredth anniversary, had the distinction of sheltering eighteen dance bands that make music one of the community's principal industries. I have sat for hours talking about New Ulm music to Fezz Fritsche, a big man with a strongly built face. Fezz would pull on a stein of local beer and tell how the bands, once the hobbies of men who worked in the nearby sandstone quarries, became highly trained organizations that now travel thousands of miles a year. The polka rhythms which dominate New Ulm music were brought from Bohemia in the seventies and have evolved into a unique style that is known far and wide as "oompah." The exponents have included Bum Bum Bauer and his Rafter Dusters, Harold Loefelmacher and his Six Fat Dutchmen, and Fezz Fritsche and his Goosetown Band. Their renditions of polkas, mazurkas, and Herr Schmidts have made the town almost as renowned for oompah as Nashville is for country music. Radio stations as far afield as Miami and San Jose, California, have devoted regular programs to New Ulm music, and KNUJ, the local broadcasting studio, announces itself as "the polka station of the nation." None, except perhaps the absolutely tone deaf, should ignore a chance to spend an evening in the New Ulm Ballroom or in the other opulent local mecca called George's, where the good beer comes from the brewery down the street and the good music is laced with the *baddleda* rhythm of a Central European heritage.

New Ulmers like to say they make the beer that makes Milwaukee jealous. Before twentieth-century distribution systems evolved, they sent out wagons, each drawn by four huge snow-white horses, to share their brew with other valley towns. The drivers were ambassadors of *Gemütlichkeit*, and wherever they went, they beckoned the people along the streets and roads and treated them to round after round of New Ulm brew. The only nearby competition was in Mankato, and New Ulmers had a way of pointing out that there the brewmasters were Britishers, who could not possibly understand the art that goes into the making of real lager beer.

There are more than one hundred and fifty thousand people in the valley, and twenty-five thousand of them live in the cities of Mankato and North Mankato at the great bend where the river perversely begins to flow north toward Minneapolis and St. Paul. Of all the valley people the most adventurous, in re-cent years, was a North Mankato farmer named Charlie Poliquin. From the river Charlie heard a siren sing and decided to see the world. One spring day he was overwhelmed by the boredom of farming and he went down to the waterside to think things over. Something about that sluggish current persuaded Charlie—though he had sailed in nothing bigger than a rowboat—that he could follow the stream to lands of which he had only dreamed. Against the protests of his young wife, he sold his farm in 1958 and began to build a vessel of his own design. A year later he had produced a boat that was twelve feet wide and seventy feet long, square at stern and prow. Covered with glistening sheet alumi-num, it looked something like a roadside diner. He named it the *See Scout*.

Charlie and the *See Scout* set sail one March day amid much attention. Hundreds of valley people thronged both sides of the river as a drizzling rain dripped earthward and washed the silver-sided floating box. Charlie got his engines going and stood at the pilot window, guiding his ship as she slipped her lines and swung into the current. He had put eight thousand dollars into his project, he said. On the cabin wall he had pinned a map on which he had traced the route of his voyage—down the Minnesota and the Mississippi to New Orleans, across the Gulf to South America; down the east coast of South America with side jaunts up the Amazon and Platte Rivers; across the Pacific, the Indian Ocean, through the Suez Canal, the Mediterranean, across the Atlantic, and finally home.

With forty-five minutes, after a voyage of four hundred yards, the *See Scout* ran aground. Small boys bounced stones off the aluminum hull. Charlie managed to get away with the help of a winch, but in nine days he had covered only three miles and was aground for a third time. "With more water I'd be in Minneapolis by now," Charlie complained. "Old timers tell me this is the lowest the river has been since 1910." The *See Scout* managed to sail two more miles before Shirley Poliquin sued Charlie for divorce and he was hauled back into court at Mankato. Of course the rugged individualist, who by this time had been derisively dubbed the Midwest Magellan, acted as his own attorney, but his wife's lawyer somehow managed to tie up Charlie's bank account. He was consoled almost immediately when spring high water floated the *See Scout* as far as Shakopee, and there—to offset the cost of his wife's lack of understanding—he opened his boat to sight-seers and was a smash box-office success. All that summer the people in the valley gossiped about the waterlogged farmer, and finally, when the Minnesota was frozen, they heard that Charlie was in New Orleans. The thirty-ton *See Scout* had sailed farther than any Minnesota River boat had ever done before—as far as Pierre Le Sueur had come in 1700—and then had sunk at its Louisiana mooring.

Charlie Poliquin, with that name of his, should have been the descendant of a *voyageur*, but we could not discover that he was, and so we moved downstream to the next big bend where that real *voyageur* Le Blanc, Louis Provencalle, had settled in 1812 and later, like Joe La Framboise, had married one of the daughters of Chief Sleepy Eyes. There is a log cabin here at Traverse des Sioux that some visitors take to be a reproduction of Le Blanc's trading post. I went inside, hoping for something —maybe the scent of plews, or the dank smell of a man who lives too long in his clothes—but it didn't seem right; the interior might have been that of a log cabin in any public park and there was little to relate to the drawings made on the spot by Frank Mayer in 1851.

There are picnic tables on the treaty grounds now. That is the way we do things in the West where the highways are flat and straight as the trajectory of an arrow and no one pauses long enough to look at the land. I mean the land the way it was, before the plow and the city, and the lawn mower that now trims even the grass of a wilderness council site. Though there is only a frame house and a barn up the rise, and a few public

facility buildings off the circular drive, it is nigh impossible to get the feeling of what this place once was. "This camp life," Mayer jotted down in his diary in 1851, "is by no means a hardship as many might suppose, situated as we [are] in a bea[u]tifully picturesque & healthy country surrounded by agreeable & amusing associates, & hospitably entertained by 'Uncle Sam.'" The artist who tried so hard (and unsuccessfully) to get the state to pay him for a painting of the parley that made the Minnesota Valley white man's territory described himself "turning to a neighboring tent where are assembled the gentlemen of French descent the traders & voyageurs, [and where] we hear the canadian boat songs . . . sung with spirit by melodious voices. . . . Seated at table I heard French & Indian spoken almost exclusively & the co[u]ntenances of foreign appearance, French, Indian and half breed, beguile me into a belief of being in some foreign land. May it not be called foreign, twenty five hundred miles from home & in an Indian country[?]"

The site at Traverse des Sioux remains unbuilt upon, but— perhaps it is too close to the highway—the imagination fails to soar and you find it difficult to believe that the drama was anything but second-rate. And maybe it wasn't. Certainly the town that followed on the heels of the retreating tribes was less than adequate, even though it was whipped into the frenzy of a boom by some of the very men who had lined up the Indians for their lesson in real estate. St. Peter, stinging from its loss of the state capital to St. Paul, conned the citizens into taking the county seat away from Traverse des Sioux, and that was the end of the boom. But while it lasted, the village of Traverse des Sioux was real enough and characteristically populated with all the types who make a frontier city.

One of these whom I like has gone into valley folklore as the Reverend Brown. In his suit of good ministerial cloth Brown impressed the citizens of the boom town with his godly looks and pious behavior. He took a claim and preached at Traverse while the community was being plagued by the knowledge that there were stores being broken into and horse thieves operating in the vicinity. Finally a span of stolen horses was found in a secluded spot and a volunteer posse decided to stand by to see who would come to claim the animals. They were almost speechless when the trap they set caught the preacher, but his guilt was clinched when a search of his house turned up a lot of stolen plunder. Embarrassed at the gullibility with which they had listened to him in church, they let him sneak away to St. Paul. There he managed to sell his Traverse claim three times, giving each unwary purchaser a deed, and then he disappeared. The sheriff went after him then and found him miles away, still posing as a minister. But in bringing the culprit back to face charges in Traverse, the sheriff had to put up one night at a hotel. One narrator of the story gives it a fitting ending: "There was no jail in town to lock the prisoner in, so the sheriff locked him in a bedroom closet and to make matters doubly sure, lay down in front of the door. Next morning, when the door was opened the closet was found to be empty and this was the last heard of Rev. Brown." Preposterous? Perhaps; but that was the kind of time it was, and Traverse des Sioux—the home now of picnic tables—was that kind of place.

I like another story about this stretch of the river—perhaps because it was told by a great-grandfather. Evan T. Jones was a pillar of Welsh society in the Big Woods and he dutifully collected the experiences of his fellow pioneers. One of his stories —he put it down in Welsh—goes like this: "At one time one of the pioneer settlers was taking a load of potatoes [another translation says turnips] to the market when the wagon got mired in a slough. Though at first he thought himself in a hopeless predicament, he was suddenly struck by a bright idea. He took off his pants and tied a knot in the bottom of each leg, making sacks of the knees. He thus carried the load across on his back, and the oxen pulled the wagon to terra firma where he reloaded, went on to the market and sold his potatoes [turnips?] at a good price. Returning home safely, he sat down to relate the thrilling experience to several generations of open-mouthed new settlers."

There were more flamboyant storytellers along the river, and in Le Sueur, the town nearest the Welsh settlement in the Big Woods, there was once a man named Ora Parker, who called himself the Le Sueur Lyre and spun out yarns that he syndicated to newspapers throughout the country. He told, for instance, of the time they found Jean La Rue stuffed away in the hollowed core of a big white oak. Seems Jean was working as a hired hand on a Big Woods farm during the Outbreak. A boatload of soldiers on their way to relieve Fort Ridgley scared the dickens out of the countryside when they began shooting into the foliage on the shore. Like everybody else who didn't see the boat, Jean figured the shots for homicidal Sioux. He ran. Climbed into the hollow oak, and whiled away the time by making entries in a diary. . . . Years later when some woodsmen found Jean he was perfectly preserved—mummified by his incarceration in the bone-dry core of the tree. His diary, the last entry dated August 29, 1862, said:

"Cannot get out; surely must die. If ever found send me and all my money to my mother, Madame Suzanne La Rue, near Tarascon, in the province of Bouches du Rhone, France."

Nobody was expected to believe the Le Sueur Lyre.

Le Sueur is one of the river's bench towns, its main street running straight on the first setback above the stream and the largest part of its residential area on the higher bluff. On Main Street there is a small frame house with classic entablature that was built, board by board, by a doctor who was one of those to go to the defense of New Ulm in 1862. The town now uses the house proudly as a library, for that doctor was W. W. Mayo, founder of the Mayo Clinic in Rochester and father of Doctors Charles and William J. Mayo, the latter of whom was born here. Down this main street, in 1902, came John Silver Hughes, a descendant of a long line of Maryland canners. "What this town needs," said Hughes, "is a corn cannery." The townspeople agreed, and in a main-street harness shop they organized a firm

that, through years of co-operation with valley farmers, grew
into the Green Giant Company, preserver of select peas and
corn that provide, in specialty food stores throughout the world,
proof of the river's lush land.

It was hot the last time we were in Le Sueur and we paused
at the bridge and watched a blue heron swooping low over a
sand bar. Then we took the old road along the riverbank to Henderson and climbed a high hill to salute Joe Brown in his last
resting place above the stream. A finger of granite rising forty
feet above the grave is about all there is to call one's attention
to Henderson's founder. In the historical museum at the foot of
the hill there were framed portraits of Brown and his wife—
nothing more. And there amid wooden butter churns and other
immigrant memorabilia I looked in vain for a rusty wrench with
which old Joe might have tinkered with his steam wagon before
that Fourth of July trial run—or perhaps for a muskrat plew

dried hard and crusty by a hundred years of waiting, its fur dust-filled and as fragile to the touch as a long-cherished scalp.

We went on downstream, heading toward Belle Plaine. Ninety-nine years before us the government had chartered the *Fanny Harris* to bring Civil War troops from Fort Ridgley to Fort Snelling, and when the steamboat hit this stretch of river it was caught in an April flood. The Rush River at Henderson was a raging torrent as it entered the Minnesota. Every brook and creek was overflowing, the countryside was inundated, and houses and fences were uprooted. Old traders said the water level was higher than it had been since the spring of 1821. It was so high at Belle Plaine that Captain Orren Smith took the *Fanny Harris* right over the left bank of the Minnesota and sailed across country. He nosed the boat between the trees, threw open the throttle and headed for a short cut. After a ten-mile overland excursion, Smith brought his vessel back into the river channel, and made the fastest time on record between Ridgley and St. Paul. That year's flood waters were so abundant that Big Stone and Lake Traverse were joined and, had it not been for a general preoccupation with the rebellion, the dream of taking a steamboat from the Minnesota into the Red River Valley might have come true.

Judith and I were sitting under a tree beside the river, drinking coffee from red plastic thermos caps, eating a sandwich. A man sat in a rowboat just beyond the bend, his line trailing in the water, and across the field of bottom land we saw a woman lying in the sun beside a white house that needed paint. She went inside as we started over the field, but a farmer in faded overalls appeared then and we struck up a conversation. He was Hedley Wolters and he had been watching the river flood periodically for nearly forty years. The last big one had been in 1952 when the state had had to close all the bridges between Mendota and Belle Plaine and when the deluge had covered the Dyke Road at Shakopee as high as a man's head. Then the Minnesota waters poured into the Mississippi and dislodged five thousand St. Paul citizens from their homes, causing the worst flood disaster in the area's history. One gets to expect the Minnesota to go on the rampage once in a while, Hedley Wolters said in the tones of a man who doesn't think a child's behavior has to be always perfect. "She's a thief," he said, squinting over at his rich bottom land. "She takes from one side and gives to the other."

She is like all rivers, capricious. But she didn't look it that day. Under the canopied trees the water was as still and gray as a mirror of smoked glass. I watched another heron take flight and remembered a story about Captain Martin Scott, who had been commandant at Fort Snelling back in the summer of 1837. He spent years at the fort and in the valley, and he was renowned as a hunter and as a deadeye shot. One of his favorite sports was doing a William Tell with an apple balanced on the head of his Negro servant, and the other was hunting along the river, followed by a yelping pack of a score or more of dogs. His skill was so sure that even the animals knew the game was up when Scott appeared. My story concerned a raccoon who sat in a tree after several of Scott's companions had aimed at him and missed. When the captain leveled his gun the raccoon looked down and asked, "Who are you?"

"Name's Scott," said the captain.

"Scott?" said the animal nervously. "What Scott?"

"Captain Martin Scott."

"Oh, Lord," the raccoon moaned. "Don't waste your ammunition. I'll come down."

Close to this stretch of river was a place once known as Little Rapids, where Jean Baptiste Faribault had had one of his earliest trading posts. Here Faribault and a neighboring trader, Colin Campbell, held some target practice that was a little different from Scott's. An Indian had come to Campbell's house beside the Minnesota to retrieve his daughter and had murdered two of Campbell's clerks, including the man with whom the squaw had been living. Campbell told the Indian that murder was something that shouldn't be done, and the Indian got so riled Campbell figured he ought to visit Faribault, just in case. Sure enough, not long after the two traders had barred the door the irate savage arrived and in a moment he was heard climbing on the roof. Campbell stepped over to the chimney, rested the butt of his musket on the hearth and pulled the trigger. The ball whistled skyward and blew away half the face of the Indian as he peered down the flue.

Like any river, the Minnesota had its share of violence when men took matters into their own hands. One winter day on the bluff where Fort Snelling stood for law and order, John Emerson, the Army surgeon, lost his temper when the quartermaster refused to issue a stove to Emerson's Negro servant, saying there were not enough stoves to go around. "You lie!" Emerson stormed. The quartermaster smashed his fist between the surgeon's eyes. Emerson whipped out a brace of pistols, and was chasing the quartermaster across the parade grounds when he was arrested by the commanding officer. The Negro who caused that trouble was Dred Scott, whose right to freedom was later denied in the famous St. Louis trial.

Gentler ways have changed the river. Charlie Poliquin is the only man of recent times to understand (or, maybe, to be infected by) the old wanderlust, the buccaneer quality that strong characters of the past invested in the slow-moving Minnesota. Those who speak of it now as the forgotten river are right. I knew a Bloomington woman who wrote in a sort of journal she kept: "The river, as we see it, has no way of telling us what an important part it had in the settlement of our state. Sometimes when sitting on the riverbank below our house I think of the names of those who have come and gone. . . ." In her ninth decade my friend, Mrs. Tapping, remembered the river when it was something more than a cherished accent in the landscape—before its vitality had been neglected and its days of glory reduced to the dim memory that admits all too condescendingly that once this ridiculously twisting stream bore steamboats. Neglect is no stranger to other rivers. Yet the Minnesota has not kept burnished the names of its great men and for that reason much of its own eminence seems forgotten.

Its natural facilities also seem lost to the minds of many who dwell along its shores. Only a few are certain that someday there will be boating for everybody, and that each of the river towns will have its own marina which, though it may not accommodate a sea-going yacht, will have moorage for cabin cruisers, outboards—and plastic canoes. We were hailed by one nautical family who had brought their twenty-nine-footer up from Louisville and were disappointed to find that they could navigate no further than Mile 14 on the Minnesota. This limitation will be removed, some river dwellers say. Commercial interests have brought about legislation to straighten some of the kinks and maintain a nine-foot channel as far as Savage. Committees promise other government co-operation to make the lovely, indolent Minnesota once again a people's river. There will be a complete restoration, some say, to cause Josiah Snelling's citadel once more to dominate the bluff at the mouth of the river. They are working hard to maintain twenty-five hundred acres in natural state as Fort Snelling State Park. When these and other historic sites are splendidly marked the river will be less forgotten. But the real remembrance of any river must be in the minds of those who cross it regularly, watch it lovingly.

Sit under the mile-long bridge where the waters meet and watch the Minnesota disappear around Pike's island. The cities —Minneapolis and St. Paul—are lost to you here. There is an almost authentic wildness. In the high air a cloud drifts; a buffalo fish nibbles at the river's surface. It seems a good time for young, blue-jacketed Zeb Pike to come along and stretch his white sails from tree to tree and whistle up Le Petit Corbeau and all his braves. The river's history begins at the river's end. Upstream, mile by mile, the echoes of the past can be heard behind the sounds of the present.

Acknowledgment

A great part of the work on this book was done in the reference department of the Minnesota Historical Society, under the watchful eye of Miss Lois M. Fawcett, whose good offices will not have been served as well as her friendliness warrants. I am deeply grateful to her for her unstinting help while I was within her jurisdiction as well as after I left it. I also owe a special debt to Mrs. June Drenning Holmquist who read the manuscript, to Russell Fridley, director, Lucille M. Kane, and James Taylor Dunn, all of the Minnesota Historical Society. The staff members of the American History department of the New York Public Library and those of the New York Society Library were helpful in many ways of which they may be unaware.

My thanks go to Mrs. Clark Kellett, curator of the Brown County Historical Society in New Ulm, and to Miss Hazel G. Meine, talented executive officer of the New Ulm Chamber of Commerce, who has never failed to come to my rescue in various projects over the years. People up and down the river were very helpful. Scott Schoen of the Redwood *Gazette* paused in the midst of putting his paper to bed to talk to us; so did my old boss, Paul Eastwood of the Le Sueur *News-*

Herald. Robert Starr of Delhi was as fine a guide as his wife was a tolerant hostess. Mr. and Mrs. Clyde Ryberg of Savage, Dr. and Mrs. W. W. Vollmer of New Prague, Fezz Fritsche and Bill Macklin of New Ulm, R. I. Gahler of White Bear, Mrs. Harriett M. Evans of Le Sueur, Evan M. Evans of Middle River, Ruth Peterson Johnson, Roger J. Jones, and Harlow Ross of Minneapolis; Wesley Dibbern, Roman Green, Gareth Hiebert, and Roy Swanson of St. Paul all have earned my gratitude.

I have dedicated this book to the memory of my mother, who began her newspaper career on the river and who should have written its story. Notes which she made in the course of her own work have added much to my research. My father, Lewis R. Jones of the St. Paul *Dispatch,* has been a partner in this enterprise, and my sister, Gwenyth Jones Spitz of the Minneapolis *Star,* devoted many hours to my great benefit. I cannot fail to mention the help of my daughter Pamela. I owe special thanks to Carl Carmer and Miss Jean Crawford, editors of the Rivers of America Series, for friendly guidance. But my insistent debt in connection with the story of the Minnesota is to my wife, Judith Bailey Jones, whose editorial contribution warrants a proprietary interest which I admit with pride, and with the understanding that any mistakes herein are mine alone.

BIBLIOGRAPHY

Books

In addition to the invaluable *Minnesota Historical Society Collections,* the following are some of the sources consulted:

Allanson, George G., *Stirring Events of the Joseph R. Brown Family.* Wheaton, Minnesota, Wheaton Gazette, undated.

Allyn, G. W., *When Blue Earth County Was Young.* Madison Lake, Minnesota, 1919.

Beltrami, Giacomo C., *A Pilgrimage in Europe and America Leading to the Discovery of the Sources of the Mississippi and Bloody River, with a Description of the Whole Course of the Former, and of the Ohio.* London, Hunt & Clark, 1828.

Berthel, Mary W., *Horns of Thunder, the Life and Times of James M. Goodhue.* St. Paul, Minnesota Historical Society, 1948.

Bishop, Harriet E., *Floral Home, or First Years in Minnesota.* New York, Sheldon, Blakeman & Co., 1857.

Blegen, Theodore C., *Grass Roots History.* Minneapolis, University of Minnesota Press, 1947.

———— *The Land Lies Open.* Minneapolis, University of Minnesota Press, 1949.

286

————*Land of Their Choice*. Minneapolis, University of Minnesota Press, 1955.

Bode, Carl, and Harding, Walter, *The Thoreau Correspondence*. New York, New York University Press, 1957.

Bond, J. Wesley, *Minnesota and Its Resources*. Chicago, Keen & Lee, 1856.

Bremer, Frederika, *Homes in the New World*. New York, 1853.

Brown, Samuel J., *In Captivity*. Mankato, Minnesota, Mankato Review, undated.

Bryant, Charles S. and Murch, Abel B., *History of the Great Massacre by the Sioux Indians in Minnesota*. Cincinnati, Hickey & Caroll, 1864.

Callender, John M., *New Light on Old Fort Snelling, An Archaeological Exploration, 1957-58*. St. Paul, Minnesota Historical Society, 1959.

Carver, Jonathan, *Travels Through the Interior Parts of North America in the Years 1766, 1767 and 1768*. Minneapolis, Ross & Haines, Inc., 1956.

Catlin, George, *Letters and Notes on the Customs, Manners and Condition of the North American Indians*. New York, 1842.

Christianson, Theodore, *Minnesota: The Land of Sky-Tinted Waters*. New York, 1935.

Coffin, Charles Carleton, *The Seat of Empire*. Boston, Fields, Osgood & Co., 1870.

Coller, Julius, II, *The Shakopee Story*. Shakopee, Minnesota, North Star Pictures, Inc., 1960.

Copp, Henry M., *The American Settler's Guide: A Brief Exposition of the Public Land System of the United States of America*. Washington, 1880.

Couès, Elliott, *New Light on the Early History of the Greater Northwest*. New York, 1897.

Day, Frank A., *Life of John Albert Johnson*. Chicago, Forbes & Co., 1910.

De Voto, Bernard, *Course of Empire*. Boston, Houghton Mifflin Company, 1952.

Donaldson, Thomas, *The George Catlin Indian Gallery in the U.S. National Museum*. Washington, Smithsonian Institution Annual Reports, 1885.

Dorsey, James Owen, *A Study of Siouan Cults*. U.S. Bureau of American Ethnology, Eleventh Annual Report, 1889-90. Washington, 1894.

Dunn, James Taylor, and Poatgieter, A. Hermina, editors, *Gopher Reader*. St. Paul, Minnesota Historical Society and Minnesota Statehood Centennial Commission, 1958.

Eastman, Mary, *Dahkotah; or, Life and Legends of the Sioux Around Fort Snelling*. New York, 1849.

Eggleston, Edward, *The Mystery of Metropolisville*. New York, Orange Judd Co., 1873.

Ellet, Elizabeth, *Pioneer Women of the West*. New York, J. C. Riker, 1852.

—— *Summer Rambles in the West*. New York, J. C. Riker, 1853.

Featherstonhaugh, George W., *A Canoe Voyage Up the Minnay Sotor*. London, England, Richard Bentley, 1847.

Folsom, William H. C., *Fifty Years in the Northwest*. St. Paul, 1888.

Folwell, William Watts, *A History of Minnesota*. St. Paul, Minnesota Historical Society, 1924.

Foote, Charles M., and Warner, George E., *History of the Minnesota Valley*. Minneapolis, 1883.

Frémont, John Charles, *Narratives of Exploration and Adventure*. New York, Longmans, Green & Co., Inc., 1956.

Fritsche, L. A., *History of Brown County*. Indianapolis, 1916.

Galbraith, Thomas, *Report to Commissioner of Indian Affairs*. Washington, Annual Reports, 1863.

Gates, Charles M., editor, *Five Fur Traders of the Northwest*. Minneapolis, University of Minnesota Press, 1933.

Gray, James, *Pine, Stream and Prairie*. New York, Alfred A. Knopf, Inc., 1945.

Gresham, William G., *History of Nicollet and Le Sueur Counties*. Indianapolis, 1916.

Hansen, Marcus, *Old Fort Snelling*. Minneapolis, Ross & Haines, Inc., 1958.

Heard, I. V. D., *History of the Sioux War*. New York, Harper & Brothers, 1863.

Heilbron, Bertha L., *Documentary Panorama: John Stevens and His Sioux War Pictures*. Minneapolis, Folk Arts Foundation of America, 1949.

——— *The Thirty-Second State, A Pictorial History of Minneosta*. St. Paul, Minnesota Historical Society, 1958.

——— editor, *With Pen and Pencil on the Frontier in 1851, The Diary and Sketches of Frank Blackwell Mayer*. St. Paul, Minnesota Historical Society, 1932.

Helmes, Winifred G., *John A. Johnson, the People's Governor*. Minneapolis, University of Minnesota Press, 1949.

Hewitt, Girart, *Minnesota: Its Advantages to Settlers*. St. Paul, 1867.

Holand, Hjalmar R., *Westward from Vinland*. New York, Duell, Sloan & Pearce, Inc., 1940.

Holcombe, Return I., Hubbard, L. F., and Upham, Warren, *Minnesota in Three Centuries*. St. Paul, Publishing Society of Minnesota, 1908.

Hughes, Thomas, *History of Blue Earth County*. Chicago, 1909.

——— *Indian Chiefs of Southern Minnesota*. Mankato, Minnesota, Mankato Free Press, 1927.

——— *Old Traverse des Sioux*. St. Peter, Minnesota, Herald Publishing Co., 1929.

Hughes, Thomas E., Edwards, David, Roberts, Hugh G., and Hughes, Thomas, editors, *History of the Welsh in Minnesota*. Mankato, Minnesota, 1895.

Huntington, George, *Robber and Hero*. Northfield, Minnesota, Christian Way Co., 1895.

The Indians in Minnesota, a Report to Governor Luther W. Youngdahl by the Governor's Interracial Commission of Minnesota. St. Paul, 1947.

Innis, H. A., *Peter Pond, Fur Trader and Adventurer*. Toronto, Irwin & Gordon, 1930.

Jenks, A. E., *Pleistocene Man in Minnesota*. Minneapolis, University of Minnesota Press, 1936.

Jarchow, Merrill E., *The Earth Brought Forth*. St. Paul, Minnesota Historical Society, 1949.

Keating, William H., *Narrative of an Expedition to the Source of the St. Peter's River, Lake Winnepeek, Lake of the Woods, etc., Performed in the Year 1823*. (Introduction by Roy P. Johnson) Minneapolis, Ross & Haines, Inc., 1959.

Kellogg, Louise Phelps, *French Regime in Wisconsin and the North-*

west. Madison, Wisconsin, State Historical Society of Wisconsin, 1925.

Lahontan, Louis Armand, Baron de, *New Voyages to America.* Chicago, 1905.

Latrobe, Charles Joseph. *The Rambler in North America.* New York, 1834.

Marryat, Frederick, *A Diary in America, with Remarks on Its Institutions.* Philadelphia, Cary & Hart, 1839.

Mattson, E. Neil, *Red River Carts Trek Historic Pembina Trail.* Warren, Minnesota, c. 1958.

McConkey, Harriet E. *Dakota War-Whoop.* St. Paul, 1864.

McWilliams, R. G., *Fleur de Lys and Calumet.* Baton Rouge, Louisiana State University Press, 1953.

Merrick, George Byron, *Old Times on the Upper Mississippi.* Cleveland, 1910.

Minnesota in the Civil and Indian Wars. St. Paul, 1891.

Minnesota River, Minn. House Document, No. 230, 74th Congress, 1st Session; House Document, No. 144, 84th Congress, 2d Session.

Minnesota River at Mankato and North Mankato, Minn. House Document, No. 437, 84th Congress, 2d Session.

Neill, Edward D., *History of the Minnesota Valley, Including the Explorers and Pioneers of Minnesota.* Minneapolis, North Star Publishing Co., 1882.

Nevins, Allan, editor, *Robert Rogers' Ponteach; or the Savages of America, a Tragedy.* Chicago, Caxton Club, 1914.

Newson, T. M., *Pen Pictures of St. Paul, Minnesota, and Biographical Sketches of Old Settlers.* St. Paul, 1886.

Nicollet, J. N., *Report Intended to Illustrate a Map of the Hydrological Basin of the Upper Mississippi River.* Washington, 1843.

Oehler, C. M., *The Great Sioux Uprising.* New York, Oxford University Press, Inc., 1959.

Old Rail Fence Corners. Austin, Minnesota, 1914.

Pike, Zebulon, *An Account of a Voyage Up the Mississippi River from St. Louis to Its Source.* Washington, 1807.

Pond, Samuel W., Jr., *Two Volunteer Missionaries Among the Dakotas.* Boston, 1893.

Potter, Theodore, *Autobiography.* Concord, New Hampshire, Rumford Press, 1913.

Riggs, Stephen Return, *Mary and I: Forty Years With the Sioux.* Chicago, 1880.

Robinson, Doane, *History of the Dakota or Sioux Indians.* Minneapolis, Ross & Haines, Inc., 1956.

Roddis, Louis H., *The Indian Wars of Minnesota.* Cedar Rapids, Iowa, 1956.

Rose, Arthur P., *History of Yellow Medicine County.* Marshall, Minnesota, 1914.

———— *An Illustrated History of the Counties of Rock and Pipestone.* Luverne, Minnesota, 1911.

Sasse, Fred, *The Dan Patch Story.* Harrisburg, Pennsylvania, The Stackpole Co., 1959.

Schwartz, George M. and Thiel, George A., *Minnesota's Rocks and Waters.* Minneapolis, University of Minnesota Press, 1954.

Sevareid, A. E., *Canoeing with the Cree.* New York, The Macmillan Co., 1930.

———— *Not So Wild a Dream.* New York, Alfred A. Knopf, Inc., 1946.

Seymour, E. S., *Sketches of Minnesota, the New England of the West.* New York, 1850.

Sharp, Abigail Gardner, *History of the Spirit Lake Massacre.* Des Moines, Iowa, 1885.

Shea, John Gilmary, editor, *Early Voyages Up and Down the Mississippi.* Albany, New York, Joel Munsell, 1861.

Shetrone, Henry C., *The Mound-Builders.* New York, Appleton Co., 1930.

Shortridge, Wilson P., *Transition of a Typical Frontier.* St. Paul, 1919.

Smith, Henry Nash, *Virgin Land, the American West as Symbol and Myth.* Cambridge, Massachusetts, Harvard University Press, 1950.

Snelling, Henry Hunt, *Memoirs of a Boyhood at Fort Snelling.* Minneapolis, 1939.

Snelling, W. J., *Tales of the Northwest.* Boston, 1830.

South Dakota Historical Society Collections, vols. 10 and 20.

Tapping, Minnie Ellingsen, *Eighty Years at the Gopher Hole.* New York, 1958.

Trollope, Anthony, *North America.* New York, 1862. Reprint edited by Donald Smalley and Bradford Allen Booth. New York, Alfred A. Knopf, Inc., 1951.

Upham, Warren, *Glacial Lake Agassiz.* Washington, 1895.

Van Cleve, Charlotte Ouisconsin, *Three Score Years and Ten: Life-Long Memories of Fort Snelling and Other Parts of the West.* Minneapolis, 1888.

Wagner, Henry R., *Peter Pond, Fur Trader and Explorer.* New Haven, Connecticut, Yale University Press, 1955.

Wahlgren, Erik, *The Kensington Rune Stone, A Mystery Solved.* Madison, Wisconsin, University of Wisconsin Press, 1958.

Wakefield, Sarah F., *Six Weeks in the Sioux Tepees.* Shakopee, 1864.

Water Resources Development by the U. S. Army Engineers in Minnesota. Chicago, 1959.

Watts, William, *History of the Red River Valley, Past and Present.* Chicago, 1909.

Welsh, William, *Taopi and His Friends.* Philadelphia, 1869.

West, Nathaniel, *Ancestry, Life and Times of Henry Hastings Sibley.* St. Paul, Pioneer Press Publishing Co., 1889.

Wheelock, Joseph A., *Minnesota: Its Place Among the States.* Hartford, Connecticut, 1890.

Willard, Daniel E., *The Story of the North Star State.* St. Paul, Webb Publishing Co., 1922.

Williams, J. Fletcher, *History of the City of St. Paul.* St. Paul, Minnesota Historical Society, 1876.

Wisconsin Historical Collections, vols. 16 and 18.

Winchell, N. H., *The Aborigines in Minnesota.* St. Paul, Minnesota Historical Society, 1911.

Newspapers and Periodicals

American Historical Review

Brown County's Heritage

Bulletin of the Minnesota Academy of Natural Science, December, 1882

The Busy West, April, 1872

Dakota County *Tribune,* July 15, 1927

Harper's New Monthly Magazine, April, June, 1859; October, 1860

Henderson *Democrat,* 1858

Henderson *Independent,* July 25, 1952

Hennepin Lawyer, May, 1941

Hennepin County Historical Society Quarterly

Journal of American History, Vol. 1, No. 2

Le Sueur *News-Herald*

Magazine of Western History, October, 1890

Minneapolis *Star*
Minneapolis *Tribune*
Minnesota History
Minnesota Pioneer
Mississippi Valley Historical Review
The Nation, August 28, 1913
New Ulm *Daily Journal*
New Ulm *Review*
The New-York *Tribune,* June 20, 1854
North Dakota Historical Quarterly, Vol. 1, No. 2
Northwest Magazine, Vol 12, No. 12

Pioneer Magazine, October 30, 1938
Redwood *Gazette*
St. Paul *Daily Pioneer and Democrat,* 1859
St. Paul *Dispatch and Pioneer Press*
St. Peter *Herald*
Saturday Evening Post, Burlington, Iowa, 1913, 1914, 1915
Scott County *Argus,* 1876
Southern Minnesotan
Swedish Historical Society Yearbook

INDEX

Index